passing for perfect

In the series *Asian American History and Culture*,
edited by Cathy Schlund-Vials, Shelley Sang-Hee Lee, and Rick Bonus.
Founding editor, Sucheng Chan; editors emeriti, David Palumbo-Liu,
Michael Omi, K. Scott Wong, and Linda Trinh Võ.

A list of additional titles in this series appears at the back of this book erin Khuê Ninh

passing for perfect

college impostors and other
model minorities

TEMPLE UNIVERSITY PRESS
Philadelphia • *Rome* • *Tokyo*

TEMPLE UNIVERSITY PRESS
Philadelphia, Pennsylvania 19122
tupress.temple.edu

Library of Congress Cataloging-in-Publication Data

Names: Ninh, Erin Khuê, author.
Title: Passing for perfect : college impostors and other model minorities /
 erin Khuê Ninh.
Other titles: Asian American history and culture.
Description: Philadelphia : Temple University Press, 2021. | Series: Asian
 american history and culture | Includes bibliographical references and
 index.
Identifiers: LCCN 2021058766 (print) | LCCN 2021058767 (ebook) | ISBN
 9781439920510 (cloth) | ISBN 9781439920527 (paperback) | ISBN
 9781439920534 (pdf)
Subjects: LCSH: Model minority stereotype—United States. | Impostors and
 imposture—United States. | Asian American students—Psychology. | Asian
 American families—Psychology. | Asian Americans—Ethnic identity—Social
 aspects. | Asian Americans—Race identity—Social aspects.
Classification: LCC E184.A75 N565 2021 (print) | LCC E184.A75 (ebook) | DDC
 305.895/073—dc23
LC record available at https://lccn.loc.gov/2021058766

Printed in the United States of America

9 8 7 6 5 4 3 2 1

to our chosen families

for our wildflower selves

Contents

Tables

passing for perfect

introduction

The Strange Case
of the College Impostor

By all appearances, Azia Kim was a Stanford freshman: living in the dorms, laboring over papers in the library, complaining about midterms on her social media account. It was nine months before the administration and her classmates caught on: Though she fit unremarkably among them, Azia had never been admitted.

For Jennifer Pan, retaking the single calculus class she had narrowly failed would have meant telling her parents that she did not have her high school diploma and had lost her early admission to college. She chose instead to pretend: to four years of undergrad and then the approved pharmacology school. Finally exposed, she hired hitmen to have her parents killed.

I've hesitated to tell people my book is about college impostors, unless I have the time to back up and explain that, yes, there is such a class of persons. In fact, there are several classes of such persons, and I am focusing on just one. The impostors that interest me may not have been admitted to their predetermined colleges, or maybe they flunked out; either way, they respond by staying the course, walking out onto thin air as if the ground had not dropped away beneath them. Above are the most famous cases in that set, but there are innumerable unsung ones. The phenomenon is literally uncountable because, like racial passing, college impostoring is by definition done in secret.[1] Those who do it have few (if any) confidants; those who are exposed rarely make the news. Yet, often enough that I half-expect it now, once I get the definition across, a listener will pipe up, "I know someone like that!" Some will even confess to it themselves, in confidence.[2] So far, they have all been Asian American, these masquerading friends of friends: sons and daughters of immigrants, passing for perfect. This book is the first to give the phenomenon a name and a classification system—but expect no epidemiological review of incidence, distribution, and determinants here. What I have for you today will not tell you about the strength of trends and makes no predictions. That not being my background, this is not that kind of study. What I *will* do is ask the puzzling questions and do my best Sherlock to answer them: Why would someone make such an illogical choice? How do they stage these lies so convincingly, for so long? And, hey, Asian Americans, what's so hard about being model minority, anyway?

this is a prequel.

Passing for Perfect is a do-over, of sorts. In writing my first book, *Ingratitude: The Debt-Bound Daughter in Asian American Literature*, what mattered to me was to explain with utmost precision how it is that Asian immigrant families bent on raising only shiny, high-income professionals may render their children great harm—and to explain it in words that my own immigrant parents would not understand. Like secret code, academese let me smuggle out what needed to be said, without detection. This plan worked pretty well, for the most part: I have never had to talk about *Ingratitude* with relatives, while strangers with the necessary motivation to read it (term paper deadlines, say) have often found their own truths in its pages. That is to say, it's the kind of urgent message one prisoner slips to another: *Live, friend! I've found a way out.* But that book being literary criticism, most who could use it would never suspect it was meant for them. Year after year, in courses like Asian American mental health or Vietnamese American experience, my students tell their stories by opening, unbidden, with remorse—remorse for never measuring up, for not redeeming sacrifices, for owing more than their lives can repay—because no one has shown them how rigged these covenants are. Yet, I've hesitated to recommend *Ingratitude* even to them: "I think you need my book," I'd have to say, "Decoder ring not included." The need I see being no less dire, this is take two, and this time, no deliberate barriers to entry.

This is a book for the desperate and for those who love them. It is for those of us who look at figures like Azia, or even Jennifer, and see something of ourselves. At the same time, it's an academic monograph, which means it takes part in an intricate conversation among scholars about its subject. I draw on concepts and arguments developed by researchers in the social sciences as well as humanities—whatever's relevant and useful, or relevant and flawed, because the idea is to build on what we know collectively and to improve it. Reaching people and creating knowledge are equally modes of fighting the good fight, and here I hope to do both at one and the same time, by telling a story worth hearing to the end. The subjects featured in this book might not have wanted their histories rehashed, it's true. But I hope they will ultimately prefer the respect of an attentive telling, and the humanity of a careful listening, over having been jeered and then forgotten.

I call this book a prequel, though, because staking its arguments on the lives of actual people does make it circumspect. Working with the published (i.e., voluntarily public) word, a literary critic can level a character, remake a world, so long as her analysis stands. In *Ingratitude*, I am relentless. *Passing for Perfect* delivers its truths but cushions its blows, so if you must see blood and bone to know your gods demolished, then maybe you will need to read the other book, too.

decoder ring

What if what seem to be outlandish and outlier behaviors are instead depressingly Asian American? This book considers life at the intersection of some demanding social, familial, and educational realities—among them, neoliberal abandonment of the middle class, "Tiger" and "helicopter" parenting, and increasingly racialized and intensified competition for admission at top-tier universities. As I write this Introduction, two proximate stories populate the media cycle: First, the Operation Varsity Blues scandal, in which moderately wealthy parents purchased fake credentials for their children's real enrollment into competitive colleges. As chapter one explains, those are a different type of impostor: Though part of the same dystopic universe, their greed is not racially-specific and hardly mystifying—fit for schadenfreude, not rapport. Second, the anti-affirmative action case against Harvard filed by "Students for Fair Admissions,"[3] which claims five of the first ten spots in my search results for "Asian Americans" in the news. In this cultural moment, scaling the Ivy Leagues is the idée fixe of success, and Asian Americans (by overrepresentation) are its very picture. This book means to trouble that perfect picture and to take its emotional measure.

My opening bid is this: Where I come from, the model minority is not a myth. This is not to say that *all* Asian Americans are prosperous or even upwardly mobile; it is not to say that we people pull ourselves out of poverty without government assistance and so can you. Those statements are demonstrably false for many Asian Americans; then again, they are demonstrably true for others. That which is partially true is not a myth (problematic or inconvenient, yes; uncalibrated or misleading, quite possibly; roundly deniable, no). But the empirical ratio is not what matters here. What matters is the immigrant auntie who buys that story, the father who works nights off the books but insists his children will be doctors, the boyfriend who walks through gilded doors pried open by generations of activism but hails America as meritocracy, the cousin who feels Harvard is her due. I define the model minority as an *identity*: a set of convictions and aspirations, regardless of present socioeconomic status or future attainability. It is an orthodox faith in what sociologists Jennifer Lee and Min Zhou, of *The Asian American Achievement Paradox* (*AAAP*), have dubbed the "success frame"—"earning straight A's, graduating as the high school valedictorian, earning a degree from an elite university, attaining an advanced degree, and working in one of four high-status professional fields: medicine, law, engineering, or science."[4] That list comprises not merely a set of goals but a framework for personhood, such that to be socially viable as Asian American—to hold up one's head at family gatherings or church socials—is to live by its terms.

Among many a second-generation Asian American this frame is *common sense*, especially as Antonio Gramsci used the term: to convey that certain perceptions of reality may seem logical, inevitable, even though they are culturally specific and serve the interests of those in power. To be model minority is to "know" (even as one may hate it) that success means hitting each of the achievement checkpoints in sequence, because *everyone knows this*. What qualifies are not the achievements themselves, mind you, but the shared sense of them. Which means, as this book draws the set, to be model minority is not a matter of income bracket or GPA (nor is generation a guarantee*). The litmus test is not whether an Asian American meets "success frame" standards per se. Only the few do (my English major exempts me, right?), while some of us toil daily at such a far cry from its lofty requirements that surely we have been excused? But that, my friends, is too easy. It lets the vast majority of us off on technicalities.[†] Because this book

---

* A note on terminology: immigrants are "first generation" Americans, while their (American-born) kids are "second generation." This because immigrants can become naturalized citizens and, therefore, Americans.

† "Model minority" and "Asian American" are not identical sets, and I don't pretend to know statistically where one ends, the other begins. But this book's focus is squarely on those invested in being, or enlisted despite themselves as,

holds that the model minority is coded into one's programming—
racialization become feeling and belief—its litmus test is whether
an Asian American *feels pride or shame* by those standards. If you
have enjoyed what Tiger parenting memes say about you (laughed
ruefully, maybe, but knowingly): Congratulations, you have tested
positive. With your click, like, and share, you affirm an identity set
apart from other racial groups: a feeling that *our bar is higher.* Or,
equally, if communal judgment can pith you, and you have needed
to walk yourself back time and again to remember that your life
has real worth: Your affliction can be managed, but it never leaves
your system.

How could so much possibly hinge on a checklist? I suppose
what has become codified as the success frame is a distillation:

---

model minorities; those to whom that paradigm is foreign are outside of its pur-
view. Asian Americans exist who have never been subject to model-minority
racialization; they are just not studied here. Still, I do hold that as a racialization
internalized, model-minority identity has a reach that exceeds its intersectional
grasp: poverty provides no immunity from its values, feelings, beliefs. Demo-
graphically, nothing inherently does. I offer for proof of concept the following
interview with filmmaker Justin Chon: His family's experiences as Korean small
business owners, whose warehouse was looted during the Los Angeles Uprising/
Sa-I-Gu, form the basis of his film *Gook*. Faulting Hollywood for its neglect of
such Asian American stories, Chon demands, "How come we're never seen as
working class . . . ? We're always [shown as] the model minority and we're pitted
against other minorities for someone else's agenda." That is, using the conventional definition of "model minority" as a checklist of stereotypical achievements,
Chon confidently absolves his family of perpetuating the racial hierarchy. The
way it sounds, the success frame could not have been further from their minds.
But, define the model minority by conviction and aspiration instead, and Chon's
family begins to sound typical of the set: "My dad's reason for being [in a Black
neighborhood] was that the rent was cheaper. . . . But my sister and I lived in
the suburbs because my Dad wanted us to go to a nice public school." (Jada
Yuan, "From *Twilight* to *Gook*: How Justin Chon Found His Voice in His Own
Painful Racial Past," vulture.com, August 25 2017, available at https://www
.vulture.com/2017/08/from-twilight-to-gook-how-justin-chon-found-his-voice
.html) And, in fact, it turns out Chon was raised in Irvine, among the children
of professors and affluent white families, at top-ranked University High School.
At the University of Southern California, he majored in business. All of which
suggests an upbringing—whatever their household income—in active pursuit of
the model-minority dream. ("Justin Chon," Wikipedia, last modified January 24,
2020, available at https://en.wikipedia.org/wiki/Justin_Chon)

These expectations are an insider's experience of racial formation;* they are the structure of model-minority feeling.† By definition, then, to be model minority is to have this very fixed sense of success and failure in common, like it or not. And yet, it is worth pausing here to marvel at how truly saturated that common sense is. For their study, Lee and Zhou purposely chose two populations that "differ enormously in . . . their immigration histories, socioeconomic backgrounds, and settlement patterns": "the Chinese, a long-standing immigrant group in the United States, and the Vietnamese, a relatively recent refugee group." Yet, they find, rather to their dismay, "despite the tremendous intergroup differences among the first generation, . . . the educational outcomes of the children of Chinese immigrants and Vietnamese refugees converge within one generation—a *vexing* pattern that we refer to as 'second-generation convergence.'" This is the paradox to which they refer. As they rightly marvel, moreover, "*most remarkable* is that regardless of class background" interviewees from the two groups "recounted the same success frame."[5] Remarkable, yes; unusual, no. The model minority converges from across groups so numerous, disparities so great, that paradox may be its only rule. Formerly hailing from a federal territory as "wards" of the United States, the Filipinx community's route to America is unlike any other Asian Americans'. Largely Catholic and shaped by centu-

---

* Sociologists Michael Omi and Howard Winant coined "racial formation" to name "the sociohistorical process by which racial identities are created, lived out, transformed, and destroyed." (Michael Omi and Howard Winant. *Racial Formation in the United States* [New York: Routledge/Taylor and Francis, 2015], 109).

† Relevant but not vital to my project, "structure of feeling" I use lightly. In the original, Raymond Williams intended it to pinpoint the experience of living through a new wrinkle in history, a social or cultural development that we may sense but not yet have the conceptual vocabulary to articulate. The term has proven quite popular—though, as here, its versatility may come of a somewhat less strict application. I like it for the spatial quality it gives to lived experience: that our feelings come to map out, like sonar, the shape and size of what is happening to us, even if, like bats, we don't quite know what we are being made to fly around. This concept is useful, I think, even with social formations not exactly newborn unto the world.

ries of prior Spanish imperialism, Filipinx have been "strikingly absent from contemporary literatures on immigration and on Asian-Americans."[6] Meanwhile, largely Hindu or Muslim, their histories marked by centuries of British rule, South Asians are further distinctive among Asian Americans for having no "direct historical connection to the United States": "no history of colonial encounter [or military engagement] that explains their presence in the U.S. today."[7] And yet, this book will be able to cite both groups' success-frame lives across wholly separate studies. Among the quotes below, some describe Filipinx students at a northern California high school; others, South Asian students in a Boston-area school district. Guess which is which.

- "My parents and my grandparents have always instilled in me that I can do whatever I want as long as I was happy. But now and then they always push, 'well you can be a doctor,' or 'do you like medicine?'"[8]
- "Anything below an A is unacceptable."[9]
- "Anything less than an 'A' was unacceptable."[10]

Such consensus comes despite material differences in the very things usually deployed to explain why Person-or-Group X is so unlike Person-or-Group Y this strangeness is hard to overstate. What it tells us about this common sense, though, is not how very true it is but how very powerful.

Just how powerful is, in fact, the very thing we need to wrap our heads around if we are to understand what drives college impostors like Azia and Jennifer. As I argue in chapter two, the academic world has no shortage of ways to make the point that humans are socially conditioned creatures: that our beliefs and actions default not to individual authenticity but to cultural norms. Still, most of the terms around this concept disappoint when it comes to making sense of choices as unreasonable as our protagonists'. Where if-then formulations and cost-benefit analyses are hopelessly inadequate, rationalist-minded explanations will not suffice. We need, here, tools that account also for the emotion of the thing: for the training and manufacture of persons on the level of fear and guilt, love and loyalty. But, what, is this structure of feelings so singular that there's no understanding it short a utility belt of literary and philosophical terms? I think quite the opposite, actually. There are those who *get* a college impostor's doomed choices on a gut level and need no outside assistance to show them how or why desperation is plausible. Though strangers, they *feel* like intimates, recognizing themselves and each other across these stories. If they need any help, it is in translating their peculiar dialect of feeling into the common tongue. But among the greater public, many find stories like Azia's and Jennifer's nonsensical and react with either bafflement or ridicule: the former is a mental impediment to empathy; the latter, an emotional repudiation of it. For the culturally monolingual, this passing for perfect is a spectacle too foreign; for the model minority, it whispers too close to home. Check in with your feelings, reader, if curious whereabouts you fall.

Concepts coined by Lauren Berlant crop up rather a lot in this book, because they are uncannily good for figuring out the geometry of a social configuration and for reading the emotional charge that animates it. A literary critic qua philosopher of capitalist life, it's as if Berlant had coined the cultural equivalent of pi and a series of correlate concepts as well; henceforth, it would be silly not to use these very handy constructs when dealing with things of a circular nature. Equally silly would be to reinvent the pi. And so, while *Passing for Perfect* taps useful theories wherever it finds them—plundering journals of law and quantitative psychology alike—it leans most consistently on Berlant's concepts of genre (along with intimate public) and of cruel optimism. In her oeuvre on American literature and sentimentality, she defines genre as "an *emotionally invested*, patterned set of expectations about how to act and how to interpret, which organises"[11] not only aesthetic productions like movies or poetry but temporal experience: how we each narrate and understand our everyday lives. The top billing emotion receives in that definition is key because, as Berlant argues to increasingly devastating effect across her own trilogy, even when we have come to know our social formation as harmful to us, a life worth wanting may still be trapped in its terms. While I do end up proposing some modifications in her concepts, they are nonetheless the secret sauce for explaining why the relationship between discourse and social being is, ultimately, not straightforward: why it is paradoxical and irrational and self-extraction is so dear.

passing . . . for model minority

Passing is not an easy commitment to make. Historically, in the racially stratified United States, to pass has meant to live or work surreptitiously as a member of a racial group not your own—and, in the vast majority of instances, thereby to stage whiteness. As a social phenomenon (as opposed to, say, a social experiment[12]), it is a choice made under duress—though, as the conditions of duress vary, so too do the manner and motivation. In the antebellum period, slaves who could are said to have "passed *through* whiteness" as a fleeting measure for reaching the free states, upon which they were apt to drop the charade and "*reject* rather than embrace the power and superiority whites claimed as their singular possession."[13] Indeed, only by acknowledging their former circumstances could fugitives hope to achieve the other part of their ends: Under a racial order in which "they could be bought, sold, and forever separated from their families" at a master's whim, escape meant at least the possibility of finding their loved ones. "Surrounded by loss, enslaved people were motivated by a desire to reunite with their families, not to leave them behind."[14]

During Reconstruction and through the Jim Crow era that followed, passing could be a tactical matter of getting white-collar jobs or attending elite colleges from which Black people were otherwise barred. In such instances, deceptions were staged within circumscribed settings or definite durations ("nine-to-five passing," say). Those at home or even in the Black community were not meant to be deceived; rather, passing was a group effort, in the sense that it required all in the know to maintain "a conspiracy of silence" from white society.[15] Even this part-time duplicity took enormous tolls in anxiety and risk. Law professor Cheryl Harris relates of her grandmother, who worked in a department store as a (presumed white) shopgirl, that "Day in and day out, she made herself invisible, then visible again, for a price too inconsequential to do more than barely sustain her family and at a cost too precious to conceive."[16]

But, of course, there were also those who disappeared into white identities entirely, a practice regarded by at least some among the Black community as betrayal and by white society as an especial threat. As a choice, it is as if the passer had taken every intimacy of friend or kin, along with communal comforts of food or song, memory or story, and placed them all on a scale, then traded them in to sweeten his odds alone. While this fully committed form of passing was thus "a deeply individualistic practice," it nonetheless rested on the cooperation of others, whose silence was purchased with nothing: "The iconic image of the heartbroken yet sympathetic black mother who must not speak a word nor lay eyes upon her white-looking child in public lays bare the painful consequences of this practice." As historian Allyson Hobbs writes in *A Chosen Exile*, "To pass as white meant to lose a sense of embeddedness in a community or a collectivity. Passing reveals that the essence of *identity* is not found in an individual's qualities, but rather *in the ways that one recognizes oneself and is recognized as kindred*."[17] It is a lot to give up, and not necessarily redeemed by the rewards accrued in its place.

Meanwhile, at the top of a racial hierarchy, a lot rides on biology as a meaningful anchor of difference and phenotype as guarantor of those meanings. Insofar as passing proves difference to be indiscernible, it attacks the foundations of power and changes the terms of the debate about race: "[Passing's] 'performance' so impeccably mimics 'reality' that it goes undetected as performance, framing its resistance to essentialism in the very rhetoric of essence and origin."[18] In other words, in successfully "hiding" genetic origins, passing "outs" racial identity itself as a matter of norms and cues, in staging and costume, habit and mannerism, speech and story: race not as what you are but how you do you. Passing champions the heresy that to be white in America is not (biological) fact but (cultural) act—as it is,* likewise, to be Black, Asian, etc. It is in this performative sense that our college impostors may be said to be racially "passing."

Passing is a loaded term, then, but one that this book, nonetheless, adopts for impostors like Azia and Jennifer, because to pass for model minority is a performance of race—even if your own. This reworking draws from concepts like "covering" (from Kenji Yoshino's *Covering: The Hidden Assault on Our Civil Rights*—in chapter three) as well as performativity (from Judith Butler's "Performative Acts and Gender Constitution," for starters—chapter two) because its premise is that social identities are a matter of what we enact. That is, we necessarily manage our mix of identities every day, performing each by its respective script (straight male, middle class, mother, student, etc.) and dialing each up or down in varying contexts, with varying success, to score prestige and mask stigma. To call imposture a kind of passing, then, is to plot it on the extreme end of a range of common, socialized practices—as opposed to isolating it as a freak mutation or individual pathology.

In that sense, this book picks up where Tina Chen's *Double Agency: Acts of Impersonation in Asian American Literature and Culture* leaves off. Chen's work is very much about racial identity as a performance—and, more specifically, as an impersonation.[19] Not only does she assert racial faking–it as normal but, most usefully, she drills down into the unfeasibility of opting out, when the role appointed to you is also the only role that will be believed of you. If "perform[ing] themselves into being *as persons recognized* by their communities and their country"[20] means that

Asian Americans strive to look and act like Asian Americans are expected to look and act, the case *may* be that they earnestly see themselves as the model minority, but the case is certainly that being seen and heard by others is contingent upon being recognized. Be it in a courtroom or at a board game, to play is to play by roles, whether well or poorly; else, you can disrupt, but you can never win. Authenticity is not the name of this game. Chen's overarching concern is that we "ordinary" impersonators not be mistaken for deviant impostors, who are guilty of stealing someone else's identity and may presumably deserve to be uncovered and expelled. But, here, my argument makes a different turn, ditching the distinction between impostor and impersonator, morally and otherwise. Because if Asian Americans are recognized as persons *by their communities and their country* only by the success frame, then whose public identity is a failure allowed to use? Whose racial reputation and likeness if not their own? I use "passing for model minority" to describe what Azia and Jennifer do because it is an oxymoron, and signals the paradox of their having trespassed by taking their assigned places, their having offended by trying so hard to please. Lying about their public identities as college students, yet at least as earnestly playing their racial part as the next Asian American, those who resort to passing for model minority are impostors and impersonators, both.

All told, then, I choose "passing" precisely for how heavy it is, with what is at stake. Because, while the conditions and contexts of duress vary, even the moral valences shift, the cost of passing is always high. So, to see it chosen is to know that the alternative, not to pass, has to have felt in each case even more intolerable. But, to see it truly, is also to know that the distance between those choices is actually so slight: Realities cleave, sure, from that moment forward, but aren't the hardest choices precisely those in which it's not clear which path is worse, and the selves we imagine either way rack with fear or pain? Performance artist Kristina Wong has probably never been a college impostor, but she could have passed for one.* In an essay about the emotional backstory to her work on mental health, she describes the rewards and punishments of model minority performance, according to which "success usually came in specific quantifiable terms like having a well-paying job, a medical degree from a reputable school, or marrying a Chinese bilingual doctor husband":

> I won't lie. Getting good grades, winning trophies, and stacking a long list of accomplishments on my college application made me feel good because it meant I had avoided my parents' idea of a failure. But most of the time, the road to the seemingly unattainable, chasing a dream that wasn't really mine, felt so totally miserable and pointless.

Despite what she calls the "agony of living" this way, though, the alternative seemed to hold no better: "To me, choosing a different path meant flunking out of school and disowning my parents."[21] Per what she had been told and told to feel, not performing her racial part might cost her her family or render her features unrecognizable in a community obsessed with face. Was this framing hyperbolic, histrionic? Hopefully, yes. Emotionally, no. Thing is, there is only one way to find out.

assimilate this.

One more thing to note about this particular kind of passing: Whiteness is not its aspiration. Which suggests the practice may be native to some more than others of the states in the union, even some more than others of the counties on the coasts. The

---

* Wong is a comedian and actor whose work is informed by ethnic studies and feminist criticism. In 2006, she wrote and began to tour a solo theater show called "Wong Flew Over the Cuckoo's Nest," inspired by CDC reports of high rates of depression and suicide among Asian American women. She graduated from UCLA "but" with an English major and Asian American studies minor.

success frame flourishes most where Asian ethnic communities are thickest: enough to seed the schools with a plurality or more of their students; enough to sustain networks of churches, tutoring services, and cultural activities. Lee and Zhou anchored their study in one such region: metropolitan Los Angeles, with special attention to the "ethnoburbs" of the San Gabriel Valley and Orange County.[22] Likewise, in "Family Secrets: Transnational Struggles among Children of Filipino Immigrants," sociologist Diane Wolf's sites were two high schools in Vallejo, California, where, in the 1990s, Filipinx students accounted for 25–30 percent of the population—and the highest average GPAs of any racial-ethnic group. Surprised by the alienation and crises she discovered to belie students' "cheerful, socially involved" appearance, Wolf gives us what reads as an early transcript of the success frame.[23] Also in the 1990s, anthropologist Shalini Shankar set her research in Silicon Valley, where high school already meant student-bodies up to 54 percent Asian American, about a third of them South Asian. She dubbed her project "Desi Land" in reference to not only the numerical predominance of South Asians but the local hegemony of Desi* identity, overachievement and all.[24] Even on the East Coast and twenty years later, Pawan Dhingra's *Hyper Education: Why Good Schools, Good Grades, and Good Behavior Are Not Enough* (2020) is based in districts over 30 percent Asian American and projected to reach 40–50 percent in "a couple of years." His sociological elaboration on how model-minority parenting "fits into the neoliberal education system" is worth reading in its own right† but serves here, along with Wolf's and Shankar's work, to fortify the foundation provided by

---

* A self-referential term for South Asian people, usually from India, Pakistan, or Bangladesh.

† Had *Hyper Education* been published earlier, no doubt it would have been well threaded through these pages. Our arguments are complementary (i.e., largely compatible)—save that *Passing for Perfect* insists on biopsying affective aspects of achievement-parenting that *Hyper Education* accepts as benign, such as "caring" that takes the form of "discuss[ing] the need to do well for the sake of the [already upper-middle-class] family" (Dhingra, *Hyper Education*, 43).

AAAP.[25] Evident across concentrations like these is a new normal: local countercultures about Asian American excellence competing for hearts and minds with mainstream U.S. racial thinking. This development has put a wrinkle in the long-standing "assumption in classic assimilation and segmented assimilation models" that immigrants use "native-born whites as their reference group when measuring their success."[26] Where "academic success has become racially recoded as 'an Asian thing,'" and also the paramount thing, whiteness can be a liability: a measuring stick neither long nor exacting enough.*

As an identity, then, the model minority is not so easily written off as wannabe-white. Which is not at all the same as saying it is politically "resistant." In Dhingra's words, "immigrant parents . . . care first and foremost about outcompeting others":[27] If they question some of the rules as being to their disadvantage, it's because they play to win. Model-minority aspirations or realities buy into privilege plenty; it is just not white privilege.[28] The vicarious glee of second-generation viewers, then, for the opening scene of *Crazy Rich Asians*[29]—in which an owning-class Singaporean family avenges itself against racist treatment by

---

* Some caveats: Anecdotally, it does seem that towns "east of California," where an Asian family may still number among the few or only, still foster classic assimilationism and classic scenes of self-hate. Having grown up that way, Wesley Yang opened his infamous "Paper Tigers" essay by admitting that he is estranged, even astonished, by the sight of his own face—Asian features he loathes to call his own. Yang has no desire to pass for model minority; he would be white, though, if he could. Yet, judging by that same essay's description of Stuyvesant, one of New York City's most competitive public high schools, even a student body 72 percent Asian does not assure the inverse experience: Even vastly outnumbered, white students there ruled the social hierarchy. (Wesley Yang, "Paper Tigers," *New York Magazine*, May 6, 2011, available at http://nymag.com/news/features /asian-americans-2011-5/) This is to say, there is no hard-and-fast rule. An isolated immigrant family might manage to manufacture communal mandate out of thin air: gossip and some Chinese-language newspapers (see Elaine Mar's *Paper Daughter* [1999]). Meanwhile, South Asians in Silicon Valley high schools play the nerds and the cool kids, too (see Shankar's *Desi Land* [2008]). Across that range, Asians may rank themselves above white or below—while being equally familiar with the hail of the success frame.

British hotel workers, by instantly buying the exclusive hotel—is not about becoming white but about besting it. Indeed, the very essentials of the success frame are wrought by a sharp sense of racial disparity: compulsory higher education? clustering in technical fields? Social scientists have found these patterns to be best explained not by ancient culture or individual talent but by a pragmatic approach to institutional racism: "racial discrimination is relatively easier to combat in technical occupations due to the availability of objective criteria for hiring and advancement." The model minority derives its best-or-bust identity directly from its racialization: "We know we are a minority in this society, and we have to do better than other Americans. . . . That's the only way we'll get ahead."[30]

Produced in such moments is something more interesting than a misplaced possessive investment in whiteness. That is a common way of characterizing upward mobility among Asian Americans—that they become "almost white" or aim to "out-white the whites"—but it is a belittling one, building in a narrative of chasing after what is not theirs and never will be. The concept of possessive investment itself, however, can be transposed to model-minority identity. When people talk about "whiteness as property" or the (cash) "value of being white,"[31] these refer to the ways that the identity confers systemic advantages, making life easier, less expensive, more profitable: A membership plan that allows one to live in neighborhoods with healthier air, water, and property values; to drive unmolested along roads well-maintained to take one to retailers with the better selection and pricing of goods; to receive smiling benefit of the doubt from security guards, teachers, and employers that one is worth their protection and their time—what kind of annual fee would this be worth to you? And if you could pass it down to your children? Those advantages are not accidents of history but the upshot of laws laid down from the federal level to the municipal, which continue to pay dividends in social inclusion/exclusivity to this day. The inference of *vested* interests is useful, though, because the having of such privileges is not a passive or innocent thing. One becomes possessive of objects that, precious, grant their holders such powers. Harris, whose law review essay opened with her grandmother passing as a white shopgirl, explains that "if an object you now control is bound up in your future plans or in your anticipation of your future self, and it is partly these plans for your own continuity that make you a person, then your personhood depends on the realization of these expectations." Being "regarded as white," she continues, is a "reputational interest" and, as such, "intrinsically bound up with identity and personhood."[32]

This is why it makes sense to say the Asian American version—a racial identity that, successfully performed, enjoys all the membership privileges listed above, with *bonus* reputational assumptions of being smart and hard working—is a possessive investment in being model minority. It is also why this book's interest in impostures of model-minority perfection is twofold: Mainly, we'll be grappling with how that identity can be devastating and (yet) unthinkable to let go of. When passing for perfect means retaining a sense of yourself and your future as well as keeping your loved ones about you, you do what it takes to pass. But we'll also be spending a little time on model-minority identity as not-unfounded pride: when it means having bested the field despite racism or cultural disadvantage, whether in one generation or two; when overachievement becomes norm and powers a new cultural dominance; and then when it curdles into more cynical opportunities of imposture, and passing for perfect is a matter of working an identity to advantage.

mixed methods, literary deliverables

As a literary critic, my strength has been in reading closely, finding patterns in words and stories, to make sense of what people do—often by drawing forth an emotional truth that loosens the knot of a paradox. This is intricate work but also pretty safe. The entirety of the literary "data" that I need to answer to is normally a closed set *before* I begin: every word fixed to page and bounded by covers. I go in with questions burning but am secured against surprise. Not so this time. Pursuing the success frame as it crosses from personal life into literary or media representation and back again, *Passing for Perfect* examines permutations of that genre in "real world" as well as fictional forms. For this book, I draw together literary analysis with personal interviews and also cultural artifacts (including blog commentary and discussion threads, high school yearbooks). The latter have given me new appreciation for how the other half researches: Starting with the news has meant that my protagonists answer to no writer's authority. Most of them have declined to give interviews, none have authored their own memoirs, and so journalists and academics alike, we trace circles around them, asking questions of people who might have seen something. This gumshoe work relies entirely on the kindness of strangers—data gatekeepers and interview subjects—for access to the further potential upheaval of what file boxes can hold and people may say.

Yet, you should know, this is no exposé. True-crime coverage loves its blow-by-blow reconstruction of cases, and tabloids live or die by their fly's-eye view of private lives, but voyeurism like that feeds the opposite of compassion, and I am leery of it. After all, this is not a project about prosecution and surpassing reasonable doubt, and so the questions critical to ask are not the same. Precisely because we deal with subjects whom society has already found criminal, or who are all too easily annulled as crazy, the harder assignment worth taking is to spot what is sane or credible.

Finally, an advisory on doubt. While inherent to outcomes in the (social) sciences, doubt there aspires to reassuringly quantifiable forms: as measured by degrees of correlation or margins of error. Such are the statistical customs of diagnosis or prediction, derived by virtue of sample sizes and data sets numbering the more, the better. With questions in the mold of "What are the determinants of the disease?" or "Does college ranking translate to income differential?" research takes averages and calibrates answers. Should you be looking to measure causality in model-minority life, studies abound—tracking parenting styles among Asian immigrants to the GPAs or mental health of their children, for example—and they can offer odds of various kinds. But this project being neither medical nor (any branch of) scientific, it is after a different kind of utility. Conclusions here aim not to define the norm but to unnerve it. My analyses incline more to deliverables such as offered by Ursula Le Guin's "The Ones Who Walk Away from Omelas," in which speculation is the order of the day, and the truth of a thing is in its outliers. In this story, the health and wealth of a shining city rest on the condition that one child always be imprisoned in a cellar and that the residents above know it to be so:

> If the child were brought up into the sunlight out of that vile place, if it were cleaned and fed and comforted, that would be a good thing indeed; but if it were done, in that day and hour all the prosperity and beauty and delight of Omelas would wither and be destroyed. Those are the terms.

Such work tests the terms of the good life—what it is assumed to be made of, what it is deemed to be worth, and how its value is calculated. Such work does not, however, diagnose or predict the difference between who stays and who goes.

This may seem like a huge shortcoming: that, while *Passing for Perfect* argues the merits of some theories and the liabilities of others, it does not ultimately adjudicate the "root cause" of deviance. Considering that I am asking you to see passing on a continuum—from the practical or mundane to the pathological or outlier—it might seem we'll arrive at a rule of thumb, by which our impostors' fates were determined or can be read. Yet were I to offer you such a handy tell, you really shouldn't take it. Because to determine in the *particular* case what ratios of parenting, racialization, or underlying psychoses led to a momentous decision is an impossible assignment. For starters, each of our main impostors have brothers or sisters, who by all available accounts kept to the conventional paths; there is not pattern enough separating siblings to codify, too much in common to parse. Certainly, a parallel can be made with what scientists can forecast about the warming of the globe, versus what they can predict about next week's weather in Philadelphia; this is a useful analogue, but also limited, because the hurdle is not merely methodological. Answering definitively why, say, Jennifer took a criminal turn is an assignment impossible not as a mea culpa for a humanist methodology but impossible for the human. Even unlimited access to her and her family in interview or diary entries could not answer us that, because who among us—however intimate with the (conscious) knowledge of our autobiographical pasts, even armed with scholarship on our political and cultural histories—can do any more than guess how we came to be ourselves and not our siblings?

So this is an inquiry after something less biography, more ethos. After all, remember, model-minority induction is not picky about whether you are firstborn or last, queer or straight, and if your parents pay for violin lessons that's great, but if you started with nothing to your name but grit, all the better. This is an inquiry into the power of a narrative: to train dreams of the self and belonging, to set the price of failure. It begins with the question, *How do well-behaved Asian Americans become people with no felt options, no thinkable alternatives to the success frame?* It looks to these outlier cases, then, not as opportunities to calculate the error rate or locate the manufacturing flaw in a production process but to expose the industry itself. Come with me to the cellar, so that maybe we can imagine breaking her out.

chapter by chapter

one | Gen(i)us

Not all Asian Americans who falsify their college enrollments do so for the same reasons; nor are non-Asian impostors uniformly motivated. Within a decade, the U.S. and Canadian press have reported at least nine Asian college impostors and fourteen combined total in white, Black, or Latinx—but these tallies point to the possibility that in *this* form of college attendance even more than the official sense, Asians are disproportionately represented. This chapter offers an overview of the college impostor phenomenon at its widest point, with the many men, and some women, of various races who have been publicly caught out at their deceptions. Motives and backgrounds do vary but not so much that they can't be grouped by types—types that fall largely along racial lines. The bulk are "scammers," con artists of, ultimately, unsurprising motives. Others, however, stage their deceptions to no material benefit, and in ways that evoke no readily recognized social tropes; these I call "shammers." By way of Sara Kim, a.k.a. "Genius Girl," this chapter shows that the model minority "passers" at the heart of this study form a species that is (unlike scammers) more irrational, more counterproductive, and yet (unlike shammers) somehow intuitive.

two | *Exemplary*

This chapter sifts through Azia Kim's case to derive the archetypal form of the model-minority impostor: its tropes and aspirations, its gestures and speech acts. What elements of her deception/practice make her recognizably, generically Asian American, even from a distance? Where imposture is another name for racialization, I pair Lee and Zhou's success frame with Judith Butler's work on performativity, and take failure for the core of passing for model minority. This chapter also examines press coverage and online debates alongside a short story partly inspired by Azia: Vanessa Hua's "Accepted." Across these texts, I make a case for the success frame as an instance of Berlant's construct of genre—a kind of life-ordering, world-building narrative—and second-generation Asian Americans as a genuine intimate public: strangers who can spot each other's stories between the lines and read each other's pain. Balancing the myth of Azia as model minority against interviews with those who knew something of the person, I strive to tell a story about her that is also a story of shared proportions: in which failure is too ruinous to admit, and acceptance too narrowly defined.

three | *Limit Case*

Initially cast in the media as a conniving woman and a "monstrous" child, Jennifer Pan became the object of astonishing empathy when it came to light that she had been the daughter of Tiger parents—and thus suddenly victim, not villain. This chapter traces the drift between normalcy and anomaly, perfection and pathology. It combines media analysis (including in-depth coverage of her case in *A Daughter's Deadly Deception*, by journalist Jeremy Grimaldi) with a critique of current social science research on deception in Asian American families. This case tests the tensile strength of the genre: its ability to order *readerly* expectations as well as Jennifer's own, about "the bargains that can be made with life."[33] This chapter also traces the concept of cruel optimism back to its DNA, by comparing the true-crime case of Jean-Claude Romand as told in *The Adversary* by Emmanuel Carrère (unemployed man murders wife and children when faked life unravels) with the inspired-by fictional version in *L'Emploi du Temps* (directed by Laurent Cantet; this version: no murders). Given that Berlant elides the former to build her concept off the latter, Jennifer's story tests the limits of the profile Berlant derives: Can a construct conceived in the mild image of "crisis ordinariness" and in contradistinction to trauma make sense of murderous violence?

four | *Bad Boys*

This final chapter stretches to broach the question of gender in college impostoring—a curious one, since scammers have tended to be men, while our better-known passers have all been women. Rather than indulge, however, in the kind of post hoc theorizing apt to leave us no wiser, this chapter turns *not* to why men versus women might end up making this lifestyle choice, but instead to how well the tropes of Asian American masculinity fare in explaining model-minority life. To view gendered performance in relief, two brief stories of Asian male college impostors are read alongside another male model-minority crime—one that went viral (so to speak) and even inspired a movie: the Honor Roll Murder, retold by Justin Lin as *Better Luck Tomorrow* (*BLT*). Among perpetrators and victim alike were Ivy League hopefuls— and the former attended Sunny Hills High in Azia's hometown. Enlisting this case enables *Passing for Perfect* to look not only at what else a model-minority performance can hide but also at the hard glint of glee with which Asian Americans savored this story of valedictorians-cum-criminal masterminds. The book culminates here—through correspondence with Robert Chan, as he serves life without parole—with perhaps its highest-resolution portrait of how it feels to be model minority.

chapter one

Gen(i)us

Passing for Perfect starts here with the college impostor phenomenon at its widest point: an overview of the women and men of various races who have been publicly caught out at their deceptions. Sorted into types according to their motives and their reception, there would be three. Ultimately, it's the third that we're after: what it is about passers, in particular, that they need a book's worth of explaining.

Scammers: Those who stand to gain clear material advantage from their deceptions, whether by way of cash money or cultural capital (e.g., awards, degrees from distinguished colleges). In some cases, this means individuals who gamed admission using false transcripts or letters, even invented names and life histories. In other cases, this set is populated by those with a criminal record—usually of a nonviolent, financial nature, such as check forgery, embezzlement, credit card fraud, theft. Of the fourteen non-Asian impostors, eleven fall into this category (78 percent). Of the nine Asian impostors, only one (11 percent). (See Tables 1.1 and 1.2.)

Table 1.1 Non-Asian College Impostors

Name/alias	Target institution	Time frame	Age when caught	Race*	Sex	Enrolled or posed	Type	Other offenses/history of deception
Patrick McDermit/ Andreas Stephan Alrea	Yale	1977	21	~White	M	Enrolled	Shammer	Turned himself in to prevent prank from becoming fraud; suffered no penalties; no other known offenses
Mauro Cortez Jr./ Maurice de Rothschild	Duke	1988–1990	37	Latinx	M	Enrolled	Scammer	Convicted for embezzlement and loan fraud while at Duke
James Hogue/ Alexi Santana	Princeton	1989–1991	31	White	M	Enrolled	Scammer	Check forgery, lifelong and compulsive theft; serial invented identities
Lon Grammer	Yale	1993–1995	25	~White	M	Enrolled	Scammer	Prior indictment for check fraud, charges for forgery; plagiarism at Yale; Yale charged with larceny for financial aid, grants
Tonica Jenkins	Yale, graduate	1997, 3 months	23	Black	F	Enrolled	Scammer	Yale charged with fraud, larceny for financial aid; later convicted for cocaine trafficking, kidnapping, and attempted murder
Edward Meinert	Harvard	1999, 2 months	~20	~White	M	Posed	Scammer	Prior conviction for and extensive history of theft and fraud
Rodrigo Fernando Montano	Rice	2002, 1 month	24	Black and Latinx	M	Posed	Scammer	Prior indictment for forgery and theft; Rice charged misdemeanor theft for meals eaten.
Kenneth Foster/ Gianluca Velissariou	USC	2005, 2 months	22	Black	M	Posed	Scammer	Prior felony car theft

Name	School	Year	Age	Race	Sex	Status	Type	Notes
Sheldon Ross	UCLA, graduate	2003 or 2004–2006	36	Black	M	Posed	Scammer	Prior indictment for grand theft credit card fraud; UCLA charged with burglary, identity fraud
Esther Reed/ Brooke Henson	Columbia	2004–2006	30	White	F	Enrolled	Scammer	Prior convictions for credit card and petty theft; serial identity theft
David Vanegas	Rice	2005–2006	20	Latino	M	Posed	Shammer	Rice charged with criminal trespass and theft for food supposedly eaten at dorms; no other known offenses
Michael Godelia	Harvard	2007	34	Black	M	Posed	Scammer	Prior conviction for criminal trespass and charges for sexual assault, burglary
Kevin Hart	Cal, football	2008	~17	White	M	Posed as recruit	Shammer	None known
Adam Wheeler	Harvard	2007–2009	23	White	M	Enrolled	Scammer	Serial plagiarism, from routine homework to applications for awards, including the Rhodes and other prestigious fellowships

This chart includes some figures of fair infamy and public fascination, along with many names of such scant mention that they were found and added here only after several rounds of "snowball" searching. Still, the list is surely incomplete, as no one seems to run an organized database of university impostors: "The National Student Clearinghouse, the main educational-credentials verification organization that works with more than 3,200 U.S. colleges and universities, doesn't even track statistics on fraud cases." (Jane Porter, "U.S. Colleges Stumped by Fraudulent Applications," *Bloomberg Business*, August 28, 2008, available at http://www.bloomberg.com/bw/stories/2008-08-28/u -dot-s-dot-colleges-stumped-by-fraudulent-applicationsbusinessweek-business-news-stock-market-and-financial-advice). Even the promisingly titled *Ultimate Book of Impostors* provides not an exhaustive inventory but only "Over 100" of the "Greatest Phonies and Frauds," including a single, solitary case from our own list. It would seem that trying to steal academic prestige does not make the grade among fraudsters. (Ian Graham, *The Ultimate Book of Impostors: Over 100 True Stories of the Greatest Phonies and Frauds* [Naperville, IL: Sourcebooks, 2013]. For James Hogue, see pp. 7–9.) Nonetheless, the twenty-three total cases listed in this book being those that our collective internet memory retains, the patterns they form are suggestive and meaningful.

* See endnote no. 9 in chapter 2.

Table 1.2 Asian College Impostors

Name/alias	Target institution	Ostensible area of study	Time frame	Age when caught	Ethnicity*	Sex	Enrolled or posed	Type	Deception/history of other offenses
Elizabeth Okazaki	Stanford; UCLA	Physics Ph.D.	2003–2007; 4 months	30s	Japanese	F	Posed	Shammer	Posed as graduate student; may have been homeless and lived in labs
Amit Kumar Sinha	UC Irvine	Medical school	2000–2005	28	Indian	M	Posed	Passer	Rented cap and gown to attend med school graduation; set off improvised explosive device and called in bomb threat to derail ceremony
Akash Maharaj	Yale	English	2005–2007	26	Indian (born in Trinidad/Tobago)	M	Enrolled	Scammer	Faked transcript and LORs, but did well in classes; later convicted of larceny for stolen credit card
Audley Yung	UC Riverside	Biological Sciences	2006–2007	22	~Chinese	M	Failed out	Passer	Set off improvised explosive device and called in bomb threat to derail graduation ceremony

Name	School	Field	Years	Age	Ethnicity	Sex	Posed	Passer/Shammer	Notes
Azia Kim	Stanford	Human Biology	2006–2007	18	Korean	F	Posed	Passer	
Jennifer Pan	Ryerson, U of Toronto	Pharmacology	2004–2010	24	Ethnic Chinese Vietnamese	F	Posed	Passer	
Abe Liu	Harvard		2010–2011	27	Taiwanese	M	Posed	Shammer	Harvard Extension student; joined Harvard social circles as Harvard College student
Birva Patel/Rhea Sen	Columbia	Engineering/Chemistry	2011–2012	27	Indian	F	Posed	Shammer	Lurked around/harassed first-year women, posing as one of them
Sara Kim	Harvard and Stanford	Math	April–June 2015	17/18	Korean	F	Claimed acceptance	Passer	

* See endnote no. 9 in chapter 2.

Shammers: Those whose motives are more idiosyncratic, less discernible. They pose for months or even years as students without any official status and, therefore, no possibility of degree. Yet neither do they seem to be working some angle on the side, any long con. I'd place the three remaining non-Asian impostors in this company (Patrick McDermit, David Vanegas, and Kevin Hart), along with three of the Asian impostors (Elizabeth Okazaki, Abe Liu, and Birva Patel).

Passers: College impostors come of all races, but only Asian shammers can or do pass for model minority. That is, the "passer" as strictly defined refers to this sliver of overlap between shammers and a much larger set: people performing model-minority identity. But because the premise of my argument is that "model minority" is a role Asian Americans are all scripted to play, I also use a loose definition by which most of us are "passers" to some degree. That I use the same term for stagings of the success frame whether everyday/normative or extreme/deceptive, shifting only in inflection throughout the book, is deliberate: I mean to make it difficult to enunciate a normal "us" as distinct from an anomalous "them." We look to the five remaining Asian college impostors because, as is so often the case, the inner workings of essential things become most legible when they go awry. Sara Kim belongs as much at the heart of this project as do Azia and Jennifer, but, her story (and the available information) being relatively brief, she makes her appearance here in the overview to help flesh out the genus, rather than occupying a chapter of her own. The last two figures, both men, would certainly bring passing into further relief here: showing it for a performance particularly irrational, especially counterproductive. You'll meet them in chapter four, however, where they'll do the most good by modeling the contrast between the strict and the broader ways of passing for perfect.

The aims of this first chapter are mostly descriptive, taxonomical. It sets the stage for the theoretical work that comes later. But if the classification system as I see it is persuasive, we will

build on the agreement that among college impostors, only passers are trying, however preposterously, to play by the rules—rules
they have internalized for belonging in Asian America. Moreover,
we'll know that such staging of model-minority success is possible to spot even from a distance: the genre of passers' life stories
clearly visible through the lenses of news coverage and the shape
of online chatter.

casts of characters

If college impostors have a classic type, the scammer would be
it. This because, well, the grifter/con artist figure is in itself a
classic type. They have shown up with their scams across centuries, continents, and social sets, but do favor lavishly wealthy
circles—because such lifestyles make for both better fleecing and
better indulging of their own flights of fancy. A casual survey of
human-interest stories nets the following in 2018: William Baeke-
land, né Jesse Simon Gordon of Birmingham, England, posed
as the heir to a fortune and bilked fellow world explorers out of
nearly a million dollars, when his own jet-setting charade seems
to have come to the end of its credit line;[1] Anthony Gignac, a
poor kid from Bogota, Colombia, passed himself off as one Saudi
royal after another, for decades, and was eventually indicted in
Miami of defrauding investors to the tune of $8 million;[2] Rus-
sian-born Anna Sorokin, a.k.a. Anna Delvey, played the social-
ite among New York's upper crust on a raft of friends' advances
and bank loans, the latter of which she sometimes pursued in
amounts upward of $25 million apiece;[3] Anna March is one of at
least four aliases for a woman who charmed and swindled literary, arts, political, or nonprofit scenes one after another in major
cities across the United States, the damage and ill-gotten gains
from which have yet to be fully tallied.[4] Compared to the above,
serial check forgers or compulsive thieves like James Hogue or
Lon Grammer, who fabricated applications and life stories for
themselves at Princeton and Yale, respectively, look very much

the small-timers: plying their trade in the halls of academia rather than on Fifth Avenue because their particular aspirations and fascinations drew them to the Ivy League.

So is there a whiff of something quaintly bookish, faintly charming about the academic grifter? After all, the shortest route to mad bling does not run through four years of coursework. Money, then, would not appear to be the primary driver for our scammers—*status* is, arguably, and self-identity. For this reason, larceny is not a requirement for scammer status in this taxonomy. (It is sufficient but not necessary.) One of the better-known impostors, Adam Wheeler has a biography dedicated to his exploits[5] but no record of nonacademic frauds or crimes. Granted, of course, the Harvard degree he nearly secured by cheating would likely have paved access to lucrative careers or more lucrative cons down the road. Indeed, he'd been mere inches from leveraging that status into highly coveted postgraduate fellowships, including the Rhodes and Fulbright scholarships, when he was caught. But let's see: A Fulbright scholarship covers travel and living expenses for the awardee and any dependents during their tenure in the award country, while a Rhodes scholarship comes with round-trip economy airfare and approximately $18,000 in annual stipend for the individual. On the whole, academic awards are not exactly cushy; what they do come loaded with are bragging rights.

It seems that, along with some prospect of material gain, academic scammers like attention. Granted, this isn't indicated in each and every profile, but, considering that the press on some of these impostors is a scant few paragraphs long, the incidence of braggadocio is striking. Generally, they are not content to have tricked the admissions office and then to lie low until commencement—though this would likely be the safest play. Instead, they embroider. Compulsively, it seems. James Hogue, already a gifted distance runner on the collegiate team (with ten years' advantage on his competitors, granted), and legitimately smart enough to ace infamous chemistry exams at Princeton, nonetheless felt the need to keep embellishing the myth/the legend of (self-educated,

Plato-reading, Nevada ranch hand) Alexi Santana: Presenting himself as "an exotic creature who wove fabulous stories about his wayward youth," he claimed, for instance, to have done ski stunts for some movie[6] and to sleep "on the floor in his room at Holder Hall."[7] To impress Yale, Lon Grammer doctored his community college transcript and forged glowing letters of recommendation. Once there, his grades hovered in the C and D range, but his fictionalizing seems not to have slacked: "Among other things, he claimed he had played minor-league baseball and was related to actor Kelsey Grammer"; peers reported that "one day, he would tell [them] he was in Mexico for three years, then he said he was in the Bahamas for three years."[8] And Adam Wheeler's downfall seems to have been a direct product of this same problem: that the status of merely being in and among the Ivy League did not sate. Over and over, he staked his public identity *above* those of his peers, even if that meant more cheating and more risk. Having transferred to Harvard on the fable of an ill-fitting first year at MIT and perfect SAT scores, Adam spent the next two years racking up highly touted poetry and other university writing awards, including "the $4,000 Hoopes Prize, $2,000 Sargent Prize and an $8,000 Rockefeller research grant, all through plagiarism."[9] While, in person, his temperament may have tended more to restraint than bluster, Adam let English-department award announcements and his fantastically inflated résumé do his showboating.[10] Still, his play for the Rhodes and Fulbright scholarships takes the cake. Faculty in an undergraduate's own department review these applications to select those worthy of advancing to the respective organizations. Thus it was that "James Simpson, a Harvard English professor, . . . [u]pon reviewing Wheeler's application, . . . discovered Wheeler had plagiarized the work of *Stephen Greenblatt, another Harvard English professor*, and notified university officials."[11] Stephen Greenblatt is very famous. Choosing his work to claim at all is high-risk behavior; within his own department, it is daredevil. So it's plausible to consider this choice an act of self-sabotage, and perhaps on some level it is, but it is also in keeping with Adam's pattern of raising the stakes for himself in a kind of unbridled one-upmanship with all of Harvard.

Such headlong self-inflation (to the point of bursting) would likely be tagged by psychologist Maria Konnikova as one of the personality hallmarks of the "con artist": "Narcissism entails a sense of grandiosity, entitlement, self-enhancement, an overly inflated sense of worth, and manipulativeness"; it characterizes "someone who can't stand to be seen as inferior, who needs to be the center of attention, and who will do what it takes to get there." Author of *The Confidence Game*, Konnikova offers a profile of grifters like Gordon, Gignac, Sorokin, and March—whose bilking of victims for great sums she considers psychopathic—as suggesting "the basic absence of empathetic feelings for . . . fellow human beings."[12] But I think to call our academic scammers that would be unfair; again, theirs is a less virulent strain of fraud. Indeed, that term is not much bandied about around college impostors, and informal consensus around Adam seems to reject psychopathology.[13] When the Harvard scam hit the press, his former high school principal was quoted as saying, "We were all thinking, 'This can't be our Adam Wheeler.'"[14] Could they be considered Machiavellian, if defined as using "aggressive, manipulative, exploiting, and devious moves in order to achieve personal and organizational objectives"? Possibly, though even that seems harsh. It's true that each scammer must have "identif[ied a] victim" and profiled that victim systematically: "who is he, what does he want, and how can I play on that desire to achieve what I want?"[15] But, for the college impostor, that victim is not one or more people; it is one or more institutions. It was Harvard itself that filed a "victim impact statement" with the court when Adam was busted,[16] because it was Harvard's confidence that he played: "What does an Adam Wheeler give them? More proof that the school is the pointy end of the pyramid in a great meritocracy, where only a select few belong."[17] Given the power differential, the would-be student seems more a check on a system than an exploiter of innocents. According to

Konnikova, "Over 40 percent [of grifters] were motivated by greed—but even more, just under half, *by a sense of superiority*, the hallmark of narcissism. They were simply better, they felt, and so they deserved more. Many reported being motivated by a sense of anger, of *being underpaid and undervalued*."[18] That is, academic scammers are driven equally by a sense of themselves as the underdog, *and* the conviction that they do not belong in the station to which they were born—that their rightful place is among a different class of people, performing social scripts that their friends and family at home would not recognize.

I take for my starting point three white male impostors in the Ivy League, in part because this neatly aligns the academic scammer with what is, again, an already recognized type in American culture—folklore and literature both. This is hardly an obscure association to make; media commentary on these cases is peppered by such insights: "Much like we admire Jay Gatsby's 'fevered strivings to reach the green light at the end of the dock, to invent a new name and a new past for himself and to win the love of Daisy Buchanan, . . . it is also hard not to admire James Hogue,' however deceptive his acts."[19] In fact, my next point is made for me in the *New Yorker*: "Self-invention is the founding subject of American literature. We celebrate the self-made man, and honor the dream of transcending one's origins; we are suckers for people who invent themselves from scratch."[20] But is this celebration capacious enough for female impostors, or people of color? Rather surprisingly, yes. Our single Asian scammer, Akash Maharaj subtracted about five years from his age and personal history, and submitted to Yale a transfer transcript full of "perfect A's" along with a professor's "glowing recommendation," both of his own creation.[21] His impostor profile most resembles Adam's, in that both enrolled fraudulently but had no other criminal records. In fact, the author of the book dedicated to Adam's (much more publicized) case directly compares them: "In a story that sounded awfully like [Adam's], Maharaj had spent two semesters as a transfer student at Yale, displayed an exuberant interest in pursuing a Ph.D. in English literature, and even won a writing prize."[22] Although Akash's racial background is identified (immigrant from Trinidad and Tobago, of Indian descent), the Yale newspaper likens him no less ardently to Horatio Alger and Jay Gatsby, saying, "his is a startlingly common story: A student who, swept up in an admissions frenzy, resorts to bending the rules to secure a spot among the elite."[23] Said quote could easily have been lifted from coverage on Adam or James.

That is, Akash's racial difference proves literally assimilable, to a quintessential narrative of what it is to be American: to come from nothing and become someone. In a culture to which Gatsby is fascinating, grifting is intelligible: behavior extreme and unethical, but rational, as a means to game a system in which status breeds status, and status is money. Said of Adam: "Like any rational economic actor, he sought to procure a diploma from the finest college, with maximum efficiency."[24] Said of James: "He simply wanted to get an education, what everybody else wants to do. It was the only way he could get into Princeton, so he got in."[25] Moreover, there's a tradition in literary scholarship that takes the Alger, Gatsby, or Benjamin Franklin figure—self-inventor, class traverser, appearance-conscious operator—as the prototype on which ethnic assimilation and racial passing are built.[26] So, indeed, remarkably little hay is made of Akash's ethnic, racial, or national identities. In that absence, his choices are granted to him as those of an individual rather than as determined by his cultural or even immigrant backgrounds. I'd venture, then, that while his hustle did not finally make Akash a Yalie, it briefly made him an honorary white male American.

unusual suspects

As a set, shammers slot into no such ready narratives. They essentially posed as students (or recruits) to no clear advantage, some for months and others for years. And, unlike Harvard (Extension) scammer Michael Godelia, for example, they didn't spend that time mining college networks to pitch "business schemes."[27] Their motivations tend to the more idiosyncratic or opaque. For starters, our earliest impostor Patrick McDermit seems to have spent a semester enrolled at Yale under alias, just to thumb his nose at the aristocracy. He imagined himself "the most amazing record possible," then played that outsize character until turning himself in to prevent the "joke [from becoming] an outright fraud." (He became instead the toast of the town).[28] The less merry stories of Kevin Hart and David Vanegas I'll reserve for later, as foils for differences in meaning between shamming and passing, compared to Sara and Azia, respectively. Meantime, I'll make the case that not all Asian Americans pretending to be college students are acting the part of the model minority, even if an elite university is their stage. Since such shammers are not trying to "pass" for white *or* Asian models of personhood, their exposure (even in the press) does not gel into racial meanings.

In 2011, twenty-seven-year-old Abe (Yi-Fan) Liu was booted from the Harvard campus, where he had insinuated himself into freshman social life for most of a semester: eating in the dining halls, crashing periodically in the dorms, and going to campus parties. It is known that he studied sports management at North Carolina State College until at least Fall 2006 before dropping out.[29] This leaves about five years unaccounted for before he began at Harvard Extension School and also began to "troll" the incoming Harvard College class on Facebook, eventually pretending to be one of them. Abe is the only one of our Asian American impostors to have given an interview when caught out, and in it he declares that his deception began with no particular plan, just as "an attempt to gain friends that spiraled out of control." The *Harvard Crimson* quotes him as saying, "The first lie is like, 'Oh, I'm a student at the College.' . . . They always want to know more, so you start telling a lot of little white lies. And then you find yourself integrated into that society.'"[30] The lies grew, not only to keep his ship afloat but also to showboat, for instance, as a "former Olympian who had played in Beijing for either the United States or China, depending on who he was talking to."[31]

Absent obvious monetary motives, the questions raised by this character choice are awkward ones: What is a man in his late twenties gleaning from his intimacy with people nearly a decade his junior? Some of the secondary reporting (commentary pieces, summaries) declares him "creepy," but most echo the title given to the original *Crimson* article: "Weld Visitor Abe Liu: I Was Lonely." Taking Abe's own explanation at face value, headlines like "'Lonely' 27-year-old posed as Harvard Freshman for Months" turn the emotional state into a personality attribute, and a notably individual one.[32] This angle could easily skew to the socially awkward Asian male, it's true—all the more remarkable, then, that it does not, leaving Abe, instead, untagged and ambiguous. Nowhere do journalists or commentators narrate him as a representative "type": not of Asian men or Taiwanese immigrants, but certainly not of America itself, either. That is, in contrast to scammers as a group, shammers are treated like one-offs: laughed with like Patrick or laughed at like Abe, but not deemed emblematic or symptomatic of something larger than themselves.

Same goes for Birva Patel, another twenty-seven-year-old escorted from an Ivy League campus. Birva posed as a junior in engineering at Columbia at least as early as December 2011 but was arrested at the end of Fall 2012 orientation. By that point, she was calling herself Rhea Sen, introducing herself as an incoming freshman, and beggaring belief with her contradictory lies and odd behavior. "She approached [young women] and all but demanded to be friends" but might later send them rambling "Facebook messages littered with misspellings and dozens of English and Hindi curses."[33] According to reports, while "nobody actually saw her in the residence halls," people did see her "running around, hiding in bushes."[34] Whether students felt threatened by her ("I felt like she was psychotic"), however, or dismissed her as harmless ("others wrote [off her lies] as the behavior of an awkward student"), her actions were construed as functions of a disordered mind.[35] What speculation there is, ends with a shrug: "Perhaps she's homeless, some conjecture—but no one really knows";[36] no cultural patterns or broader narratives seem to stick. Granted, Birva was apparently so patently terrible at this that she made all impostors look bad: "College impostors aren't a new phenomenon, but they're always so much less driven and enterprising in real life than in, say, some billionaire's memoir about bootstraps, elbow grease and spit shine."[37] But we know that to be an unfairly broad dismissal: For one thing, its disappointed writer seems to have had scammers in mind, and Birva doesn't qualify; for another, shammers just don't reward generalization.

For four years in her thirties, Elizabeth Okazaki claimed to be a graduate student in physics at Stanford and loitered about campus. Not until 2007, in the media firestorm following Azia's removal, did Stanford administrators decide also to oust Elizabeth, who packed her things and immediately tried to start a similar (though, ultimately, much shorter-lived) sham at UCLA. At the Stanford Varian lab, the oddness of her presence had been an open secret. She horned in on conversations between researchers, despite clearly having no concept of theoretical physics; if questioned about her affiliation to the lab, she claimed to be dating various graduate students at various times (news to them). There's uncertainty as to whether she was homeless but none regarding the fact that she was not authorized to be there: Except for the instance in which security found her in possession of someone else's card key, she left doors propped open for entry, compromising the security of equipment and people.[38] That no one saw compelling need to expel her until bad press loomed may speak to a generous threshold for the "loopy" in that particular space or to her savvy navigation of higher-education institutions and their norms. For UCLA, she concocted a "project on the philosophy of music," and it was the philosophy department that granted her affiliate status; this comprised very nominal affiliation to the university and courtesy

library access . . . via her own BruinCard. With that slender pass-
port, she occupied the library for "up to eight hours a day, and
[used] recreational facilities, where she would store some of her
possessions"[39]—arguably the incarnation of resourcefulness but,
again, to what end is anyone's guess. Aside from the campus settings, it's hard even to say what is academic about Elizabeth's
shams. Certainly, she was after no degree, but, unlike Abe and
Birva, neither did she seem to yearn for college-life membership:
No one counted her a friend; no one related that she had attempted
to befriend them. It's as if she was in it for the infrastructure—
computers, hot water, and the like—and research universities were
simply well-stocked hubs with weak barriers to entry.

Implausible though it may be—that deviance exhibited by people
of color consistently *not be cast* in racial terms in Western press—
narratives about the shammers above include neither explicit nor
slyly "coded" theories about race or culture. As a surprising whole,
discussions of Abe, Birva, and Elizabeth seem satisfied that each
is aberrant, weird—a conclusion that is not an explanation. At
best guess, racial effects seem present in the negative: a shallow-
ness of curiosity, a lack of intrigue regarding the backgrounds or
personas of these outliers. Their press coverage is relatively limited (on average maybe four pages apiece of Google results), and
none of them is deemed worthy of a profile piece investigating
their childhoods or psyches. Of course, this is not to rule out *any*
role race might have played to begin with, in how these "visible
minorities" were perceived; we haven't sufficient information to
do much ruling out of anything. And it may seem fair to attribute
some administrative nonchalance around Elizabeth's unautho-
rized presence to race-colored glasses—to wit, "the Little Asian
Woman theory, wherein because one is little and non-threatening
in appearance one is safe and should be allowed to roam freely
in a secured building."[40] . . . But then again, meet Sheldon Ross.

A minor operative on our scammer list, Sheldon is a Black
man who posed as a math graduate student at UCLA. During

this time, he is said to have "infiltrated UCLA life: he wrote an article for the *Bruin Standard* and a submission to the *Daily Bruin* Viewpoint section, played rugby, . . . was elected editor of *Nommo*, an African American newsmagazine,"[41] and joined the Bruin Republicans. The ruse about being a student seems to have folded quickly, yet he was not prevented from continuing to sneak into the Student Media publication offices and squatting all weekend. He is not known to have feigned coursework; he *is* known to have urinated in disposable cups around the office overnight.[42] Sheldon was discovered there several times over a period of three years, but, defying any expectations about perceptions of race/gender and criminality, "he was simply asked to leave. It wasn't until [July 2006] that the police were called"[43] to arrest him for the first (not the last) time. At the time of his arrest, he had an "outstanding felony warrant in Alameda County for grand-theft credit card fraud"; at his trial, the operations manager for the UCLA Student Media Center testified that Sheldon had stolen "a door from [their] office, along with a hard-drive and some money out of the desks."[44]

Now that doing quite literally anything #WhileBlack is demonstrably apt to be criminalized, it's hard to believe that Sheldon's story took place merely over a decade ago, and not a science-fiction universe away. Yet his scam seems to have subsisted narratively in a nonspace that was neither upwardly thriving (and allowed as white) nor criminally threatening (and shut down as Black). That is, while his larceny makes Sheldon technically not a shammer, his behavior and Elizabeth's have a great deal in common—not least that neither was performing a recognized racial script. On Sheldon, Google yields only three solid, individual results, all from the *Daily Bruin*. This story of a thirty-six-year-old Black man with a police record, who lied about who he was and loitered at a university for several years, while doing nothing terribly criminal or productive, then was eventually charged with petty theft, was not found newsworthy by a single outside media source. Perhaps, like other shammer stories, it made no sense.

There is little point second-guessing, of course, why a particular incident was not picked up in the press, but it may be nonetheless enlightening to consider what the general principles are for this type of thing. Budding journalists learn basic priorities by which news outlets decide to pick up a story via lists like the following:

1. Timeliness
2. Conflict
3. The unexpected
4. Routine typifications
5. A preference for big "names" and official viewpoints
6. Superficial acquaintance-with information (as opposed to a more analytical knowledge-about)
7. Objectivity[45]

All college impostor stories meet the first three criteria as well as (in the form of big-name schools) the fifth. Those that also meet the fourth thereby satisfy all top five qualifications in a row—but, as college applicants well know, to qualify is not necessarily to be chosen. Still, of those that do go viral, all have number four to their name. (See Table 1.3.)

Table 1.3 Search Results circa 2018

Impostor	#4	Search results
James Hogue	✓	19 pages of Google results and counting, a book, and a movie
Adam Wheeler	✓	25-plus pages of Google results and a book
Azia Kim	✓	13-plus pages
Jennifer Pan	✓	16 pages, a book, TV news and several crime programs, and a true-crime podcast episode
Sara Kim	✓	7-plus pages in English, in addition to coverage by at least six major South Korean newspapers and unenumerated television footage
Abe Liu	⊘	5-plus pages
Birva Patel	⊘	2-plus pages
Elizabeth Okazaki	⊘	3-plus pages
Sheldon Ross	⊘	3 hits

The magic, when it happens, arguably has to do with items three and four together. Seemingly contradictory, their conjunction is actually key: News is understood to be more persuasive, more compelling "if it represents events that fit our models without being completely predictable." Combined, these values dictate that "the most unexpected or rare events—*within those that are culturally familiar and/or consonant*—will have the greatest chance of being selected as news."[46] While Abe, Birva, and Elizabeth are lightly dismissed as anomalies, press and ensuing discussions of "passers" indulge extensively in "routine typifications" of model-minority culture. And while, again, it's dicey to speculate on cause and effect between these patterns, turn from the scammers or shammers to our first actual specimen, and the difference is hard to miss. Passers do what they do for reasons economically unfathomable, but emotionally transparent—if not transparent to media then to fellow model minorities in the making.

saying too much

For maybe a week Sara Kim was "Genius Girl"—darling of the South Korean and then Korean American press, apple of any Ivy-minded parent's eye. It was spring of her senior year at Thomas Jefferson High School for Science and Technology (TJ) in Virginia, and Sara had made a batch of false claims, including to a 4.6 GPA, a perfect 2400 SAT score, and to "math research . . . so revolutionary that she was receiving calls from both Harvard University and Stanford University" to woo her, along with efforts by Harvard alumnus Mark Zuckerberg himself.[47] But the crux of her madcap charade was (per the June 2015 announcement in *Chosun Ilbo*, "one of South Korea's biggest newspapers") that:

> Kim initially opted for Harvard, but Stanford wanted her too and struck a deal with Harvard to create a unique program for her. She will study at Stanford during her freshman and sophomore years and then at Harvard for

her junior and senior years. She can then choose from which school she takes her bachelor's degree.[48]

To back up the story of what would have been an unprecedented offer, she forged wincingly bad acceptance letters and, later, missives from renowned faculty and admissions officials defending her against doubters. As none of these forgeries could yield admission to either school, Sara's exposure was always a matter of time, but likely the end was hastened by the lie's quick leap from family fib to international news. The *Korea Daily* learned of the story through a connection to her father, an executive based in DC for a South Korean gaming company. This led to "wall-to-wall," "breathless coverage in the Korean media," hailing Sara as the girl "who made her parents immensely proud."[49] While it's fair to wonder what Sara could hope to gain from "an obviously unsustainable lie,"[50] among those who knew her there was no mystery: "The answer seems obvious to students and teachers [at her school]: overwhelming pressure to succeed from parents and unrealistic expectations from the teens themselves."

TJ is a highly selective magnet school "very popular in Northern Virginia's Korean community," among immigrant and expat families alike. As the region's high-tech sector, that part of the state does have a high concentration of ethnic Korean and Indian residents: upward of 20 percent in the county, compared to about 7 percent in the state.[51] Still, in fall 2016, the school's entering class was 70 percent Asian, telltale sign of a certain kind of academic culture: one personified by a "senior who earned a 4.57 grade point average, aced 13 Advanced Placement tests and founded a national non-profit before her 18th birthday," earning her "admission to all eight Ivy League schools, *a story that made national headlines.*" TJ's director of student services explained its atmosphere by using that classmate as a frame of reference, no less: "We celebrate the accomplishment of students who get into all eight Ivies. . . . That's the bar."[52] Behind this royal "we" is patently a Western school administration "caught up in the 'prestige'" generated by its star pupils.[53] Meanwhile, for some commentators, the Kims' status as South Korean nationals made for quick work: blame that culture's "unhealthy obsession with academic elitism," file the incident away as part of their pattern of "academic forgery cases."[54] But, clearly, the media itself—Western as much as Eastern, international and domestic—was part of the problem. On the selfsame pages of articles denouncing unhealthy academic pressure, it was common to find web links to "related" reading with headlines like these: "Son of Immigrants Accepted to Every Ivy League School: Where He'll Attend in the Fall" (YahooParenting); "Harvard Tops List of World University Rankings" (*The Independent*); "Kim Tae Hee Reveals How She Got into Seoul National University" (Soompi).[55]

In fact, citizenship status be what it may, Asian American readers were swift to recognize Sara's struggle as their own. To Jeff Yang, the *Wall Street Journal*'s then-columnist for things Asian American, Sara is an "example of a young Asian American pushed to the limits and beyond by the stress of academic success at all costs, measured in greatest part by the name of the college that offers acceptance." To anchor the demographics of the pattern, Yang drops a few more examples:

> Chinese American senior Mira Hu, who had been dropped off to take the SATs by her parents, went missing for nearly a week after declaring she was "overwhelmed" by the pressures she experienced to succeed academically. She was a senior at San Marino High School, a top-performing Southern California school with a student body that's two-thirds Asian American.
>
> Palo Alto's Gunn High School—rated the 4th best STEM school in the nation by *U.S. News and World Report*, with a student body that is 44% Asian—has been rocked by a string of suicides, including four deaths over just the past six months. Three of the students who took their lives were Asian American.[56]

What makes these examples so on-point is Yang's care to note the composition of the student body at each of the high schools in question. Sociologists Jennifer Lee and Min Zhou would, I think, be impressed. The "success frame" they describe ("earning straight A's, graduating as the high school valedictorian, earning a degree from an elite university, attaining an advanced degree, and working in one of four high-status professional fields: medicine, law, engineering, or science") as defining Asian American identity is weightiest in schools where immigrants' kids form the demographic default and the dominant academic culture. Both San Gabriel Valley and Silicon Valley, home to San Marino and Palo Alto, respectively, are to Lee and Zhou prime examples of ground zero.[57]

But this is not to say that Yang and other readers saw schools alone as driving desperation like Sara's. Readers were unabashed about filling in the blanks of her story with material from their own family lives. From a crop of discussion forums:

- I'm Korean myself, and I know a lot of my friends were pushed into going into the best high schools and best colleges. Along the way, my friends and I would get beaten by our parents and basically told that if you don't get into the best, you're basically failing. That does play a huge role in this, I feel like. That pressure to do the best is a big motivating factor. . . . I tried for med school, partly due to family pressures, and I failed. I mentioned going into nursing school, and my parents just immediately asked me to reconsider. My mom told me afterward she was crying all night.[58]
- My parents are guilty of this too . . . The obsession with university ranking and league tables. . . . People laud over the Tiger Moms of Asia but in actual fact this is nothing more than human beings imposing their own selfish desires and ideals on their offsprings, more often than not to fulfill some dream that they themselves

have not managed, or to raise the social status of their family to something accepted by a society, which itself is completely devoid of originality when it comes to measuring success.[59]

Since the publication of Amy Chua's memoir, *Battle Hymn of the Tiger Mother* (2011), "Tiger Parenting" has evolved into popular shorthand for what is essentially success-frame parenting, associated with Asian immigrant families. Its hallmarks are intense discipline plus scant consideration to the niceties of a child's well-being. While this chapter leaves aside, for now, theoretical discussion of success frames, Tiger moms, and the like, it should already be clear that what Sara inspired are "routine typifications"—abundant discussions of cultural type and racial form. And that the shammers did not.

That is, despite expectations that "people immediately assume it's parental pressure when the kid is Asian,"[60] the evidence is manifestly to the contrary. Even in the face of superficially quite similar situations (Asian impostor, elite university), Abe, Birva, and Elizabeth elicited not *less* of the above-style comments from press and readers; they elicited *none*. Garnering *zero* speculation regarding family, parenting, academic or cultural pressure, their ruses did not hail as racial conventions, racial performances. Reader comments in the *Crimson* mused about Abe being a reflection on Harvard's relationship with its Extension School or debated the journalistic standards of the *Crimson* versus the rival *Independent's* reporting of the story; comments on other sites primarily wondered about the security breach and crowed their schadenfreude.[61] His cultural meaning, though, was evidently nothing readers were interested in exploring. Discussions of Birva often dwelled on giddy descriptions of past encounters with her and her strangeness. The more sympathetic commenters expressed pity for her presumably desperate plight.[62] But no one expressed *em*pathy; at best her story elicited magnanimity, not affinity. As for Elizabeth, her story seems to have generated very little online discussion, aside from some spirited sparring among physicists because one called her a "science groupie." At Stanford, one source "suggested that Okazaki likely was looking for somebody in the physics department to provide for her. '. . . I think she wants a sugar daddy. If she can latch onto some grad student . . . , I think she thinks that the professor's wife would be just the lifestyle for her.'"[63] She may have been the object of sexist watercooler talk, but of racial typifications, no.

Not that the case for Sara's racial passing is limited to how others write about her. An impostor's motivation is pivotal to this argument, and the categorical difference with hers can be gleaned from two key comparisons. For one, until Sara, we had only known Asian impostors to be in their late twenties or even thirties, busily disclaiming four to nine years of their ages so as to pose among undergraduates (primarily) as peers. This holds true even for our scammer Akash (twenty-five at the time of his transfer to Yale), though less so for Elizabeth (in her thirties): Because graduate school has a less conventionally defined age range, deviation from the average is less meaningful, presumably requiring less specificity from her about that particular lie. Still, there is a marked and meaningful age gap splitting the Asian impostors, because, as people out of sync with their generational peers, whatever the shammers (and Akash) were trying to achieve cannot be described as *conformity* to an orthodox timetable. As readers would know implicitly, American society's standard life stage for the late twenties is not to be a college student (and there is no "standard" expectation to attend graduate school in physics, much less to do research in philosophy—Elizabeth's cover stories). Maintaining the illusion of normative progress, therefore, cannot be the shammers' aim. After all, what was each doing during the four years that are conventionally spent in college? Was it not already obvious to family members, childhood friends, any interested observers from home that these young people had stopped marching in time? Even supposing they had carried off serial college charades, how to explain starting undergraduate over again at twenty-seven?

This means that age is not incidental in the taxonomy of impostors, factoring into both personal motivation and (public) perception. Azia, Jennifer, and Sara were all graduating seniors—about seventeen or eighteen years old—when they began their college charades. Time was of the essence: Their lies uniformly allowed these passers to *remain in alignment* with their high school peers, appearing to adhere to normative educational progress. What this tells us about the success frame is *how horribly rigid* it is. Yes, it counts all but the most prestigious universities as failure, that's no news: To immigrants with limited knowledge of the United States, higher education, or both, a liberal arts college with no name-recognition among equally uninformed relatives would look worthless, wasteful. What's news here is, when success is the delivery of perfection, perfection brooks no delay. "Not only was a specific educational track critical to the success frame from the perspective of immigrant parents, but parents also strongly disapproved of and *admonished any deviation* from it."[64] Indirect routes are deviation; lagging is deviation. The success frame permits no such luxuries as a "gap year" in order to reapply to the Ivies, or two years of community college before a transfer to Berkeley. Sure, deviations of this sort can and do happen, and those for whom the admission letter or transfer eventually materializes do recover some grace. But, in the grim (indefinite) interim, they are failures. They stand out from among their peer groups as rejects; it is not every seventeen- or eighteen-year-old who can bear to don such a scarlet letter.

Very much related to this is the second quality distinctive to passers. Whatever the drama they are each performing, scammers and shammers generally do not intend it for the home-viewing audience; passers do. Exhibit A: Four of the scammers and two of the shammers chose false identities to go by; of the passers, none did. An alias is not the only way to introduce a firewall between one's present and one's past, but it is rather the industry standard. Even among those who don't scramble their names, it is still safe to say that for anyone with a prior criminal history, having folks back at home privy to current campus activities would increase risk of exposure—so add seven scammers (including Akash) to the tally of those likely to keep their former friends and loved ones in the dark. And, accordingly, there is barely any mention of family to be found in news about these sets of impostors. Many of them are adults well beyond the age of parental supervision, granted, so perhaps it is understandable that for most—including Abe, Birva, and Elizabeth—their upbringings don't come up. But so little is said about college-aged Adam's parents *even in the book* about him that one Amazon reviewer felt compelled to ask, "What were his parents doing while this was happening?"[65] What little is divulged about scammers' and shammers' hometowns and backgrounds is usually packaged as nonexplanatory (bafflingly so) or uninteresting. James's parents are depicted as decent and caring, utterly normal, people: "What the parents of Wyandotte County wanted for their children was a life that would allow them to spend weekends with their family and then to wake up Monday morning, put on a suit, and drive to the office in a shiny new American-made car."[66] His impostor ways are a narrative mutation. There are exceptions to this implied parental nonrelevance: David Vanegas's mom, for discussion in the next chapter, and Kevin Hart, whose story comes shortly.[67] But typical of media treatment of the parental role is the *Yale Daily News*'s profile of Akash, which mentions his parents' professions (high school teacher, banker) but says nothing of their having influenced his choices, much less of their having been implicated.

In terms of "home" viewership, Sara's turn in the spotlight is not actually so far removed from everyday life for Asian Americans who genuinely attend Harvard. This is what anthropologist Christine Yano gleans from the student stories she collected while teaching there: that having landed the role of a lifetime, students find themselves performing not only for a public of "high school classmates, school districts, [and] hometowns" but also for an ethnic and communal network that "can even extend overseas" to "relatives [who] may not know exactly what goes on at the college campus, but . . . understand well that this particular campus counts."[68] Sara's circumstances, however, afford an uncommonly good view of the active role parents play in priming these audiences. Hers promoted and then defended a narrative they clearly relished telling. Both parents joined Sara in granting interviews to print, radio, and television news outlets overseas and in the United States. "[Sara] 'answered the phone one day and it was Zuckerberg, so she was surprised,' her mother told the Korean publication Newsis." It was, in fact, her father who supplied her childishly written admissions letters to reporters. One, supposedly composed by a dean of admissions, reads in part, "Also, originally, in the acceptance package for Harvard, there are a lot more documents but I had to take some out due to the other research papers given from your professors."[69] When challenged about the veracity of the story, the Kim parents, like their daughter, doubled down, indicating that they'd look to sue their doubters for defamation. The shame-faced public apology that Mr. Kim eventually issued to Korean papers may have been excessive in taking sole, personal blame, but it was also an insufficient statement of the problem: "Everything is my fault and my responsibility . . . I regret having pushed my child into deeper sickness."[70] This states his guilt as failing to recognize his daughter's particular pathology—not as having raised her into a harmful (and widely validated) mindset nor as having taken it for victory laps when it metastasized. As her parents took the stakes of her lie global, it would have been ever more wrenching for the girl to stop that juggernaut with the truth.

To see this more distinctly—the parents' role as well as its public perception—we look to another contrast. On the Friday in 2008 before high school seniors could begin to sign college athletic scholarships, Kevin Hart called a press conference. In front of local media, school administrators and students, and his family, he pulled on a Cal cap to signify that he would sign with UC Berkeley's football team. The hoax began to unravel almost immediately. Had it been real, his Division-1 scholarship would have been a historical first for his small rural school and an enormous financial relief for his family's modest means. One reporter describes Kevin's father "during the momentous school assembly" as "holding back tears." But press coverage at the time includes no quotes from the parents, who were mentioned only as part of the audience before things fell apart, and who afterward declined to comment, citing an investigation.[71]

Some commenters took the cultural hype around college football to task for this hoax:

> Maybe the family wanted to believe. Maybe the school staff and the locals went along with it, because . . . the glory of being recruited was too seductive to question.
>
> And therein lies the problem. We have turned college recruitment into an entertainment seduction. Why on earth do we allow high school athletes to call news conferences to announce their college choices? . . . Do we do the same for chemistry majors?[72]

Others wondered how Kevin's parents had allowed the charade to happen, accusing them of negligence: "Nationally and locally, people blamed his parents for being naive about college recruiting, for being utterly out of touch, for being too detached."[73] But, across the board, Kevin's football dreams are assumed to be his own, not those of "the hardworking father and mother who trusted him."[74] This is a far cry from the reproachful speculations made about Sara's parents—and a striking contrast given that both teens were high school seniors pretending to recruitment from prestigious colleges. Again, it would be foolish to imagine that race does nothing to color these perceptions—and yet, again, it would also be unwise to overlook the real differences in evidence. In none of the coverage leading up to or immediately after Kevin's press conference do his parents assist, much less take the lead, in telling the story. During his finest moment, they sit outside the spotlight and never take the mic to preen for the press. Whatever this may say about the Harts, it underscores by contrast the Kims' appropriation of their daughter's story, their eagerness for the glow of her putative success to bathe them. To whatever extent Sara's achievements were about her parents, then, equally so must her "sickness" be.

the plot thickens

Judging by Sara, then, this is how we know a passer: Her primary audience is her loved ones, and her performance is powered by widely held expectations. She lies to meet the terms of their love, because falling short is too punishing an option—but small lies spin quickly out of orbit when one's finish line is really a horizon: "Regardless of what they have achieved, they (or their parents) know someone who has achieved more."[75] So, while to the untrained eye, Sara's press conferences and phone interviews may look identical to Kevin's, or like a version of the showboating that Adam or James indulged in, remember: In a culture of overachievers, "we celebrate the accomplishment of students who get into all eight Ivies. . . . *That's the bar.*"[76] To the Kims, being parents of the "Genius Girl" felt just about right. Fundamentally, then, passers lie not to serve their own dreams or as cover for their ulterior ends—but for the time and space that the lie itself buys. Even when there is no foreseeable outcome but disaster, they pass for model minority for a little bit longer—for however long they can—because they have absorbed the success frame not as a means but as the end-all of being an Asian immigrant's child.

Finally, we know a passer by how much of themselves Asian American readers see in her. To abuse a cliché, who better to appreciate the artful application of a model-minority résumé than others who know well the same work of beautification and concealment? Granted, viewing these cases only through the aperture of media coverage puts a hard limit on what we can, factually, determine. On the other hand, that frame is itself data: snapshots of the meaning-making such events trigger, via narratives told and retold by publics who found them worth passing along. Publications knowingly tend their "lexical cohesion," selecting stories "to fit into a consistent worldview and longer narratives of social belonging and identification."[77] Presented to a mainstream readership, however, figures like Sara, Azia, and Jennifer may appeal *either* because they seem to reflect "socially-shared norms, values, and attitudes" *or* because they seem to embody alien values such that "it confirms our negative schemata about such persons or" cultures.[78] Among *non*-Asian readers/writers, the genre of these stories seems indeterminate: They might be curios, parables, comedies, tragedies. . . . But, as I show in later chapters, which deep-dive into the commentary around Azia and Jennifer, within Asian American readerships there is a high current of feeling that (though endings may surprise) this type of story they know.

Note that, analytically speaking, "genre" here should also begin to take on its proportions from literary scholar and philosopher Lauren Berlant's work, as not merely conventions that organize stories but conventions that organize people:

> To call an identity like a sexual identity a genre is to think about it as something repeated, detailed, and stretched while retaining its intelligibility, its capacity to remain readable or audible across the field of all its variations. For femininity to be a genre *like* an aesthetic one means that it is a structure of conventional expectation that people rely on to provide certain kinds of affective intensities and assurances.[79]

That social roles like student or girlfriend are learned, that they come with (detailed) scripts and (repeated) norms has been a matter of common sense because of its general acceptance in sociology and psychology, since at least the early twentieth century. The notion that social *identities* like gender and race also work like verbs rather than nouns—that one *does* femininity rather than *is* feminine, that one *performs* race rather than *embodies* it—this is of more recent vintage, traceable most to philosopher Judith Butler's work in the late 1980s. Coining the term "performativity," Butler made it possible to see the perpetual work that goes into being recognizably the things that one supposedly was born. Performativity also explained that it is possible to fail at one's presumed identity and to reap the consequences.

To this, Berlant adds narrative and longing. She uses "genre" to flag the types of stories we tell ourselves about how the world works, what places are ours within it, what makes sense and will likely happen from here. Moreover, our hopes and hearts are bound up in these rules for the plots of living:

> A "genre" is an emotionally invested, patterned set of expectations about how to act and how to interpret, which organises a relationship between the acting and interpreting subject, their feelings and impressions, their struggles and their historical present. Genres also organise conventions about what might be hoped for, explicitly or secretly, and the bargains that can be made with life.[80]

And, here, as with novels or movies, genres are story forms we share. Like members of a reading club, we become adept at their conventions, adroit at picking up on them and rating one storyteller's iteration against another's: moving or unconvincing, predictable or ingenious. So, to live a given social identity as genre is to look to its formulas for codes of conduct and modes of explanation and to be legible to each other as its creatures.

Genre and its logical extension, cruel optimism, are mighty concepts, in ways the next two chapters increasingly enumerate. For this first pass, suffice to say that whether people or choices "make sense" is a matter of which plots they are bent on following. In *The Female Complaint*, Berlant demonstrates the loop within which femininity as a genre holds its would-be subjects: sold love (romantic, normative, sentimental, utterly conventional) as life's true meaning, driven to crisis by its ongoing insufficiency, and persuaded to persevere because love is the thing that will prevail. Across her seven chapters, Berlant shows sentimentality taking narrative hold of one realm of disappointment or failure after another—whether political, racial, or personal—and rerouting its anger or agency into generic explanations, generic (holding) patterns of response. Much the same can be said for the genre of model-minority identity. Whatever the arena of conflict—poverty or workplace discrimination, social isolation or emotional despair—to persevere as model minority is the "logic of rescue."[81] Utterly conventional, strictly normative, its vision of the "good life"[82] is reachable only via the Four Paths of Professional Virtue.

Among those tuned to this frame of reference, stories of fellow travelers are met like versions of the self at a casting call: all auditioning for the same part. In blogs, in chatrooms, in opinion or human-interest pieces long and short, were Asian American voices who answered to Sara's, Azia's, and Jennifer's stories as if someone were taking roll. But for Abe or Birva, Elizabeth or Akash, no. Scammers, we abhor or admire, as those who broke the rules or bested the game. Shammers, we see as players in a comedy, maybe laugh at their expense. But, in fellow travelers, we who have passed the same way read our own racial tragedies, narrowly averted or yet to come.[83]

chapter two

Exemplary

On May 24, 2007, just two weeks from the start of spring quarter final exams, the *Stanford Daily* reported that someone who had "seemed like a pretty typical Stanford student" had been posing as a freshman since New Student Orientation.[1] Explaining that she "was temporarily out of housing due to a technical mixup," Azia Kim initially managed to persuade a pair of roommates to allow her to stay with them, crashing for two full quarters in Kimball Hall. In April, she finagled her way into a vacancy on the ground floor of the Asian American theme dorm (Okada), which room she entered each day by climbing through a window she purposely left ajar. Azia crafted and tended her deception with the fastidiousness of an undercover agent: She learned the exam schedules for courses she claimed to be taking, "going as far as to buy textbooks [and] study with friends for tests she would never take," and posted of stress or excitement to her Xanga blog with the rhythm of classes. The audience for this ruse was, therefore, not only—and arguably not primarily—the Stanford freshmen; it included her sister, her parents, their extended family, and also friends and church members back in Fullerton, California, where she had graduated from what the *Daily* referred to as "one of California's most competitive high schools." No reporter was able to obtain interviews with Azia or her immediate family, so none could shed light on some fairly basic facts about the ruse: What, for one, did she tell her parents about tuition payments? But still the story caught quickly—careening from the campus paper to national news in under a day—with a narrative frame that implicated race, named culture.

This chapter is about Azia, but it is also about a story of shared proportions: in which failure is too ruinous to admit and acceptance too narrowly defined. Picking up where chapter one left off, I next argue that Azia is exemplary of our particular sort of college impostor: the sort passing for her own racial type. In other words, this profile dwells not on what made Azia an outlier at Stanford but on what allowed her stunt to go unchallenged for so long. "Exemplary" begins with media accounts and responses, combined with a short story that fictionalizes her exploits. Public record captures some of the facts of the case, along with something of the genre and its readers: an "intimate public" that shares the narrative logic of her story, even if they themselves manage a more conventional plot. Starting as herself a reader of this genre, author Vanessa Hua backtracks the saga to its logical beginnings, such that her story "Accepted" furnishes us with one fully rendered imagining of how a person might come to be in Azia's predicament. Interviews have a part to play in this chapter as well, and we will get to them. Conversations I've had with people who knew Azia during high school and at Stanford afford certain glimpses of her beyond what appeared online: enough to confirm the collective wisdom in some ways and to test it in others. Nonetheless, the crux of the argument here has less to do with who that individual was (a biography this is not) than with what her story tells us.* After all, as a literary critic it

---

* Endnotes in this and remaining chapters periodically include supplemental instances from a collection of first-person essays on the condition of being Har-

has been my MO to look to novels or films for imprints left by the cultural moments that produced them. Even (or especially) when fictional, narratives are like amber for belief systems, emotional investments, social norms. In cultural studies, the work of identifying clichés of representation generally comes just before denouncing those representations as false: hostile, biased, misleading. In ethnic studies, it is a disapproving truism that readers always have their race lenses on. But this chapter holds that to see racial meanings, or to be attuned to clichés, is not always to see or hear what isn't there. Sometimes it is to receive the intended message, to recognize what has painstakingly been made visible.

about the reader

Azia's story was found newsworthy by publications as varied as *Fox News*, *Inside Higher Education*, and LaFlecha.net (a Spanish-language blog covering science and technology). Major outfits sought interviews with the resident assistant in charge of the Okada dorm during Azia's stay, Takeo Rivera, who obliged the *San Francisco Chronicle* but, as the press grew more wolfish, declined to appear on CNN.[2] Outlets attempting to do reporting sought commentary from Azia's peers in high school or college or from members of the Kims' church, and those interviewees who spoke on record gave positive, puzzled endorsements of her. Her youth pastor, Bert Yun, declared her "a motivated and diligent teenager," of whom "any deception would be 'out of character.' 'Why would she do that?' he asked. 'She's a very good person.'"[3] High school classmate Huy Nguyen, reported to have "just completed his freshman year at Harvard," described her as "brilliant," "hard working and a straight shooter. . . . 'She's one of the nicest people,' he said. 'She works so hard, and she wasn't terribly competitive. I don't understand how

---

vard undergrads. While bracketed from the main argument when redundant, that very redundancy bears some note, as attesting to the continuity between the Icon and the Impostor: *both* of them playing the part of "those who have achieved what every Tiger Mom (and Dad) wants." (Yano and Akatsuka, *Straight A's*, 9.)

this could have happened."[4] The overall portrait of Azia that thus emerged in the press, while fragmentary, is not idiosyncratic; it sounds commonplace and, in its vagueness, widely applicable. In other words, Azia seems to have been a studious, churchgoing Korean American who got into Stanford: Except that that statement contains three truths and a lie, she would be, as the internet remarks, garden-variety.[5] It is difficult to imagine a more textbook example of "the most unexpected or rare events—within those that are culturally familiar and/or consonant."[6] No wonder articles about Azia often opened, as if despite themselves, with this rhetorical cliché:

> Azia Kim was like any other Stanford freshman. She graduated from one of California's most competitive high schools last June, moved into the dorms during New Student Orientation, talked about upcoming tests and spent her free time with friends.
> [paragraph break]
> The only problem is that Azia Kim was never a Stanford student.[7]

One after another, reporters writing up this story staged it so as to recapitulate their own (presumable) surprise and perform the story's newsworthiness: Azia is the routine typification that defies expectations—personified.[8]

Admittedly, even as traditional journalistic outlets may thoroughly racialize a story, they are as a rule reticent about naming race—so much so that, while covering many of the impostors of the previous chapter, reporters often left race or ethnicity for readers to deduce from circumstantial details like surnames or photographs. And rather than cite racial narratives openly, such articles often allowed quotes selected from interviewees to do their racialization in code.[9]

> Several students [at Stanford] suggested it was because of intense pressure to gain admittance to one of the coun-

try's most elite universities. . . . [A freshman who lived in the same dorm is quoted as saying,] "I think she had told her parents, and she perpetuated the lie so far that she actually had to come to the campus to stay here."[10]

Readers tended not to be so coy, readily connecting the dots of familiar cultural scripts. Case in point, a question that appeared in a "live online discussion" about overachievement-style parenting:

> Often Asian Americans are labeled as an academically elite, hyper-driven group in America. Asian parents are accused of too aggressively promoting the academic excellence of their children at the expense of more "all rounded" activities like sports or a social life, etc. Do you think this rhetoric also embeds culturally-specific notions into classroom definitions of success?[11]

This discussion, hosted by the *Washington Post* in 2006, consisted of a Q&A with the author of *Harvard Schmarvard: Getting Beyond the Ivy League to the College That Is Best for You*.[12] Submitted by a reader of that major metropolitan newspaper, the question above speaks to what such a highly-educated and relatively affluent readership "knows": that is, it taps the social and linguistic lexicon that a paper like this shares and strategically builds on with its readers. Indeed, textbooks in journalism are matter of fact about each publication—whether tabloid, broadsheet, or blog— depending for its survival on cultivating such "lexical cohesion," entailing the "ability . . . to fit into a consistent worldview and longer narratives of social belonging and identification."[13] Which is to say that while editors and writers at papers including the *Los Angeles Times*, *Seattle Times*, and *San Francisco Chronicle* opted out of using identifiers like "Asian" or "Korean" aloud, their way of humming keywords does not make the narrative less racialized. Whatever the reason for their caginess, it does seem clear that news reports did not *need* to cite the cultural scripts explicitly in order for their readers to draw the connections.

Because connect, readers did. Taking to the blogosphere or to discussion forums, they declared this an Asian American cultural narrative. That is, they gave it what media studies would call a model-minority frame, where framing is "the process of 'selecting some aspects of a perceived reality and mak[ing] them more salient in a communicating text . . . to promote a particular problem definition, causal interpretation, moral evaluation, and/or treatment recommendation' for the described phenomenon."[14] This reading trended on discussion boards:

> Both of the guys I knew who considered Stanford THE ONLY SCHOOL were Asian as well. I would guess, based on that and the fact that they have an Asian-American dorm, that it might be kind of a big thing for Asian descent kids.[15]

It bubbled up on personal parenting blogs:

> I couldn't help but think of possible cultural factors when I read this story. Asians have the "model minority" burden, they are expected to be ideal students and high achievers.[16]

And from all over—interview sources, comment sections, scattered discussion and response pieces—but with conspicuous consistency across established Asian American blog publications, came a diagnosis of Tiger parenting:

> • Although the article does not specifically note it, I am going to guess that the student, Azia Kim, was rejected by Stanford but was too ashamed to tell her parents, who undoubtedly had huge plans for her going to such an elite school like Stanford. . . . [S]he obviously felt

desperate under the weight of all the pressure and expectations foisted upon her by her parents and by American society's image of Asian Americans as the supersmart, high-achieving "model minority."

- Kim's desperation to attend an elite college crushes me. She probably needs . . . "help," but mostly in order to live down the shame of 1) not getting into a great college, 2) her own unreasonably high self-expectations and I would venture to guess, her parents.'

- While it's pure speculation, I can't help but wonder if parental pressures are involved here. Vong's article cites a number of anecdotes about the heavy academic demands of Asian immigrant parents. "For the bulk of Asian parents it is all about succeeding, and there is no middle ground." "Oftentimes Asian immigrant parents don't know how to give positive reinforcement or show their kids that it is OK to make mistakes."[17]

To be sure, the body of online commentary about Azia is motley and cacophonous, as online commentary everywhere is. But the chorus represented here is also clearly discernible from within that noise, as an aggregation of readers who see between the reported lines of her story a distinctly Asian American experience—oftentimes, their own.

Such a baldly racial framing might seem hasty or irresponsible were it not for the context provided by the previous chapter's discovery: that reporters and readers of college impostor cases overall have proven surprisingly restrained in its use. The mere conjunction of Asian person + Ivy League longings has proved insufficient to trigger cultural scripts: Out of nine Asian impostors, coverage of four invoked no race or family speculation whatsoever. This is especially remarkable considering that said "coverage" includes social media such as blogs and Reddit threads, an online world hardly known for its measured or discerning discussions. But the beauty of these types of informal and viral media is that they aggregate comments direct from an "intimate public"—a concept that I think serves well here, even though using it means taking some liberty with Lauren Berlant's original definition.

A cultural theorist out of literary criticism, Berlant invented the term by way of explaining how a given strain of mass-market narrative (e.g., chick lit, self-help books, fashion magazines) forges its audience or woos its niche into being. The focus of her book *The Female Complaint* is squarely on commercial "women's culture" and its way of taking women's felt sense of a "share[d] worldview and emotional knowledge"—a sense "derived from a broadly common historical experience" of, well, gender oppression—and turning that into a marketing opportunity. Readers who see their lives reflected in the stories and advice dispensed by "women's culture" are strangers yet imagine themselves bonded over intensely personal matters: sex and disappointment, domestic strife and bodily insecurities. . . . That paradox makes them an "intimate public," an identity much like "fans of *XYZ*" in that, however ardently held, it is unfortunately a marketing construct: They are consumers hailed by their common sorrows, drawn to pay over and again for catharsis or sedation. These hits of *feeling heard* or *feeling part of something bigger* are absorbed into readers' ongoing "'bargaining' with power and desire," however unsatisfying the results. Hers being an argument about the culture industry, Berlant is necessarily cynical about consumers' feelings of "recognition and reflection" in objects designed to part them from their money.[18] Under lights this harsh, self-identification can't much exceed interpellation:

> An intimate public operates *when a market opens up* to a bloc of consumers, *claiming* to circulate texts and things that express those people's particular core interests and desires. . . . [P]articipants in the intimate public *feel as though* it expresses what is common among them, a subjective likeness that *seems to* emanate from their history and their ongoing attachment and actions.[19]

Putting insistent distance between the feeling and its credibility, Berlant seems to shut down not only the marketing apparatus that uses human desire for connection in bad faith but the very connection itself. Mightn't that be unnecessarily dismissive? Does the tendency for a feeling to be exploited mean it surely expressed nothing, corresponded to no social truth? Can a group that, in fact, has core interests, histories, attachments, and actions in common not coalesce like an "intimate public" if hailed by something else—something that does not come by way of product development but nonetheless makes readers recognize themselves as not alone? That media narratives about Azia, informally circulated, have been enough to make perfect strangers blurt, "I've seen that" and "Palo Alto, we have a problem" suggests, if anything, that the commonalities are (like those around gender oppression) truly here to be triggered.[20] If what's key is that such "a world of strangers . . . be emotionally literate in each other's experience of power, intimacy, desire, and discontent,"[21] then I'd say an intimate public is functionally what we have here.

That this kind of social organism can emerge among Asian Americans not by design but by circumstance is thanks to an extreme standardization in experience. And thanks to Jennifer Lee and Min Zhou's *AAAP*, evidence of that standardization is finally more than anecdotal. As they updated and recalibrated model-minority paradigms[22] for the twenty-first century, sociologists Lee and Zhou found young second-generation Asian Americans to be measured by a tightly defined "success frame": "earning straight A's, graduating as the high school valedictorian, earning a degree from an elite university, attaining an advanced degree, and working in one of four high-status professional fields: medicine, law, engineering, or science." Not only is this frame essentially the "model-minority stereotype" circa now, it is also what the children of Asian immigrants *themselves* understand (reductively, problematically) as the definition of Asian cultural identity. Granted, this checklist does not enjoy the same reverence in all immigrant families and *statistically* has held more sway in the economic-migrant communities of South and East Asia than in the refugee communities of the U.S.-Viet Nam War.* Still, its dominion in Asian America is far-reaching: its believers hailing from an implausible multiplicity of life chances and immigration histories, and where it appears it is unmistakable. Evidence of the success frame is abundant across studies of other Asian American ethnicities, communities, and locales—and its sheer orthodoxy is, in fact, one of the findings Lee and Zhou themselves marvel at: "Most remarkable is that regardless of class background, the Chinese and Vietnamese recounted the same" lockstep elements, and "regardless of whether our . . . interviewees agreed with the constricting success frame, each was keenly aware of it."[23]

Given the saturation of this model-minority "brand," it really isn't much wonder that subjects who have been socialized to measure up to it are quick to spot others doing the same. They are discerning readers of the success frame both because it is exceedingly conventional/legible and because they are emotionally literate members of a common intimate public. Faced with assorted Asian college impostors, readers en masse reacted differently to shammers than to passers, because only the latter are engaged in recognizable racial performance. A quick review from chapter one, in which we pegged those passing for model minority (strictly speaking) by the following indices:

---

* It's been observed, for example, that even in the high school years, "when Hmong parents come to [parent-teacher] conferences, they are primarily concerned with their children's behavior, not their academic performance"; the community may actively discourage higher education for its girls in favor of family responsibilities (Bic Ngo and Stacey J. Lee, "Complicating the Image of Model Minority Success: A Review of Southeast Asian American Education," *Review of Educational Research* 77, no. 4 [December 2007]: 429). In such a case, were a young woman, say, to make her way into college against her elders' disapproval, or take the MCAT despite the memory of a guidance counselor's dismissiveness—hers would be a different story. Not a wholly unrelated one—no Asian American is immune to model-minority racialization, even if only to be found deficient by its expectations—but not the same as a college impostor's.

- The impostor's deception comes with no upside of material gain or advantage—only opportunity costs, for all the risk of eventual disgrace.
- Her primary audience is at home: family, friends, and community members for whom the illusion of seamless academic mobility is so extravagantly maintained.

Still, what does such passing look like as a daily practice, for eight long months? How did Azia convey herself as the kind of person who, *of course*, belongs at Stanford, despite all the questions her lack of papers would seem to have raised? What details of her story clued readers in, as expressive of model-minority identity? But, for starters, just what is racial performance anyway?

about the performance

"One is not born, but rather becomes, a woman," Simone de Beauvoir famously said. On that distinction has been built radical insights into the nature of social identities—even those that look and feel like biological givens—as actually a matter of practice and presentation. Best known of these theories is Judith Butler's performativity, in which gender might be usefully likened to a show: femininity or masculinity being not set facts but *effects* available only if staged.

> Gender is not passively scripted on the body, and neither is it determined by nature, language, the symbolic, or the overwhelming history of patriarchy. Gender is what is put on, invariably, under constraint, daily and incessantly, with anxiety and pleasure, but . . . this continuous act is [often] mistaken for a natural or linguistic given.[24]

Performativity bids us see the perpetual work that goes into being recognizably the things that one supposedly was born. Even for those who are cisgendered, to become a heteronormative woman (or man) in a given culture is to learn the dos and don'ts of what one says, how one sits, what one wears; to become practiced in the proper replies and the attractive sets of hip or chin; and to habituate oneself to the spaces and tasks befitting a good mother (or father), a potential wife (or husband). It is perforce to *perform* these scripts, movements, and functions from one moment to the next—much like a live show needs the lyrics sung and the choreography danced in order to go on. It is also to risk performing badly with each scene, risk failing at one's presumed identity and reaping the consequences. Finally, it is to rehearse these conventional specifications in hopes of mastery but also legibility: By definition social, a successful identity needs to be an intelligible one. Call them conventions, tropes, or acts of "stylized repetition"[25] . . . they are the code in which social identities are both transmitted and received.

Race here works likewise. One is not born, but rather becomes, a model minority: this being the social identity that American society demands of the biologically Asian subject. For all that heterosexuality is differently done from place to place, the local archetypes feel timeless, inexorable to most practitioners. (See the over fifteen million copies of *Men Are from Mars, Women Are from Venus* that have sold to date.[26]) Likewise, the model minority is "identity as" what Butler would call "a compelling illusion"[27]—a folding of first the Japanese then the Chinese then East Asians then South Asians then some Southeast Asians and sometimes all Asians in America into a single character type—hardly plausible yet widely embraced as true of the self or reflective of the community. Of course, quantitative social science has shown time and again that said shiny stereotype does not describe the "average" Asian American, much less all of them:

> Main arguments include: 1) The methods of statistics analysis that supports [*sic*] the stereotype are often flawed; 2) The myth fails to recognize the increased evidence of Asian underachievement, dropout, and socio-economic

gaps; and 3) it fails to address the vast inter- and intra-group differences.[28]

Debunking arguments generally stop there, on the premise that facts will shame the devil: locate its disparities, its faulty algorithms, and the stereotype will lose its power to deceive. Except that's not how model-minority racialization works. As literary critic Min Song recognizes, its power is less stereotype, more *expectation*: "Expectations are certainly ascribed, but they also require active identification to be made fully into a set of ideas with material meaning in one's life."[29] Expectations of the self (i.e., identities) are not so susceptible to debunking because discrepancies are part of their process.

In one of the few empirical studies so far to ask whether Asian Americans *see themselves* by the lights of the model minority, the finding was "[in] fact" yes. In a survey of 704 university students, researchers found that the 119 Asian Americans generally "perceived themselves as more prepared, motivated, and more likely to have higher career success than whites" (an assessment that their peers across all racial groups endorsed)—even though judging by their actual GPAs and SAT scores, these Asian students' academic performance was no better.[30] There is, in other words, rather a lot of daylight between these students' achievements and the social ideal they nonetheless hold up as their identity: rehearsing it to themselves, presenting it to (each) other(s). And that is perfectly commonplace; it is how normative identities are done. Precursors to Butler, sociologists Candace West and Don Zimmerman characterized "gender [as] a socially scripted dramatization of the culture's idealization of feminine and masculine natures, played for an audience that is well schooled in the presentational idiom."[31] We are none of us the living paragons of our genders, but, even the heteronormative and cisgender of us strive perpetually to mime the part, to *pass ourselves off* as irreproachable, because to do otherwise is to endure mockery or discipline. "Performing one's gender wrong initiates a set of punishments both obvious and indirect."[32] Performing one's racial script wrong can be similarly punishing, as Azia's readers intuited: "I am going to guess that [she] was rejected by Stanford but was too ashamed to" admit it, given "the pressure and expectations foisted upon her by her parents and by American society's image of Asian Americans as the super-smart, high-achieving 'model minority.'"[33] This frame highlights the model-minority performance's compulsory nature, as something difficult to stop doing: Much as heteronormativity laminates gender onto sex, dominant American and ethnic cultures consort in naturalizing "Asian" and "model minority" as one. How can you be the former and not the latter? What the hell are you, then?

Understanding this, we may realize that Azia's long deception does not necessarily start with a lie. In the beginning was the impossible truth. And in the short story inspired largely by her, that is just how Vanessa Hua conceives the fateful moment. Narrating in retrospect, Hua's Azia character (renamed Elaine) confides that, while reeling from her rejection letter,

> I hadn't meant to lie, not at first, but when Jack Min donned his Stanford sweatshirt after receiving his acceptance (a senior tradition)—I yanked my Cardinal red hoodie out of my locker. When my AP English teacher . . . stopped to congratulate me, I couldn't bring myself to say, not yet. . . . I didn't want to disappoint her.
>
> Another week passed, and I posed with Jack for the school paper. . . . I showed my parents the article as proof of my acceptance.[34]

Misstep 1: subject performs a conventional action; Misstep 2: subject omits a controverting fact. Active lies come later, but by then she has already been damned by her silent desire not to disappoint.[35] This is the split in the road that will lead Elaine to her compromising position on the windowsill of a dorm room—taken not by veering off track but, ironically, by dressing the part, saying her lines, and staying true to what she is expected to do: Be the model minority. Make the unattainable look accessible. Pose for public proof of the racial ideal. Make the shared illusion of identity that much more impenetrable.

Though originally trained as a journalist, Hua chose in writing "Accepted" to work as a novelist: She had absorbed some of the news coverage of Azia but declined to do further digging or attempt interviews. In Elaine, she created a composite character, drawing lightly from news accounts of two other Asian American college impostors she remembered having come across—both of them passers (and both reserved for chapter four). Her objective lay decisively not in reportage ("This is not their story," she says, "this is mine, this is my character") but in what she calls "imaginative empathy":[36] finding a way into the backstories of figures dwarfed by their circumstances, such that the foreign or risible can become familiar or relatable. This locates her reading/writing practice on the same epistemological plane as that of the bloggers and commenters mentioned earlier: all strangers alike in the same intimate public. Of privileged information regarding Azia's personal history, they have none; regarding the racial performance they perceive, however, they have insider knowledge and outstanding consensus. In Azia's case, Asian Americans can name the success frame from the first notes of the tune—if and when they are schooled in that "genre" not only as narrative convention but as operating system.

about the plot

This expanded concept of genre comes to us also from Berlant's *The Female Complaint*—together with her later book *Cruel Optimism*, a reckoning with the dark magic of story in social compliance. We know genre in film or literature as horror or fantasy, as mystery or romance . . . each category of narrative ordered by its own unmistakable rules, populated by its familiar cast of characters, obliged to its own concept of what makes an ending good.

Taking it from here, Berlant suggests that the world-building power of narrative logic does as much to shape lives as it does to shape art. After all, science of many stripes says we are a species of inveterate storytellers: Some say it is how our brains are wired (to make sense of experiences is to put them to story); others say it is how our societies are bred (a culture's legends or parables being like its DNA, the code by which it replicates). Often, it is said that storytelling is the thing we do that is qualitatively human.[37] Clearly, if stories do so much more than entertain around the fire, then so do genres, those being the grooves that train not only our cultural plots but our temporal experiences.

As borrowed from Berlant, genre writ large is "an emotionally invested, patterned set of expectations about how to act and how to interpret, which organises a relationship between the acting and interpreting subject, their feelings and impressions, their struggles and their historical present."[38] While all the pieces of that definition are necessary, it may be most useful to start with "organises a relationship." The academic world has no shortage of terms for addressing the notion that socialized subjects filter or interpret information and experiences through culturally patterned, prefab templates of meaning. In fact, it's worth clarifying how the sociological definition of "frame," lightly referenced by Lee and Zhou in "success frame," includes most of the above components, but how genre captures the college impostor's plight more fully. As used in sociology, frames refer to "'schemata of interpretation' that enable individuals 'to locate, perceive, identify, and label' occurrences within their life space and the world at large." By providing rules for what is relevant then principles for how elements are strung together, frames tell us what counts as data then what compels as meaning. Classic examples of this include whether the unpurchased items in a purse are deemed a matter of shoplifting or absentmindedness, whether a gynecologist's conduct is experienced as clinical or creepy—depending on "frames" of prosecution/defense, expertise/power.[39] This sense of "frame" is quite compatible with the media studies definition; in either case, genre is more robust. Whereas frame generates a given reading of a situation, genre dictates *what kind of story this is*, and, therefore, how that reading maps onto points before and after: Tragedy? Revenge fantasy? Where has the subject been headed and what is possible for her from here? That is, genre organizes an ongoing relationship between the subject, her historical/material circumstances, and her patterns of interpretation/response. "Genres also organise conventions about what might be hoped for, explicitly or secretly, and the bargains that can be made with life."[40] To live in a world that a genre has built is to ration one's desires by its math and choose one's path by its formulas for an emotionally satisfying ending. To inhabit a genre with an intimate public is, therefore, to share not only a frame of reference but the very logic that governs what it is to have a life.

What Lee and Zhou call the success "frame," then, I move we consider an instance of genre. Genre, because one does not toggle between operating systems like frames at an eye exam. Genre identifies nothing less than *the kind of story one is striving to live*: what clichés one looks to as protagonist, what lines and character traits, what plot points and in what sequence. In this genre of hyperachievement, we all pretend to be the same superhero, because no one wants the truth, beauty, or possibility of our secret identities. Lee and Zhou are very clear that "for no other [racial] group is [success] defined as getting straight A's, gaining admission into an elite university, getting a graduate degree, and entering one of the four coveted professions: doctor/pharmacist, lawyer, scientist, or engineer"; their interviewees felt strongly that "doing well in school [etc.] not only is the expectation or obligation but also has become racialized as 'acting Asian' and the Asian thing."[41] This racial performance is compulsory, genre reminds us. Those who fall short in any particular—who attend a "lesser UC," say—feel themselves to be not only "failures" or "outliers" but ethnically or racially inauthentic. But, most of all, the work of genre is the cultivation of emotional investment and the neat pruning of hopes, so we need it to make sense of a young woman so vested in a threadbare plot that she can imagine fulfillment in no other.

about the role

To review, then: Azia's imposture met both key elements of passing. (1) She stood to gain no undergraduate degree from her efforts, making her investment of time and effort irrational in economic terms. Whatever needs it answered are, therefore, also likely to have been irrational—in the dual sense of emotional (rather than material) and illogical (because a genre that funnels every teenager it can into maybe a dozen schools and four professions is illogic itself). (2) Press accounts suggest and interviews confirm that, while at Stanford, Azia took no risks with her stock image as a model minority and staged it mainly not to impress her peers but for the regard of her home-viewing audience. For a young woman who had nothing but free time, and no one anywhere by way of confidant, she displayed a degree of self-constraint baffling except as a continuation of a racial performance she was long accustomed to—and from which she did not now dare deviate.

Item one likely needs no further explication; circumstances speak for themselves. To see item two, however, we could use a little help, which luckily we have by way of a foil. What might it look like to pose innocently as a college student—that is, to sham, not scam—but without any interest in approximating the model minority? Why, it might look something like the story of David Vanegas: a Latinx college-age impostor with no criminal record and no enrollment status, whose caper bore enough parallels to Azia's that I am not the first to think of comparing them. Claiming to be a sophomore transfer from the University of Texas or sometimes a graduate student, twenty-year-old David spent over a year on the Rice University campus, "eating in Rice's dining halls, hanging out with students and attending classes. Some nights, he crashed in friends' dorm rooms when he was too tired to go home."[42] While he was not able to score his own room, David's run at Rice was of commensurable length to Azia's at Stanford. And when caught out, the reason he gave for his deception "was that his mother was ill and he didn't think she could stand the disappointment of his not being a Rice student." David thus seems to meet both criteria for "passer," which, in fact, prompts an article giving a rundown of four impostors to pause and wonder the following about him and Azia, together:

> But what motivates someone to go to school and attend classes without any prospect of getting credit?
>
> Jerald Jellison, a former USC psychology professor who specialized in the study of lies, said some charlatans take on a new identity to hide a criminal past. But impostors like Vanegas typically begin their charade *to win approval from someone important, such as their parents.*[43]

The conflation of David's and Azia's motives doesn't hold, though. I'd maintain that the situational case where one bends over backward to avoid distressing an ailing parent is different from *trying to win approval from someone important*, period. Context matters. The former reads as a stopgap and the act of a loving (not beleaguered) son. The latter is open-ended, suggesting an ongoing effort that ratcheted up to some rather desperate measures.

Even were we to allow that Azia's and David's deceptions could in broad strokes be identical, their day-to-day performances were nothing alike. Regarding Azia, one article after another reported along these lines:

- Kim tried to keep a low profile—the *Stanford Daily* article does not mention her taking part in any clubs, although she did make friends in the Stanford dormitories and pretended to study for exams.

- Azia Kim, 18, said she was a human biology major and spent many evenings doing homework.
- [Kim] seemed to do her homework, often working late into the night on school papers.[44]

Such consensus makes the following generalizations about David stand out all the more:

- [Vanegas's] schoolmates began to notice odd things about him, like he never seemed to have any homework.[45]
- A lot of [Rice students] could recall seeing Vanegas . . . playing Nintendo in a dorm common area.[46]

This is a juxtaposition not about work ethics but about the great disparity in what these two young people felt to be at stake in lying to every loved one and every stranger. After David was busted, his previous behavior struck some as that of a man with nothing to do, nothing to prove: "You get to go to parties, you get free food, you get to hang out with people that are your age and have fun. Pretty much, [Vanegas] did nothing. He's being a bum."[47] No such conclusion was likely ever drawn about Azia: Having procured for herself nearly nine months of continuing financial support, freedom from parental oversight, and absolutely nothing by way of obligations, Azia spent her free time and disposable income in the campus library, approximating a Stanford freshman's devotions to textbooks and keyboards. There is no mention of her dating, shopping, boozing, or party going (pastimes noted about various other impostors, including Elizabeth Okazaki and Abe Liu). Residents and student staff at her dorm in the spring recall her at no residence hall socials or spirit activities, of which there were many. The press did discover that Azia had joined the Army ROTC at nearby Santa Clara University;[48] more on this later. Aside from that curious military training, I know her only to have joined a Korean drumming group at Stanford for at least part of winter quarter[49]—so modest a social indulgence it can't have raised an eyebrow had word of it come to family friends, church deacons, or relatives back in Fullerton.

It may seem that one's everyday activities are hardly theatrical, being full of habits taken for granted rather than choices made for viewers, to perform a thing like race. Yet performance scholar Ju Yon Kim reminds us that racial performance *is* mundane, that what we're guilty of racializing is nothing if not these prosaic patterns: from "how people walk, speak, eat, or hold their bodies" to their "daily routines." "Although reading a newspaper in the morning," she explains, "might seem quite different from physical tendencies such as an accent or a gait," both such habits "at the limits of conscious action" are implicated in the everyday of *acting* racially white, say, or not. The day-to-day of *acting* model minority, then, is a matter of "activities like completing one's homework, preparing for exams, and practicing musical instruments"—and doing so, Kim notes, "excessively, automatically, ceaselessly"—in other words, to the exclusion of much else.[50] Between David and Azia, only one is engaged in posing not only as an undergrad at an elite university but, specifically, as an "Asian student," a racial form that circulates in American history as coolies and automatons: "Asian workers and students, maintaining themselves at little expense and almost robotlike, labor and study for hours on end without human needs for relaxation, fun, and pleasure."[51] If she was relatively extreme in performing this to the letter, that is, of course, because without an actual (admissions) letter, Azia's high-wire act had no safety net.

So, she did not call attention to herself. Unlike James Hogue or Adam Wheeler, Azia did not tell increasingly fantastic tales or vie for ever-higher prizes. Unlike Abe Liu or Birva Patel, she sought no social inclusion, risked no intimacies. Whereas indications are that the first two characters were compulsive liars, driven insatiably to elevate themselves above the crowd, by all reports Azia either meant to or was content to blend in. The Human Biology track she claimed—"perceived as *the* 'Pre-Med major' for Stanford"[52]—ensconced her unremarkably among the campus Asian Americans. So long as she was lying, Azia might have claimed as prestigious a major as she liked; she opted out of the more rarified limelight of any "techier" and more impressive STEM.[53] Neither did she aim to stand out in physical presentation: Azia is said not to have worn makeup, and to have dressed primarily in jeans and sweatshirts, attire described by several dormmates as "nondescript."[54] As for relationships in those nine months, aside from the pair of roommates who eventually tired of lending Azia their dorm-room floor, she is remembered neither by the press nor by interviewees to have had particular friends. She is not said to have dated anyone. Let's think about this, then: The prodigious energy Azia invested in this performance cannot have been for the sake of strangers whose notice she hoped mainly to avoid. Stanford was her stage but not ultimately her audience.[55]

the show must go on

Such a desolate daily life to inflict upon oneself. We have genre to speak to the depth of Azia's commitment to the illusion; how might we understand its implausible success? Assuming her Stanford-acceptance fiction began in spring of senior year of high school, twelve months is a long time to lie and also a long time not to get caught. Did Azia mastermind an airtight story, brilliantly keeping her explanations straight? No, actually. There were inconsistencies, not always minor: to some people, she presented herself as a sophomore rather than a freshman (likely to explain something else that did not fit), leading to conflicting versions of a basic data point.[56] How is it, then, that her stories went so long unchallenged? Takeo, the resident assistant, suggested that for one, Stanford cultivates an exceedingly trusting culture, central to which is a student-authored honor code dating back to 1921. Like most (schools with) honor codes, Stanford prohibits cheating of all kinds. Unlike most (schools with) honor codes, Stanford prohibits proctoring: "The faculty on its part manifests its confidence in the honor of its students by refraining from proctoring examinations and from taking unusual and unreasonable precautions to prevent the forms of dishonesty mentioned above."[57] No doubt cultural priming this strong can make people less apt to suspect or investigate. Still, on Azia's part, her imposture may also have been relatively easy to sustain because what she was impersonating was . . . herself.

By any classic understanding, impostors like Azia are hardly "passing" at all. Having stood neither to improve her fortunes nor to upgrade her racial standing, Azia's project fundamentally does not seem to have been about the crossing of social barriers. In what sense, then, is the concept of passing even useful here? On one level, the analogy is simple: if drawn from sociologist Erving Goffman's work on stigma, passing may be succinctly defined as "the management of undisclosed discrediting information about the self."[58] And, sure enough, by deception, Azia sought to hide her rejection by Stanford. But what's more interesting, and hopefully clear by now, is that by keeping her apparently within the "success frame," deception allowed her to "pass" for a second-generation Asian American, *as that racial identity is now defined*. Scholars of historical race passing maintain that "since it is possible to pass only because that thing is already invisible, passing is therefore less a matter of hiding something than of refusing or failing to acknowledge something."[59] In practice, "race norms work through assumptions of" the privileged category, so, where whiteness is that category, "subjects are immediately assumed to be white in the absence of any telling marks of 'color.'"[60] But likewise, in the absence of any disclosed discrediting information, Azia is assumed to be a full member of her own visible, privileged racial set. Indeed, to consider Azia's ruse as passing is to understand a key difference in racialization and hierarchy in schools today versus in 1966—both in the United States and (importantly for the next chapter) in Canada: *Maclean's* published an infamous essay decrying the University of Toronto as "Too Asian," by which they mean a school "that is so academically focused that some [white] students feel they can no longer compete or have fun."[61] In "ethnoracially diverse contexts," where Asian immigrant families have reached a critical mass, Lee and Zhou find that Asian American students "looked not to native-born whites but to high-achieving coethnic peers or siblings as their reference group when measuring their success" and, indeed, that other racial groups concur with this new academic hierarchy. That study of the new second generation thus jettisons the map on which whiteness is the destination for upward mobility—making a fundamental break from both classic assimilation and segmented assimilation models.[62] In other words, the traditional prototypes for assimilation and passing are inadequate and inaccurate to the social models and personal stakes of the hard-driving immigrant's child. For Azia, racial masquerade is not a matter of trading up for whiteness but of preventing the loss of her identity as model minority. Her mechanism is, thus, not the calculated pursuit of gain but the rather more primal avoidance of ruin.

This is to say that Azia's long lucky streak at Stanford may have had something to do with her project of "passing" or impersonation being not entirely different from the next Asian American's—who is, therefore, only "passing" in a looser sense. Here I borrow elements of "impersonation" from Tina Chen, to explain a claim much less sensationalistic than it may sound. In *Double Agency: Acts of Impersonation in Asian American Literature and Culture*, Chen draws a distinction between imposture and the subtle thing she wants us to see. Per that distinction, the impostor is an identity thief of sorts: "adopt[ing a] public identity that is understood to belong to someone else." Imposture is an act of deception, "the object [of which] is to fool others." What impersonators attempt, by Chen's contrast, are public identities that are *supposed* to be their own: They "perform themselves into being as persons recognized by their communities and their country," a kind of performativity with emphasis on duress and inauthenticity. Impersonation is about donning one's assigned racial "mask"—

externally imposed, often stereotypical, and ill-fitting though it may be—in order to have a place at the table. So, all of us who are Asian and would-be American muster shows of commonality and unthreatening relatability to reassure anxious observers that we belong—even as the very need to sing for our suppers reinforces the hierarchy that makes us at best guests (not family, much less hosts) at this table. I perform second-generation acceptability as I shop for groceries each week: smiling at other shoppers, bantering in perfected English about wine, standing politely in line. Likewise, however "confined, lonely, and defeated" she may feel there, a Chinese American undergrad conducts herself through Harvard thus:

> Surrounded by people who only told success stories, I felt that my stories must only reflect success, too. I became a performer in all aspects of my life. I performed roles as an Asian American, a premed, a Harvard student. Running around from class to lab to extracurricular activities, doing all the things I should be doing, I felt as though I had become an actress in someone else's play.[63]

As racial subjects forced to impersonate our own authenticity, Asian Americans are not liars . . . but we are all caught in the act. Chen's sympathy for impersonation comes, however, at the expense of imposture: "To be identified as an impostor is to be named a fake, to be called out as a pretender who doesn't belong to whatever group is evaluating the performance in question, to be somehow found inauthentic."[64] Yet, this opposition crumbles poignantly in Azia's situation: *Consider that her performance of self the day* before *she received her rejection letter and that performance on the day* after *she opened it may not have changed in any specifics*; it's just that a distant committee had since reclassified her a fake. Azia was, indeed, "pretending" to an identity writ small (as a Stanford student) but writ large as "model minority," this is also the *only* racial identity assigned and allowed to her—and it is the identity that was formerly as much hers as any other Asian American impersonator's.

behind the curtain

Why, then, Azia? If her circumstances were so common, how did she come to make a choice so extraordinary? Admittedly, what answers I have for this question are far less definitive than I would have liked. When the story broke, and to this day, members of her intimate public have been sure of one thing: It was high-pressure parenting that drove her to it. As myself a member of that intimate public, I was tempted to agree—but, as a researcher, it's a theory I have been careful here not to endorse absent real corroboration. Proof (or disproof) would most likely have entailed my interviewing people close enough to the family to speak to their domestic life: the Kims themselves, of course; barred that, someone from their circles of confidants during Azia's high school years. But, in the decade since she became a human-interest story, Azia and her family seem to have vanished. To make an internet presence go so utterly dark, she has most likely changed her name. Those former contacts I have been able to interview, she hasn't communicated with since her exposure, and it appears her family likewise does not want to be found. As a scholar rather than a reporter, it is not my place to smoke them out of hiding. Despite the years since the press coverage did its damage and my best attempts to convey honorable intentions, many of those I've approached—key players and bit players alike—have been skittish to reply. Whatever their cost-benefit calculations, such reserve even now hints that this debacle carries a long half-life.

The broad reticence has been disappointing to me, yes; debilitating, I think no. Maybe even the opposite. Being held to observation points outside the home has helped keep this chapter mindful of its case study not for the plot—a mystery whose culprits we may or may not have guessed correctly[65]—but for the genre. Aside from Takeo, one of the two student staff tasked with the actual packing and removal of her things from the dorm room, and her youth pastor at Cornerstone Church during her high school years, the people I've interviewed about Azia and cite here include:

- The Okada dorm resident assistant who brought up questions about Azia at a morning staff meeting; that very night she was escorted off campus. This resident assistant wishes to remain anonymous.
- Trent, then-freshman and resident of Okada. Trent also participated in the Korean drumming group that Azia joined Winter quarter.
- Anne, Okada staff resident fellow, supervisor to the resident assistants. Anne handled the administrative back-and-forth that established the facts of Azia's stay at Stanford.
- Hannah, a high school classmate for four years at Troy High School and two years at Parks Junior High School previous to that.

Their observations made possible some important fact-checks— while nonetheless holding us at enough of a remove from the story's center that its truth still contains multitudes. For instance, though he worked closely with Azia on multiple projects before she graduated, her youth pastor could not speak to the particulars of her family dynamics, not having received such confidences from her, her younger sister, or her parents. However, he did push back strenuously against attempts to characterize her parents as having pressured Azia too much, or having caused all this. "I think that's too much simplified," he said, more than once, and declared from experience that "when teenagers [are] having a family problem with their parents," observers can tell; such tension is visible. But in Azia's manner to her parents he saw no sign of that.[66] As they say, absence of evidence is not evidence of absence—but it should give a researcher pause. For Azia's story,

it serves as a reminder that there's more than one possible route
to this ending, well within the genre. Sifting hypotheses proves
meaningful only after we have taken full stock of our givens,
however. So let's begin with what is known, then what can be
extrapolated, to see where it all leaves us.

The burning question about Azia's family: Did she have Tiger
parents? Answer: Unknown. Knowns about her family are as follows: Indeed immigrants, her parents owned a small business, in
the vein of a dry-cleaner or garment factory. Azia spent junior
high in a section of Fullerton with a large enough working-class
Korean population to have something of an ethnic gang problem. The Kims were members of a Korean church, where her
father was a part-time associate pastor.[67] What might be deduced:
That the Kims lived well inside a community of immigrant social
norms, assumptions, and values—the very kind of demographic
to have a mind-meld around the success frame. That as small-
time entrepreneurs, Azia's parents worked hours well before nine
and after five. And as working-class immigrants, they may have
had no higher education themselves; if any, it was likely in the
old country. Their grasp of the educational machinery here would
have been spotty and sourced heavily in "hearsay from friends
and family members . . . rather than social science evidence"
or research.[68] Drawing parallels between Azia's parents and her
own small business–owning Korean immigrant mother, Hannah
remarked, "My mom pushed me to all these things, but at the end
of the day, if she saw an acceptance letter, she probably wouldn't
even really understand if it was real or not."

The burning question about Azia's schooling: Was she a
success-framed student? Answer: Yes, though not necessarily by
the measures that come most immediately to mind. The classmate who vouched for Azia to reporters as a "brilliant person
even though she didn't get into the Ivy Leagues"[69] fit the bill
in much more obvious ways: Huy Nguyen was well-known at
Troy as among the best of that senior class. He and a partner had

taken third in the national finals of the Siemens Westinghouse Competition in Math, Science and Technology, per write-ups in the *Orange County Register* and the Troy yearbook.[70] Voted "Most Likely to Succeed," he followed up Harvard undergrad with Harvard medical school, and, eventually, a career in ophthalmology. To compare Huy's yearbook footprint to Azia's is to realize that their respective college applications were more than a little different—and yet, the dreams that governed them remained very much the same. A genre accommodates infinite variations on its themes; we look at two here, because to know a genre is to heed its variations and still recognize its core.

For holistic views of a student's life at school, yearbooks are terrible; for capturing the lives of any but a school's stars, they are next to useless. But, because the kind of content they document is also the sort of thing colleges ask for, Troy's yearbook staff have essentially compiled for us trace evidence of their classmates' model-minority performance. In 2006, the yearbook indexed Huy as a member of the school paper, vice president of the Math Club, and copresident of the following clubs: Ocean Science Bowl, Medical Science Club, and French Club. Counting his senior portrait, as well as the popularity vote and Siemens write-up mentioned above, this totals eight mentions. Azia does not seem to have sat for her senior portrait, and so, counting her listing as copresident of the Refuge Christian Club, she appears once. The paucity of extracurriculars doesn't seem to have been a fluke; in junior year her sole appearance is her class picture. Sophomore year proved only slightly more active; that edition lists her as a member of the school orchestra and Junior Varsity swim team, even including a brief interview:

> Reflecting by the pool deck, Azia Kim remembers her 2-year struggle to improve in swim. When she joined Swim last year, she wasn't the best athlete. If asked, she admitted, "I pretty much stunk." But through encouragement from a friend to join a private team, her swimming

improved, which gave her motivation to do better. "I
didn't want to be as bad as I was before," she commented.
Her progress had opened up social doors, also. "The best
part is at meets when I have free time and get to talk to
friends," she stated.[71]

The interview is endearing, but not the narrative of an over-
achiever. Truth be told, this is overall a strikingly slender high
school profile, especially considering that, instead of ramping up
for college applications, it seems to have gone dormant in the
critical years. I admit I was surprised by the data, having expected
to find evidence of diligent box-checking according to the King
James Guide for Getting into College. I had anticipated a record
something like Huy's. How else to explain Azia's apparent inability to unfix her sights from the Promised Land?

Well, once again, context matters. Picture your stereotypical
American high school with its storied social hierarchy: the jocks,
the burnouts, the nerds. . . . Local terminology may vary, but as
anthropologist Sherry Ortner observes, "These social categories
have been found in most high schools in most parts of the country for virtually the whole of the 20th century."[72] On one end is a
"'leading crowd,' who enthusiastically participate in, and receive
the sponsorship of, the school"; on the other, a "'rebellious crowd,'
who reject the hegemony of the school and in turn feel largely
rejected" by it;[73] and milling about the sidelines, those either "singled
out for their superior academic performance" or "viewed primarily
as having low levels of social skills."[74] Classically, students sort into
a small set of identities by a combination of class background and
individual temperament, and, like at Hogwarts, race or ethnicity
play little role in the sorting calculus. Or, at schools with just
enough Asian students to cluster, their racial dispensation is, of
course, as nerd: "while images of all groups [have] a component of academic orientation and/or performance, the group image of Asians
focuse[s] on their academic achievement"; other students think
of them "as 'short' and 'wears glasses,' . . . quiet and not athletic."[75]

Neither of these configurations describes Troy. What we know about American high schools has only started to account for public schools like that or San Marino High, jewel of the wealthiest of suburbs in Southern California's San Gabriel Valley: student population 24 percent White, 58 percent Asian.[76] These are top-performing schools, and the kind that Lee and Zhou have in mind when they say that, there, the new hegemony is Asian American.[77] In such places, the *nerds* are Asian kids, yes: ethnically Asian names crush the honor rolls (and that's even granting that mixed-race kids may not have identifiably Asian surnames). But in such places, the *jocks* are Asian kids, too[78]—and, moreover, they are often the *same* kids. On the "Senior Standouts" pages, Asians have claimed all but a few spots, including everything from "Class brains" to "Best dressed."[79] My point here is not that such students have "broken" a stereotype; nothing so tired or blandly contrarian. Rather, as sociolinguist Penelope Eckert defines the jock figure, his essence is actually "an attitude—an acceptance of the school and its institutions as an all-encompassing social context, and an unflagging enthusiasm and energy for working within those institutions." This opens up the possibility that an "individual who never plays sports, but who participates enthusiastically in activities associated with student government, unquestioningly may be referred to by all in the school as a Jock." So, my point is that in aiming for the Ivies—pursuing their racial role to their utmost ability—Asian American teens have ironically *redrawn* the social categories. The Asian faces pictured in the Fullerton or San Marino papers for winning academic contests and sports championships alike—"seen as serving the interests of the school and the community, representing the school in the most visible areas"[80]—become the actual definition of jocks *by way of being nerds*. In a minority-modeled school like this, the implicit bar (or even norm) is not to specialize—not to be the best jock *or* nerd you can be, much less to embrace one's burnout identity—but to excel at everything.

As brutal as that standard sounds on the whole, I suspect that at Troy the pressure was worse. To say "Troy High School" is

Table 2.1 Troy High School Student Demographics by Program (2005–2006)

Program	Black	White	Latinx	Asian	Total students	% API
Regular	26	379	245	203	853	23
TT	3	129	28	153	313	49
IBT	6	183	29	652	870	75
IB	1	20	1	63	85	74

actually not enough information; Troy is three schools in one: an International Baccalaureate (IB) program, a magnet school called Troy Tech (TT), and the regular/"college prep" track, with graduating classes of about six hundred per year.[81] Eighth-grade hopefuls to the magnet school must undergo an examination that its website describes as "similar to the SAT I Math and Critical Reasoning exam,"[82] along with an equivalent English portion. Teens admitted to TT may, if they have successfully completed enough honors coursework in their first two years, be permitted to attempt the IB Diploma Program (those on that track are designated IBT in the table above; those successfully admitted, IB). The stratification is stark (it is public knowledge who falls where) and a kind of de facto segregation: According to Hannah, it was painfully obvious that kids who (like her and Azia) tested in from all over the region were nearly all Asian; the ones from the neighborhood, taking the regular track, were basically everybody else. In their graduating year, for instance, the school-wide demographic breakdown can be seen in Table 2.1.[83]

To grow up Asian here was, to the nth degree, to have racial identity ingrained as inseparable from model minority. To grow up Asian here was to live inside a success frame as artificial as a Hunger Game and, in its own way, vicious—because, of course, only one of the tributes can claim valedictorian each year, while the honor roll of 4.0+ GPAs runs three columns wide, fifteen pages long.[84]

So, it is certainly possible that Azia's parents forced her to apply to TT, that they would accept nothing less than the most-prestigious case scenario, or that they would not hear when she struggled, doubted, missed the mark. It is possible, say, that they often lectured her about their sacrifice, the family honor of certain colleges and the unacceptable shame of others. And, certainly, that would explain her seeming inability to say aloud that the thing required of her would not come to pass. But what if they had taken a less active role than that—not steering the slow disaster, but more complicit and complaisant in its course? Supposing Azia had simply been privy as relatives and community elders gushed about one teen's achievements or jeered about another's, and overheard as her parents clapped or laughed along. How would the message land differently? Would their standards sound meaningfully more optional? Suppose that, being unsavvy consumers of American education, Azia's parents had no real idea what TT life would be like for her when they bade her apply—and no real resources to support her when the curve began to stretch beyond her reach. Would its tracks seem any more yielding or its rankings feel any less total a judgment of her value? And, what if, a watchful daughter, Azia had known her parents sometimes skip meals, juggle their bills to keep the lights on both at home and at their very small business, but always they feed their children? Suppose that the family sometimes spoke of Stanford in wistful daydream, as the kind of game changer that would redeem these aches and pains. Sometimes, Bert Yun insisted to me, a parent may say something in a whisper but the child hears it as a roar. "How the children receive [it can be] bigger than how the speaker . . . who has authority" intended it, he said, and I can imagine this: the message amplified by the echo chamber in which it travels.

There are many routes, in other words, by which Azia might have arrived at that moment of finding her new truth impossible. Remember, after all, that the success frame is remarkable precisely for its ability to "make sense" to Asian immigrant families of amazing assortments—across class backgrounds, immigration histories, educational and cultural capital, countries and cultures of origin. What would seem to be insurmountable demographic distinctions are no hindrance to those who would gladly align their personal and familial histories to model-minority plots.[85] Moreover, the fact that Azia's route does not necessarily chart with our most blithe guesses actually teaches us more about the power of the genre than a more rote example would. Had her parents clearly been Tigers of the worst stripe, had she herself been an impeccable student, we would need worry only about kids like this—those scaling the highest heights of the success frame, under threat. But Azia's story is made of experiences far more basic and widespread. Murmuring in one ear, a gratifying sense of inclusion in this status group, which allows one to move through school and community life as if anointed by model-minority logic: *You are one of the gifted or industrious*, it purrs, *who will go far in life.* Shrilling in the other, a nerve-racking sense of precarity—*Not good enough*, it hisses, *What a fraud*—as one is acutely aware in every encounter that one may be exposed for one's slips or mediocrities and disqualified. To be clear, I think it is the nature of the success frame to keep even its best and brightest feeling like impostors. Perfection by definition demands a facade, because it is humanly impossible: "even those who earned GPAs of 4.0," Lee and Zhou note, "pointed to others whose GPAs were even higher."[86] My point here, though, is that this corrosive cocktail of feelings is standard-issue to success-framed students, wherever on the hierarchy they may fall—and so long as they are trapped within the logic of this operating system, it primes them for variously desperate measures.

And this, finally, is what I've come to believe about Azia: that the decisive factor in her desperation wasn't which path, in particular, delivered her to that split in the road, but how many paths she could make out before her, to choose from. I believe that she saw only the single road through the success frame—which she had been walking all these years among her friends and peers—or a cliff. (And like Wile E. Coyote, she stayed her course until the one became the other.) After all, this was not someone in the habit of pushing her boundaries or making end-runs around them. What her peers saw in classes and hallways at high school—Azia with hair in a ponytail or worn straight in a blunt cut, face presented without makeup, attire innocent of fashion trend or sex appeal—was someone "probably really respectful, obedient to her parents," who wants to "keep them happy."[87] This is a theme in her racial performance: Azia's rendition of the model minority included no donning of props or artful cosmetics, no acquiring of contraband. She did not attempt to signal one identity to one audience, a different version to another. She played the script straight.

So straight, you might say, that it is downright ironic to call her an impostor—she who was not self-inventing really at all. Once at Stanford, simultaneously impostor and impersonator of her own identity, Azia performed a singularly unlayered deception. Returning to Tina Chen, we learn that, even though a cultural "mask," the image of self that the impersonator assumes daily is "one that doesn't necessarily fall away to reveal some inner, essential truth of personality."[88] For Azia, this seems to be true even though the mask wasn't merely metaphorical; it was also operational. Behind her pretense, there are no indications of an alternate self, a different aspiration. This gets us to the heart of that otherwise baffling vacuum of rational motivations: What did Azia mean to gain from her ongoing pretense? She neither stood to receive a degree (from *any* college, and so opportunity costs are high), nor was she doing what teenagers are generally understood to do when lying to their parents. Of her known activities, the only one to bear explaining is ROTC: it alone seems more than stock model-minority. But whatever other attractions that program might have held, it did entail this:

> In her self-assessment [required by ROTC] . . . Kim reported earning A's in Stanford English and Humanities classes, an A- in economics and a B in chemistry.
>
> She reported that she earned an 86 out of 100 on her Feb. 5 economics midterm and a 94 on her Feb. 1 math midterm. [89]

For these grades, the ROTC "awarded her a special Dean's Award ribbon for her uniform,"[90] allowing her to live out her dream more fully: to be *reputed* not only as a Stanford student in a STEM major (ostensibly on track for one of the four approved professions) but as one on the honor roll. Floating inside a bubble she wrought at great cost, Azia held in her hands extraordinary freedom to reinvent herself. But the buttoned-down and unimaginative existence she chose seems to have been, quite literally, her fantasy life.

There's a story her youth pastor tells that encapsulates what he knows to be true of Azia, her goodness, and her value. It's actually not much of a story: no drama, no conflict whatsoever. Youth in their church were encouraged to help out with retreats or other projects, and Bert figured out quickly whom he could entrust with growing responsibilities, whom he could not. While some clamored to lead praise or join the media team—jockeying for glory in front of the camera or for power holding the mic— Azia volunteered for the paperwork, to organize retreats and other events. In rooms full of hormonal teens, she did not fuss and required no management, emotional or otherwise. "Let's say I give her the work, and then that's it. It's done. Others, I give them the work, it's not done, and then I have to go talk [to them] again, or sometimes they reject the work." To Bert, Azia is someone "you know you want to work with"; "Someone like her, maybe three or four around you, then it will be very smooth" when important things need doing. Her pastor saw her regularly as "very good mannered to her parents," being considerate and kind to others, such that "her joy was others' happiness, you know?" To hear her jeered in the press as a con artist hurt him. He tried to defend her then and gave an interview with me mainly to do so again, even though, granted, he had not managed to make any more sense of things. "I don't know what happened there, because Azia is [a] faithful, dependable, stable and good person, like through the Bible study she takes notes, even though you don't have to."[91]

Dear faithful notetaker, wherever you are in the world now, I hope you are well.

chapter three

Limit Case

S ix months after Jennifer Pan was found guilty of first-degree murder in her mother's death and attempted murder on her father's life, *Toronto Life* magazine published the definitive profile piece on her case. It included the following passage:

> The more I learned about Jennifer's strict upbringing, the more I could relate to her. I grew up with immigrant parents who also came to Canada from Asia . . . with almost nothing . . . My dad expected me to be at the top of my class, especially in math and science, to always be obedient, and to be exemplary in every other way. He wanted a child who was like a trophy—something he could brag about.[1]

Written by a business reporter and former high school classmate, that July 2015 profile radically transformed the conversation around a daughter's heinous crime. Early coverage of the trial had echoed the prosecution's presentation, that Jennifer "planned the staged home invasion to murder her parents for separating her from her boyfriend of six years, who [sic] she 'relentlessly, obsessively' loved." In fact, the prosecutor folded years of Jennifer's prior deceptions into that story of a vindictive, thwarted love affair: "Pan's parents . . . didn't consider [boyfriend Daniel Wong] worthy of their daughter. . . . So Pan lied, pretending to attend university to become a pharmacist, when she instead lived in Ajax with Wong and his parents."[2] When her police interview was introduced into evidence a month later, elements of a success-frame narrative did make their way into media reports (including high parental expectations, classical music training, teenage depression, and cutting/self-harm), but they didn't stick. Jennifer expanded on that backstory in her subsequent testimony: notably that, disillusioned and despairing of being rewarded for her actual achievements, she first began forging her report cards in ninth grade—two years before meeting Daniel. She also claimed to have made several attempts at suicide after her lies were uncovered. But it is difficult, granted, to take the word of a murder suspect on the stand, much less one with a history of deception, and the gist of coverage toward trial's end tended still to "What she did for love: Kill."[3]

The emergence of Karen Ho's profile piece, a one-two punch of credible journalistic and first-person account, had the surprisingly powerful effect of reversing the Pans' positions of villain and victim in the eyes of the public. Though, to be clear, some defining story elements stayed untouched even as the narrative switched poles: Jennifer's parents were cast, beginning to end, as stock figures of the refugee turned model minority. Ho's opening sentence is interchangeable with that of innumerable other write-ups: "Bich Ha and Huei Hann Pan were classic examples of the Canadian *immigrant success story*." She continues, "They lived frugally. By 2004, Bich and Hann had saved enough to buy a large home with a two-car garage on a quiet residential street in Markham. He drove a Mercedes-Benz and she a Lexus ES 300, and they accumulated $200,000 in the bank."[4] But starting

here, Ho intervenes in the genre, interrupting what had been presented as obvious logic, an inevitability: that, according to earlier
coverage, *"as refugees from Vietnam, they wanted something better* for their daughter and son—higher education, degrees, solid
careers."[5] In other words, their immigration history had been supposed to determine and (naturally) explain the expectations the
Pans placed upon their children. To defy such expectations would
be sheer perversity; to repay them with violence, monstrosity. A
liberal fairytale of Westernization and upward mobility, *that* plot
could not assimilate a murderous conclusion into its heroism, its
family telos. However, the version that Ho offered, redrawn as
more of a model-minority dream than an American or Canadian
one, took the sharp turn with sudden ease. Add Tiger parenting
and, judging by readers' outrage turned understanding, the violent ending makes new generic sense.

In thinking us through Azia's story, I shifted arguments about
immigrant parenting to the side because we had nothing more
than projections to go on. In Jennifer's case, though, questions of
family loom front and center: It was them, after all, she meant to
kill. But what we learned about racial performance in the previous chapter we do not leave there. Indications are that the script
for playing Asian Canadian reads very much the same as that
for playing Asian American. This is surprising, given that as a
racial term and history, the model minority is identified with a
specifically U.S. context: devised during the civil rights era as
a redemptive spin on World War II Japanese American intern-
ment, extended in the 1960s to Chinese and, eventually, other
Asian ethnicities to stifle activism against systemic racism. Yet,
Canadian racial discourse has come to show a strange affinity
for this paradigm. Although scholarship on the model minority remains scarce in Canada, the popular press has been leak-
ing it into mainstream consciousness since the 1980s. In major
newspapers such as the *Toronto Star, Globe and Mail*, and *Mon-
treal Gazette*, "columnists continue to perpetuate the discourse
of Asians as being 'academic giants' [and] 'math whizzes'" such

that some hold that "an originally American discourse is now fully interspersed within the discursive field of Canadian liberal democracy."[6] In fact, Asian Canadian scholars like Eleanor Ty adopt the term in their own work, observing that "the concept has become transnational" and that Asian Canadian youths need not ever have heard the words *model minority* to live lives indistinguishable from the success frame:

> A recent sociological study conducted in Toronto [found that] . . . South Asian youths between eighteen and twenty-six . . . experience[d] guilt, shame, parental influence, and psychological stresses in their career decisions or educational choices. Parents preferred professional careers, such as engineering, medicine, and law. . . . Many immigrant parents have high expectations and . . . desire that their children have careers that would make their own sacrifice and hard work worthwhile.[7]

Likewise, I have argued elsewhere the improbable versatility of this racial form: able to defy seemingly imposing differences in historical context and material circumstance to replicate its patterns of high achievement and intergenerational conflict.[8] So this chapter addresses model-minority paradigms without belaboring the national border. The assignment this time, however, is very much to grapple with "parenting" and "racialization" as terms twinned[9] in the success frame genre. After all, only when it turned out to be a story about parenting did Jennifer's case become recognizable to the general public—and meaningful to Asian readers among them—as a story about race.

This case tests the tensile strength of the success frame as genre: its ability to order readerly expectations, as well as Jennifer's own, about "the bargains that can be made with life."[10] The sheer fact that empathy coalesced around this story is profound and demands explanation: On what grounds and for what gain would members of her intimate public announce themselves as sharing the upbringing, much less the sentiments, of a (would-be) patricide? There were no such outpourings for other impostors with serious criminal charges; it was as if the pleasure of seeing oneself in these impostors (mainly scammers) was categorically disabled by larceny or assault, much less by murder. This chapter proceeds on the strength of two key narrative accounts: Karen Ho's piece of long-form journalism, "Jennifer Pan's Revenge: The Inside Story of a Golden Child, the Killers She Hired, and the Parents She Wanted Dead"; beside the true-crime book *A Daughter's Deadly Deception: The Jennifer Pan Story*, by court reporter Jeremy Grimaldi, who covered the ten-month murder trial. The latter is useful, certainly, for its alternative vantage point—Grimaldi describes his own book in an interview as "a tale of a very private culture, and we got to see child-rearing techniques inside a strict Asian family."[11] His "we" clearly occupies no intimate perspective; quite rather, it assumes the hegemonic white Canadian one. The book represents, nonetheless, a wealth of information. In its writing, Grimaldi studied the copious court documents, conducted what interviews he could, and did a journalist's due diligence. Until I discovered his book, this is work I had thought to undertake myself: Jennifer having ignored my several requests to communicate with her, investigating had seemed the only avenue forward. But, whatever my disappointment at being unable to hear from Jennifer directly, it is a relief not to be chasing down leads. Had she been willing to sift through her past with me, I'd have thought it fair to go about asking others to do the same: relive memories, reopen wounds. . . . But according to Ho and the Correctional Service Canada, Jennifer has granted not a single interview since her arrest. Her past may be public record; her present is not, and I am glad not to try to make it so without her consent, the wounds in this case being not entirely figurative.

Had this inquiry revolved around interviews, as originally conceived, it might have angled itself at more personal history, waded between being privy and being beholden to what the tragedy's cast would each have us believe about their roles in it.

What's emerged instead is a level removed from the mire—at which distance this chapter seeks not gaps in what happened (the essentials of which are not in debate), but gaps in *making sense of* what happened. We have on one side a sense of recognition and validation so bone-deep that perfect strangers declare of Jennifer, *There but by the grace of god go I*:

> I grew up in a town with many households similar to Jennifer's. . . . I also falsified report cards. I told lies to my parents about programs and classes I got into and really didn't. . . . [H]ad I not been able to achieve what I did [after high school], had I not been able to satisfy my parents, I might have [continued lying].
>
> [The] line is thin. . . . At any point I could've come across people or information that pushed me closer to Jennifer's story than my own. I would never kill my parents. . . . But there are so many more stories of second generation Asians that don't make the news for homicide—instead for suicide.[12]

We have, across the chasm, a white female clinician in Connecticut who "diagnosed" Jennifer (by remote, at Grimaldi's behest) as a sociopath.[13] Also on that far side, however, I'd place well-intentioned social science that strives to explain the success-framed child's plight yet stumbles (arguably, where stakes are highest) at the irrationality rather than instrumentality of desperation: Favoring a kind of positivism, current theories of deception—whether in intergenerational or racial contexts, to manage scrutiny or stigma—can make out little of this case, even though it often makes intuitive sense to the very populations they study. Finally, I locate across the gap Lauren Berlant's construct of *cruel optimism*. As clearly apt as that concept proves for explaining Jennifer, its usefulness gives out before the end—by flawed design. This chapter returns to the moment of cruel optimism's genetic engineering to recover, and to reckon with, its violent DNA.

for want of a nail the shoe was lost

In November 2010, Jennifer was twenty-four years old and living in her childhood home, under strict curfew and aggressive inspection. Her lifestyle seemed to have stalled out at late adolescence, and there was at least one solid reason for that: though unbeknownst to her parents, she had never completed high school, having come up short by a single course credit. The easiest remedy should have been to retake that sole course in summer school, at the end of senior year; her early admission to Ryerson University would still have been forfeit, and she might have had to do a stint in community college while waiting to reapply, but that sort of thing is possible to manage without losing too much time. Except that that sort of thing is not possible without losing too much face, and so it was not the easiest remedy at all. As a course of action, above eminently rational plan would have raised questions: *How could a lifelong straight-A student fail a calculus class?* Pull a loose thread and it might all come apart: that she had been doctoring her report cards since ninth grade—elementary school graduation having been the moment that the world broke faith with her, and she stopped running herself into the ground after its empty promises of meritocracy.

You see, Jennifer prior to high school was the real deal—and something of a legend for it. "She was one of those students other teachers were always talking about," the elementary school secretary remembered, while a former teacher declared, "I would have taught her from junior kindergarten to grade eight if I could have."[14] Her academic performance was such that, at middle school graduation, "Jennifer expected to be named valedictorian and to collect a handful of medals for her academic achievements"[15]—even as, meantime, she seriously pursued (and ranked in) both piano and ice skating. Her teacher at Scarborough's New Conservatory of Music attested that "Jennifer reached a proficiency level in piano that . . . she has only seen a handful of times" in forty years; in figure skating her parents groomed her to compete at the national level, with designs on the 2010 Winter Olympics in Vancouver. She came by none of this easily. Her eighth-grade teacher recalled an alacrity that reminds me of Azia: how Jennifer "whipped out her agenda before he even got that evening's assignments out of his mouth," and "if she received a mark that she didn't like, she'd never complain, but sought out advice for the next time and then she'd do it. She would take it to heart." This sentiment was echoed by her piano teacher: "She was a perfectionist. When I was telling her there was a mistake or we had to change something, she'd listen. When I saw her next, she fixed it." And, what she did on the ice, she managed despite both severe asthma and eyesight so poor that without the glasses she could not wear while skating, she could "see shapes but no definition."[16]

All of her pursuits were prestige generators: individual endeavors in which ability was publicly recognized with "awards, prizes, and trophies." None was of her own choosing (she would have liked to try out for track, but such a team sport and school activity was not allowed), yet Grimaldi reports that Jennifer "developed a passion for both" piano and skating, such that "goals she said were originally her father's soon became hers."[17] So well internalizing her father's master plan may have made her a true believer—but it can't have made the effort entailed much less punishing. She started piano at age four and pursued figure skating until perhaps eighteen, when she tore her ACL. "Some nights during *elementary school,* Jennifer would come home from skating practice at 10 p.m., do homework until midnight, then head to bed. The pressure was intense. She began cutting herself—little horizontal cuts on her forearms."[18] So when *this* girl, who had not been named eighth-grade valedictorian despite her every expectation, then sat through that entire graduation ceremony without being called up for a single award, something broke.

If only more had broken. Instead, she contained the rupture and kept up appearances that next year, then the ones after: Yes, of course, she would plan "to do two years of science, then transfer over to [University of Toronto's] pharmacology program, which was her father's hope." Yes, of course, she was still her parents' "golden child," their portable trophy. This performance continued despite the increasing gape of opportunity costs, also not of her choosing. In the picture Ho painted, those costs had as of high school become more conspicuous, to both Jennifer and her peers:

> Hann was the classic tiger dad, and Bich his reluctant *accomplice*. They picked Jennifer up from school at the end of the day, monitored her extracurricular activities and forbade her from attending dances, which Hann considered unproductive. Parties were off limits and boyfriends verboten until after university. . . . By age 22, she had never gone to a club, been drunk, visited a friend's cottage or gone on vacation without her family.
>
> Presumably, their overprotectiveness was born of love and concern. To Jennifer and her friends, however, it was *tyranny*. "They were absolutely controlling," said one former classmate, who asked not to be named. "They treated her like shit for such a long time."[19]

Her family approached parenting like a competitive sport; what child could afford honesties about failures where winning was everything?

so close and yet so far: theories

It is due time to address Tiger parenting head-on, and so I will— but hopefully without allotting undue time or credit to the author of that particular term. When Yale Law professor Amy Chua published *Battle Hymn of the Tiger Mother* in 2011, she packaged and branded a body of shared experiences, a kind of open-source cultural code, with true marketing genius. Chua's memoir neither originates nor studies anything with authority, however; merely sells it in bad faith. The (inter)national attention her book received came at the expense of its intimate public[20]—and, indeed, of any reader susceptible to its stockpile of unfounded pronouncements and reckless advice, trademarked with the Ivy League affiliations of its author. Having inveighed against the book twice in print already (once by blog and once via academic forum[21]), by your leave I'll not repeat myself here. Suffice to say that, handy though it unquestionably now is to have "Tiger" as shorthand for model-minority moms and dads who insist on the success frame, *Battle Hymn* itself contains no proprietary knowledge that we need—and its author has continued to discredit herself sufficiently that little point remains in debating the value(s) of her account.[22]

What now goes by Tiger parenting (which I'll refer to interchangeably as success-frame or model-minority parenting) has been the focus of decades of studies in psychology and sociology. That work has tagged and sorted much of what circulates as common sense or personal history among second-generation Asian Americans. For instance, it is fairly well accepted that, among the four classic parenting styles charted by developmental psychologist Diana Baumrind, Asian immigrant parenting tends to fall into the Authoritarian quadrant. (See Table 3.1.)

But whereas, studying white American households, Baumrind linked the Authoritative style alone to all things good and cautioned that Authoritarian parenting leads to a host of undesired outcomes (passivity, hostility, poor academic performance, etc.), those who have applied her model to Asian American (and other nonwhite) families have seen markedly different patterns emerge. Specifically, they've demonstrated that in Asian immigrant households, Authoritarian parenting correlates to strong academic performance.[23] Armed with this, psychologist Ruth Chao has flagged the four categories as having been drawn on a Western bias and sought to recast Chinese immigrant parenting, for one, not as dysfunctional but as Confucian—that is, expressing an alternative set of norms and virtues.[24] Yet, the work in this subfield has itself been biased, as recently recognized by researchers themselves:

Table 3.1 Baumrind Parenting Styles

Parenting styles	Supportive	Unsupportive
Demanding	*Authoritative* Parent recognizes her own special rights as an adult but also the child's individual interests and temperament. Uses reason as well as power to achieve her objectives. Is not ruled in her decision-making on group consensus or the individual child's desires; but also does not regard herself as infallible.	*Authoritarian* Parent attempts to shape, control, and evaluate the behavior and attributes of the child in accordance with a set standard of conduct, usually an absolute standard. Values obedience as a virtue and favors forceful measures to curb self-will where the child's actions or beliefs conflict with what she thinks is right conduct.
Undemanding	*Permissive* Parent presents herself to the child as a resource for him to use as he wishes, not as an active agent responsible for shaping or altering his ongoing or future behavior. Allows the child to regulate his own activities, avoids the exercise of control, and does not encourage him to obey externally defined standards.	*Neglectful* Parenting is indifferent and characterized by minimal effort. Parent may be inconsistent in affection, emotionally unavailable, or unaware of the child's developmental needs and may neglect discipline altogether or use strict disciplinary practices sporadically.

Sources: Diana Baumrind, "Current Patterns of Parental Authority," *Developmental Psychology* 4, no. 1 (January 1971): 22–24; Lisa Pellerin, "Applying Baumrind's Parenting Typology to High Schools: Toward a Middle-Range Theory of Authoritative Socialization," *Social Science Research* 34, no. 2 (June 2005): 286–287.

There are, however, a number of gaps in current research on parenting in Asian-heritage families. . . . [T]he image of the "model minority" has dominated scholarly and public discourse on Asian American children and adolescents. Subsequently, theory and empirical research on Asian American children has focused predominantly on their educational achievement. This emphasis, however, overlooks their psychological and social well-being. As a

result, the role parenting plays in Asian American children's education has been well established in the literature. In contrast, much less research has focused on how
different types of parenting may influence the psychoso-
cial development of Asian American children and adolescents.[25]

The problem with this lopsided research platform, though, is more
fundamental a glitch than the leaving of "gaps" in the path of knowledge, gaps that need just a targeted application of bricks to fill.
The problem with this focus on educational achievement is that it
is tautological: It takes a high-performing group, asks what makes
them tick, then concludes that this wiring is adaptive and func-
tional because the group is high performing. As a follow-up question, the attention to "gaps" asks after the undesired side effects
or costs of this manufacturing process (these being core concerns
in process improvement). Though better-intentioned, the latter
does not begin to consider whether the device being fashioned
for market is a prudent aim for human potential, or the industry
itself an ethical claim on human performance? Whether perhaps
what makes pursuing the success frame so costly is not merely its
means, but its ends? A meaningful critique of the "model minority" must ask harder questions. If the only permitted endpoint is
itself dehumanizing, then achieving it entails the constant stunt-
ing and pruning of one's wildflower humanity, one's nonquantifi-
able self.

Read through the online comments of those who empathized
with Jennifer, and the outlines of this harder critique start to
emerge: "My mother was the coldest, the harshest, the most eager
to push me to my limits just so I could be competitive with the
children of her prestigious friends. It wasn't even about me," one
reader puts it. Another confides,

I'm the son of Chinese immigrants. . . . I used to think
my upbringing was extremely strict, but the reality is that

it's about the same as most immigrant families. . . . I was actually depressed enough to self harm, and most of that came from the pressure to live up to the Asian stereotype that many of my friends were meeting. . . . I did honestly have thoughts of life without my parents, but I was always repulsed by those thoughts. . . . That could have been me if only, I dunno, my parents hadn't constantly reassured me that I was more than a trophy case.[26]

A story's intimate public can do a researcher an excellent service by boosting signals, amplifying patterns. The longer quote appears in a Reddit thread devoted to the Ho account, in which discussion of the trophy is something of a lightning rod, drawing ten mentions across nine people. Their undercurrent is this: "[Asian] immigrant parents' main interest is not in academics per se. Instead, [they] care first and foremost about *outcompeting* others."[27] That they compete, however, not on their own merits but on their children's can feel like this: In dreamlike scenes from a short film by Georgia Lee, "Asian American children have become their parents' pets and are made to perform—play piano, achieve high SAT scores, greet their aunties in Chinese on command. Tightly leashed . . . (literally) by their parents, these children have become pet automatons in a stifling and nightmarish world of familial obligation and scholastic pressure."[28] As an emotional symbol, the trophy expresses both a standard of this child-rearing cottage industry and the damage *inherent* to using that standard for love.

This is not to suggest that all the members of Jennifer's intimate public viewed her with kindness or saw her with clarity; far from it. Grimaldi describes a scene at her trial in which an audience member "is asked how the testimony about Jennifer's rigid upbringing affected him;" he answers, "It's no more strict than anything I was raised with." Likewise, "Numerous female journalists of Asian and South Asian background leave the courtroom singing loudly from the same songbook, remarking how much stricter their upbringings were. 'That's nothing! My dad used to . . .' is heard more than once."[29] Similar sentiments could be found even among readers of Ho's profile, apparently laboring under the notion that familial relationships follow a simple arithmetic: measurable inputs of violence produce predictable amounts of suffering. If this were so, siblings within families would reliably suffer and respond to abuse in uniform degree and kind. We know that's not how it works. There is no linear equation that predicts, let alone justifies, murderous returns on torment or tyranny, and to suggest as much is fatuous—but to be fair, success-frame parenting is a particularly unreadable form of violence. It was the entire mission of my first book to explain this: that the intensive surveillance and unbounded control in such a household—based on granting the child no rights over her person or future, no valid desires or feelings save to be the best child of her parents—look like no big deal from the outside. In fact, because it produces such obedience and high GPAs, such parenting seems to many beyond reproach. But to be utterly unable to speak one's mind or choose one's circumstances for eighteen, nineteen, twenty-four years and counting is brutalizing, and it can break you. Nothing bruises, nothing bleeds, but you may begin to wish that it all would—may begin to carve an SOS into your flesh yourself—so that someone might know you are losing your mind.

So a casual observer of Jennifer's case can't be judged too harshly for trivializing her claims of pain. More often than not, well-turned products of Tiger parenting will even trivialize their own, dismissing their heartaches and hunger pangs as they have learned diligently to do. The scholarship does not necessarily fare better; even researchers can underrate the force carried by things that take no physical or measurable form. In a human-development study of the effects of Baumrind-type parenting styles on "adolescent disclosure," for example, researchers in the *Journal of Child and Family Studies* asked nearly two hundred teenagers to rate how often they clashed with their parents and to categorize the parents' manner of enforcing rules for a range of eighteen activities. This data was graphed against how much the teens professed to tell their parents about their activities and where-abouts, and how much they believed their parents know. Across its racially mixed sample (37 percent Asian American; the remain-der Latinx, Arab, white, and Other in descending order), this study found that despite seeking the tightest control, Authori-tarian parenting reaped the most conflict and the least actual knowledge of a child's doings. Certainly, this stands to reason: to disclose defects is to risk being subjected to more of the "coer-cive" control that is an Authoritarian parent's specialty, including "shaming, ridiculing, interrogating, demanding without explana-tion, and threatening." Yet, because this research doesn't disag-gregate its racial data, we can't know whether Asian American Authoritarian families might look different on close-up (as other studies have suggested): A trophy child does not defy her Tiger parents; resistance is a defect. And the clash not had—aborted or unthought—is not counted. "Have you ever had a conflict or disagreement with your [parents] about this issue?" the interview-ers asked, and "How angry would you say these conflicts are?"[30] Perhaps they have never read *The Joy Luck Club*: "Well, I don't know if it's explicitly stated in the law, but you can't ever tell a Chinese mother to shut up. You could be charged as an accessory to your own murder."[31]

What's more, though, whatever findings may come of the above study, its premises limit their utility. The *Child and Family Studies* article gauged parental responses to activities as divided into four social domains:

> "Personal (i.e., actions or choices that involve individual taste or preference)," deemed to include Physical appearance, Platonic friendship, Extra-curricular activities, Bed-time, Expenditure of allowance money, and Future career;
> "Prudential (i.e., actions that harm the individual actor but not others)," including Smoking, Staying out late at night, Homework completion, Academic grades, and Dating;

"Conventional (i.e., rules and rituals intended for social order, efficiency, and predictability)," under which is slotted Chores, Participation in religious family rituals, and Table manners; and

"Moral (i.e., actions that entail harm to others)," which includes Helping and sharing, Fighting with siblings, Lying, and Damaging others' property.[32]

Parents were pegged as Authoritarian or Authoritative, for example, based on their style of regulating these activities: whether they responded with Punitive or Responsive, Coercive-Demanding or Rational-Demanding practices, say. But the study did not test the validity of the domains themselves, instead taking it as bedrock that "both adolescents and parents agree (in diverse cultures)" that, on the one hand, moral, prudential, and conventional activities fall under parental jurisdiction, but, on the other, "parental authority in the personal domain should be limited because adolescents' ability to assert autonomy in this domain is essential to identity development and sense of individual agency."[33] This is cute. And not just because some of the items under "Personal" would appear, in a model-minority household, comically missorted. (Recall Hann's directive that Jennifer's future career be pharmacology, or Amy Chua's infamous list barring her daughters from playdates and "choos[ing] their own extracurricular activities,"[34] and it seems fair to wonder what types of families researchers consulted to populate this domain.) The disconnect begins with the very premise: If there are domains in which a parent's authority is limited, and a child's autonomy is a value to cultivate, we are no longer operating inside the moral order of success-frame parenting. Because inside this universe there is but one domain and it is Moral (i.e., actions that entail harm to the parent): inhabited either by the obedient child, who is good, or the disobedient child, who is bad. To apply a rubric that assumes four social domains to Authoritarian families without regard to race is thus to risk incoherence for results. At a minimum, it is to miss the distinguishing features of an authority whose jurisdiction is total. Where the very idea of bounded parental domains is an affront, anything can be grounds for the abject opprobrium due the wicked.[35]

It is, in varying stripes, this boundless quality that escapes the existing research on disclosure and deception in Asian immigrant families. Even among psychology studies in specific search of ethnic differences, research designers may gaze squarely upon patterns distinctive to model-minority formation without seeing their import or the need to account for them. And research instruments that don't recalibrate to the forms of zero peculiar to success-frame parenting risk false negatives. A study comparing disclosure to parents across Chinese, Latinx, and white American teens, for example, noted in its literature review that "obligations to assist, respect, and support the family are stressed in both Chinese and Mexican cultures, although they are expressed *primarily in terms of academic achievement and aspirations among Chinese youth*."[36] Although not something to treat as an article of faith (itself needing quite a bit of nuance), that prior finding points to a possible skew in Chinese immigrant households, such that the usual things won't necessarily be in the usual places. But, careful though they are to note that, the authors of this *Child Development* article do not recalibrate sufficiently to capture disclosure across the range of deviance/compliance on this potentially Tiger scale. Working off the four social domains, the researchers include twenty-four activities in their survey but only two pertaining to academic achievement. Neither of these directly queries achievement: "Whether I finish or turn in my homework" and "How I feel about my school work and grades."[37] Like the Dow Jones or Nasdaq of high school, GPAs and test scores are the highly watched indexes of a model-minority teen's life, so to ask subjects not a single question about how they report when the quarter goes badly is to pass on measuring the most salient forms of deviance.

Nor did the following observation, from the study's own data, seem to stand out: "Some teens (23%) did not engage in any of the prudential activities (40%, 12%, and 14% for Chinese, Mexican, and European origin, respectively)."[38] Presented without further interpretation in the Methods section, these figures seem to be considered something less than findings, and there is some truth to that: The survey's six questions about smoking, drugs, parties, alcohol, cutting class, and unprotected sex netted no data on the habits of disclosure for nearly half of its Chinese American respondents—arguably a rather dismal reflection on the alignment between instrument and intended phenomenon of study. Once again, researchers seem to have been looking for the usual things in the usual places, to little avail. But whereas the previous false negative came of catching nothing in an indifferently placed net, this one comes more of being calibrated to see no finding, when to have caught nothing is extraordinary. Think about it: four out of every ten of these second-generation Asian Americans had nothing to hide or disclose by way of socially risky or deviant behavior. Instead, they may—even when running a marathon of dishonesty, say, an everyday campaign of nondisclosure—be guilty of none of the classic delinquencies. It is a sign of better-attuned scholarship to be, in fact, astonished by such "*limited* range of rebellion." Interviewing Chinese American college students who had chosen majors in knowing defiance of their parents' wishes, Vivian Louie was struck by their incommensurate sense of their own deviance. She cites the example of a young man who "saw himself as a rebel for not going into pharmacy, as his parents wanted him to do, [but] was thinking of pursuing an advanced degree in the social sciences."[39]

Granted, the secret boyfriend makes Jennifer's deception less ascetic than Azia's, but, in the scope of her everyday activities, Jennifer is still a poster child for self-restricted rebellion: her free time spent in the same daily devotions. "She would pack up her book bag and take public transit downtown. Her parents assumed she was headed to class. Instead, Jennifer would go to public libraries, where she would research on the Web what she figured were relevant scientific topics and fill her books with copious notes."[40]

Such simple details, but they told some readers plenty—based on things specific and familiar to success-frame upbringing:

> Hey I had my share of sitting in a library (while I was skipping class due to an hour long commute). I guess it's an Asian thing.
>
> Thinking back I could have been doing something fun.
>
> - Wow . . . that didn't even occur to me to be weird until reading your post. . . . She wasn't partying, she didn't go on a hike—she went to the library. Christ . . . [41]

There is something remarkable here, and it should speak pointedly to investigators as well (about directions for future study at least, but also) about assumptions that inform the present research. After all, this (un)finding troubles the framework assembled at the beginning of the study, in which

> youth who desire more autonomy but face strict parental control and strong expectations for obedience may strategically manage information *to get their way*. Thus, in situations of *disagreement*, Latino and Chinese teens may be more likely than European origin teens to conceal information from parents to avoid upsetting their parents, getting in trouble, or disrupting family harmony.[42]

That narrative is likely fair to most teens—perhaps as much as 77 percent of them on average. But it cannot account for perhaps four out of ten model-minority children who lie or omit not primarily because they disagree with their parents' values or vision for their future but because they share that vision and can see no other. It is not an accurate narrative of them whose everyday activities—even the deceitful doings—are a function not of trying to get their *own* way but of trying desperately to live up to their parents'. Claiming to have received loans or grants so as not to accept "tuition" money from her parents, and never having gone to a club or gotten drunk in all her would-be college years, Jennifer ran herself an austere scam, with little in the way of material or other gains. While she secretly picked up some part-time jobs, visited her boyfriend at his university, and taught piano lessons on the side, none of this suggests much self-indulgence. It bespeaks instead a warped dutifulness, even obedience, as she continued to cultivate for her parents the illusion that she was the daughter they wanted: going through the motions of the career path *"which was her father's hope."*[43] Though it is an underlying consensus in the body of scholarship, the standard-issue narrative of autonomy and defiance cannot begin to describe Azia or Jennifer's plight: the all-or-nothing of passing for model minority.

what opportunity costs

Historically, of course, "passing" comes from America's slavery past. For those fugitive slaves whose appearance made it feasible, being taken for white made for better odds of eluding capture. After abolition, being able to assimilate was a matter of safety and survival but also of setting a different future for one's descendants than one's ancestors had had.* The price of passing completely, however, was unspeakably high and remained so for generations: "Those who pass have a severe dilemma before they decide to do so, since a person must give up all family ties and loyalties to the black community in order to gain economic and other opportunities."[44] For Adrian Piper, African American artist and philosopher, the history of passing in her family is of loss and its long wake. Her personal essay "Passing for White, Passing for Black" dwells for some pages on her father's sister, an accomplished woman who married into a prominent white family and (in the late 1950s,

---

* See the introduction for an expanded history and discussion.

perhaps) "proceeded to sever all connections with her brothers and their families, even when the death of each of her siblings was imminent." Piper writes that her aunt's "repudiation of us" cut deeply and not only the once but afresh with each milestone and reminder: "To read or hear about or see on television her or any member of her immediate family is a source of personal pain for all of us."[45] In this archetype of racial deception, a lone actor forsakes all the people she comes from.

But suppose now a scenario in which the unit of passing is not the individual but the family, and its destination not whiteness but the model minority.* In her interviews with second-generation Korean Americans in New York City, sociologist Sara Lee found that working-class subjects who hadn't finished college were apt to experience the model minority as a "falsely ascribed image" and to live with a deep sense of shame and inadequacy for it that "came from their parents." That is, it's their parents' shame they internalize, because insofar as "first-generation Korean immigrants define their prestige and status within their coethnic community through the academic achievement of their children," lineage is rank-ordered by the higher degrees of descendants. The weight of pedigree conveniently shifts away from the past (working class) and onto the future (elite). Dealt the stigma of second-generation underperformance, then, some families pass. One of Lee's respondents shared that at Korean functions she lies about her schooling—*because her mother did so first*: "[My mother] says I go to NYU and that I'll be going to Yale. . . . Obviously, a lot of parents do this."[46] Her phrasing leaves unclear whether "this" means parents falsely claiming a child's acceptance into a prestigious school, in particular, or parental inflation of children's achievements, in general, but regardless the gist is this: the passing that seemed so outlandish at the beginning of this book turns out to be an extension of the commonplace. *Obviously, a lot of parents do this.*

---

* See chapter two's discussion of the new racial hierarchy in academic standards.

Now further suppose a scenario where leaving one's people is not the price of racial masquerade, but racial masquerade is the price of staying. Across Sara Lee's study and Lee and Zhou's, subjects who did not make the model-minority cut came to feel that "they did not belong to [their respective Asian] American community."⁴⁷ Worse, their personal disqualifications are also their parents' social jeopardy, as we have seen. So, among Asian immigrants' kids, disownment is a punch line. In their natural habitat—engaging in social media expressions like *High Expectations Asian Father*—this intimate public handles disownment as part of the meme:

- "Onry 96% in Maths Test," one reads: "I HAVE NO SON."
- "Your sister get B on math test? CONGRATULATION. YOU ONLY CHILD NOW."
- "Asian that doesn't do science? ORPHAN."
- "Asian grading scale: A = Average, B = Bad, C = Catastrophe, D = Disowned, F = Forgotten Forever." ⁴⁸

As memes go, some are "inside joke[s] that the whole Internet gets."⁴⁹ They activate shared knowledge, and in so doing consolidate the group as an identity.⁵⁰ This is easily one of those. In fact, scholarship on meme culture has described *High Expectations Asian Father* specifically as an instance of "ironic, sarcastic performance of certain kinds of normativity experienced throughout childhood and teenage years".⁵¹ Each share, like, and riff cosigns the understanding that model-minority standards mark the boundaries of the family, if not legally then socially. That is, the child who "fails" academically/racially may well find herself under house arrest even as she is banished. In her famous memoir, Maxine Hong Kingston, herself an immigrants' daughter, heard her parents speak of an "outcast table" in their childhood homes and filled in the blanks from her own experience: "the powerful older people made wrongdoers eat alone. Instead of letting them start separate new lives . . . , the Chinese family, faces averted but eyes glowering sideways, hung on to the offenders and fed them leftovers." She deduces that her aunt, so shunned she had become a No-Name Woman, nonetheless "must have lived in the same house as my parents and eaten at an outcast table,"[52] in a purgatory of disgrace. Disownment is a punch line; it is also a parenting practice. But it is no way to live.

Meaningfully, perhaps for Jennifer, legal theory (albeit the American set) has not yet taken into account that "passing" can take this form for the model minority: a lifelong impersonation of Asian racial forms, under duress. In the early 2000s, Kenji Yoshino's famous law review article and subsequent popular book on "covering" did call attention to a variation on passing, one more performative and not classically/necessarily "racial." As first coined by sociologist Erving Goffman, covering refers to a subtler way to manage stigmatized identity, having to do not with donning a false face but with downplaying one's own features: making them carefully inoffensive to those in power. Covering queer identity might mean not holding hands with one's same-sex partner at social functions; covering racialized identity might mean adjusting one's accent or speech, shearing one's dreads, or avoiding fermented foods at the office. A professor of constitutional law, Yoshino argues that institutional and systemic demands to cover—for example, by employers or school administrators—constitute a "hidden assault" on the civil rights of protected groups. Covering in this sense is forced assimilation, as "an effect of discrimination as well as an evasion of it."[53] Rightly so, yet his premise wherein covering is costly bears expanding. Yoshino holds that "covering is work," a kind of emotional labor with psychic tolls, inequitably distributed. The effort entailed in "bending over backward all the time to avoid making white people uncomfortable" becomes an "exhausting burden," and the watchfulness needed to rein in every racialized or stigmatized behavior is tantamount to "living [a lie]."[54] In her own law review response, Jean Shin argues that for Asian Americans, more specifically, covering takes the form of tamping down "ethnic or 'foreign' behaviors, while projecting their arguably more desirable status as model minorities."[55] Insofar as projecting model-minority status is an exhausting lie, however, it is so among coethnics and in the home as much as anywhere else. Indeed, in the Tiger family there is nothing mutually exclusive about the model minority and the ethnic; the former does not equal assimilation versus the latter's authenticity.[56] The proud Chinese/Korean/Vietnamese family that vies together, lies together. But such high expectations come with an unrelenting demand for covering: There is no alternative space in which not to excel, none in which mediocrity does not offend, least of all with one's parents.

If I've belabored the distinctiveness of success-frame as home-life, it's because the sort of things that seem regularly to elude research design—unbounded, unquantifiable, undisclosed—may hold the very difference between the calculated and the desperate, the sympathetic and the absurd. I dare say it's around these things that, even in the book that gave the "success frame" its name, legibility stops. In their chapter "Success at All Costs," sociologists Jennifer Lee and Min Zhou devote a section to an "outlandish" story: the single interviewee out of eighty-two whom they discovered to have misrepresented himself extensively. The researchers list depression and nervous breakdowns as among the mental health tolls that *other* interviewees "pay when they cannot meet [or reject] the success frame." But what they consider the "cost" or the "payment" in deception is unclear. We learn that "Garrett," son of a Hong Kong immigrant mother and white surgeon father, found himself attending a "safety school" when, to his shock, his stellar grades from an exclusive East Coast boarding school and 1560 (out of 1600) on the SAT failed to yield admission to any Ivy. Rather than abandon the success frame, however, "[t]hroughout the interview" Garrett claimed to have full scholarship offers from two law schools—impossible because he had dropped out of college. Prompted by his "jittery" and "defensive" manner, researchers took the unusual measure of verifying his account; they reported incredulously that he had lied "in order to look better in front of the interviewer, whom he had never met and most likely would never see again." To wit: an anonymous, volunteer subject had adamantly deceived them to no practical benefit whatsoever. While clearly quite struck by the illogic of this, however, the researchers offer thoroughly pedestrian explanations for his motives. Citing a social psychology finding that performance-oriented students may lie about test scores to preserve their appearance of intelligence or ability, even to peers they had never met, Lee and Zhou conclude that Garrett "lied about his accomplishments in order to save face . . . , to mask shame about his 'failure,' and to buttress his self-worth in front of another."[57]

That explanation may suit the more garden-variety deceptions just fine—the self-serving benefits of telling nosy neighbors that one's child is enrolled at Yale rather than community college are self-evident. But it provides little actual insight into the *compulsive* quality of Garrett's behavior, and the ways it shades into Azia's or Jennifer's. For that, we look to Lauren Berlant, philosopher of American life via literary and cultural criticism.

imagine no possessions . . . I wonder if you can

It is hardly coincidence that Berlant discerns the liberal-capitalist subject's fantasy life—its perverse obstinacy, its appalling meagerness—in part through the story of an impostor: The protagonist of the film *L'Emploi du Temps* (directed by Laurent Cantet) is a business "consultant" who, having lost his job some time ago, spends his days asleep in his car or killing time in parks and diners while spinning the fiction of a prestigious new post. His is a heightened enactment of what Berlant calls cruel optimism: "when something you desire is actually an obstacle to your flourishing. It might involve food, or a kind of love; [or] it might be a fantasy of the good life," like a success frame. What makes an attachment cruel is its mockery of the suitor's bid for well-being on its terms, along with his inability to quit them. Berlant sees cruel optimism in modes of living such as the U.S. obesity epidemic, for example, but elaborates on it most in the form of the "heterofamilial, upwardly mobile good-life fantasy": that blueprint which, despite receding from possibility for ever larger swaths of the population, maintains its grip on first-world imaginaries and global dreams. In Vincent, who cannot give up the social position he seems allergic to, Berlant finds her textbook example that subjects "might not well endure the loss of" their cruel object because, even though it harm them, "the continuity of its form provides something of the continuity of the subject's sense of what it means to keep on living on and to look forward to being in the world."[58] Though not much given to explaining himself, Vincent muses at one point that the only thing he had liked about his job was the driving, alone on the road for hours: "I felt so good in my car I had trouble leaving it."[59] He would drive past his exits, and appointments, leading eventually to his sacking. This impulsivity we have seen somewhere before, its short-sightedness not so inexplicable. Consider that Vincent's solitary satisfaction with the position is couched not even in terms of any family life or social belonging it afforded, let alone in the work itself; its pleasure consisted of a limbo during which all social roles were suspended, yet all were met. His every role galls him, but in these amber stretches he lives the dream.

That is, Vincent's life before the firing is already a condition of cruel optimism, in the latter of two senses that Berlant lays out: "a relation of attachment to compromised conditions of possibility whose realization is discovered either to be *im*possible, sheer fantasy, or *too* possible, and toxic." Having lost the paycheck that had kept this good life fed, it would not have been difficult for him— a white man with private school networks and a wealthy, connected father—to find a fungible position. It would, indeed, have been *too* possible, and so he keeps driving. Bade choose between seeking more of the toxic same or perhaps something different, he leans into his toxic good-life as literal fantasy because "fantasy is the means by which people hoard idealizing theories and tableaux about how they and the world 'add up to something.'" Though the "object" of the fantasy may not be what he wants, he cannot let go; without the single genre by which he understands himself to matter, neither he nor the world means anything. Berlant characterizes this Vincent of the diegesis as in a state of impasse: "a space of time lived without a narrative genre, . . . after the dramatic event of a forced loss, such as after a broken heart, a sudden death, or a social catastrophe, when one no longer knows what to do or how to live and yet, while unknowingly, must adjust."[60]

Undoubtedly, as a prototype for cruel optimism, Vincent's crisis and impostoring yield concepts true and useful to model-minority life. Yet, insofar as cruel optimism can take two different shapes, Berlant's protagonist does not embody both, and insofar as he exemplifies the good life as *too* possible rather than *im*possible, he does not stand for Azia or Jennifer. It is perhaps due to her interest in "crisis ordinariness" and a generalized condition of precarity that Berlant's choice of impostor depicts such mild desperation: crisis as prerogative, and optimism considerably less than cruel. Consider: on being busted, Vincent cannot bear to face his father, whom he'd bilked of 24,000 francs for a fictional second home. Despite this, the story closes with his acceptance of a new senior position on the strength of his father's name, following this assurance from the old man: "It's not serious. Money problems can be worked out." Not only is his safety net sound but all will be forgiven: "You don't have to explain anything," soothes papa, "This will be forgotten in a month."[61] The fantasy, like a collapsed circus tent, shall be raised again intact. In fact, despite financing his vacation with a one-man Ponzi scheme that gulls friends and family out of tens and hundreds of thousands of francs, Vincent faces no discernible legal repercussions at movie's end. If crisis ordinariness can come with such impunity, we should all be so unlucky. Nothing in Azia's or Jennifer's cases, by contrast, suggests that they receive or indeed expect any buffering from the full fallout of their choices. And those very different estimates of their respective precarity would seem to inform how carefully each treads water. With other people's savings, Vincent splurges: 125,000 francs on a new car he takes off-roading; a cool 500 francs, over his wife's objections, to buy his teen son's good opinion. Both girls, on the other hand, spent their borrowed time and money sparingly, seeming even in impasse to work more than play. (Although then still young enough to sponge off her parents, Jennifer seems to have worked her pizza parlor gig like her life depended on it: She "was one of the best servers at the restaurant . . . a manager's dream, being able to serve seven tables at a time, always professionally, managing her time so the food came out promptly, and she made few mistakes. She took plenty of shifts and often worked five nights a week."[62]) Vincent we meet napping rather than climbing through a window to bed, while his job even before he lost it (per the press release: "drab, middle-management"[63]) would have been by success-frame standards *already* a public failure. An impostor he certainly is; a cruel optimist, mildly. The model minority he is not.

crueler optimism

Lurking behind Cantet's character, however, is a murderer, on whom Vincent is loosely based. The story of Jean-Claude Romand broke in January 1993, when firefighters pulled him from the blaze of his home in Prévessin-Möens, France, and found inside the bodies of his wife and two children. In the previous forty-eight hours, Romand had murdered each of them, then driven fifty miles to shoot his parents at their home, and returned to stage a perfunctory suicide. It quickly unspooled that the man everyone had thought to be a leading figure in medical research at the World Health Organization had overslept a final exam in his second year of medical school and, instead of arranging to sit for it later, spent the eighteen years since in charade. Between his life and Jennifer's, then, are eerie parallels: the misstep made irreversible, the course set to devastating dead-end. In bypassing

Romand for his fictional counterpart, however, Berlant does not require her model of cruel optimism to account for the expanse between those points: from crisis very ordinary, to violence on a monstrous scale. This is unfortunate, as there is much to explain:

- While I'd never resort to murder, I can definitely say the thought of not having parents around has crossed my mind a few times, especially during report card season. "<Insert Evil Rival Student Name Here> can do all these things, why can't you?" is often that arrow that pierces through the tiniest of cracks in your psychological armor and words sting. Heck, they can hurt forever.[64]
- This story did a number on me, because my life used to resemble hers. I come from an Asian family, with a lot of that immigrant parent mentality. I was an exceptional student in high school, getting scholarships for university and having my pick on which to attend. And then it went downhill from there. . . . I failed, then tried again, then failed, then tried again . . . I failed the third time. But I didn't tell anyone . . . pretended everything was okay, and then told everyone I graduated. . . . I don't have any sympathy for Jennifer Pan because I feel like I was in her shoes. After her parents found out, her dad reacted similar to mine, so did her mom. I used the opportunity to get my life back, she used it to wreck hers.[65]

Even those readers who condemn Jennifer for her patricide do so from a place of recognition, proximity. For the success-framed child, the road to murder, while certainly less taken, is clearly not so far from home.

Not that this chapter is about to posit Romand as a model-minority subject, nor his reasons and drivers as echoing Jennifer's line for line. Cruel optimism is more versatile than that. But it is also (inter)personal in ways that Berlant's bird's-eye view will not acknowledge—by design. While her tremendous work has been in the theory of emotions and affects, the intellectual traditions she draws from are rooted "less in works of psychology than in works of Marxist thought."[66] This means that she is by definition interested in discerning how feelings are mass-manufactured, on the macroscale, by forces of capital and politics: how human populations are emotionally engineered to be fit for labor, disposable for profit, tractable for governing. This feeling she has named cruel optimism, then, is an invention of neoliberalism: Fantasy lives were not this meager nor obstinate until it had become a matter of course that all things bright and beautiful, all creatures great and small, all things wise and wonderful—the market sets the value of them all. This is not to peddle conspiracy theories; Berlant warns us explicitly away from casting neoliberalism as a sentient (or sovereign) force with "coherent intentions that produces subjects who serve its interests." But, while sage, that care not to anthropomorphize what is structural is best balanced with a care not to strip intent from personal choices. That is, look to the microscale of individual workers, consumers, students, or households, and we find that *subjects* with coherent intentions may yet produce others who actively serve neoliberalism's interests.

Little has been written of Romand's natal family. In his true-crime book *The Adversary*, novelist Emmanuel Carrère describes a quiet and upstanding clan of foresters, "respected for their austere and stubborn character," but he can hardly be said to pry. We hear that Jean-Claude learned young not to share his feelings nor disclose sadness, so as to avoid upsetting or disappointing his parents; this resonates, but without benefit of examples it is hard to know what to make of it. We learn that his parents had expected he'd go into forestry but seem to have accepted his choice of medicine with good grace: "A bit worried at the beginning, [his father] was soon naively proud of [Romand's] success."[67] It's a respectful distance Carrère keeps, rather like that extended to the families of scammers and shammers as a whole (see chapter one): Their upbringings glossed as unremarkable, even blameless, such impostors come across as narrative mutations. Likewise for Berlant, Vincent's parents rate no mention, and so her analysis does not challenge this impression that the criminality comes from nothing in the family—is visited upon the parents as on any other bystanders. But Vincent's Ponzi grifting is modeled on Romand's, the men in both versions financing their fantasy lifestyle by destroying the lives of others. It is, in fact, the impending collapse of the Ponzi scheme that triggers the sequence of murders, meaning the economic and familial crimes are hardly unrelated. How, then, could we take the impostor's financial violence in response to precarity and exposure as economically, socioculturally, and historically meaningful but his interpersonal violence as meaningless anomaly?

There is such a thing as neoliberal parenting,[68] and what alarms have rightly been sounded about it in recent years have to do with its embracing and folding that economic value system into its definitions of the successful child, the successful family. Of course, raising a family in an era marked by the privatization of societal responsibility for children takes one form for the already impoverished (for whom the stripping of social infrastructures and safety nets means the abandonment to bare life), and another for those who fear to become them. It is the latter we mean here: Describing what it is to "bring up neoliberal baby," a legal scholar explains: "As financial language creeps into the terminology of our closest relationships, the middle class child [has become] a parental investment. . . . The terror behind the frantic aspiration of 'intensive' middle-class parenting is a fall into the social abyss reserved for 'losers.'"[69] That this is possible appears obliquely in a *different* section of Berlant's chapter—one built on an intergenerational story of striving: "Franck, the 'baby,'" she writes, "embodies the familial investment in upward mobility"; he is to his parents "cultural, social, economic capital."[70] What is normalized in immigrant families as "discussions" about the need to repay parental sacrifices and excel "for the sake of the family"[71] are thereby shrewd, not benign. Note what feelings come into play—when neoliberalism is addressed in the context of family—which are not named in all the pages of *Cruel Optimism*: Terror. Franticness. Family gives neoliberal abstractions love and flesh, tooth and claw. For the model minority especially, familial intentions narrow the sights for normative survival; familial intentions raise the stakes for failure. Take basic terror and ratchet that high-wire act to medical school, Stanford, the Olympics. How terrified is the father who makes the social abyss a child-rearing tool: fail him and free-fall into disownment. How frantic is the child who claws back.

To keep the focus of this chapter steady, I have tried not to get tangled in the details of a second high-profile murder case. My aim, rather, is to deploy Romand's story only so much as warranted to expand the use of cruel optimism: as routing the dreams of households no less than individuals and thus as permeating relationships no less than identities. So expanded, it may contain even violence beyond the pale as *inter*personal/intimate and *im*personal/structural, both. This because, as always, my quarry haunts a range that rational or functionalist models, cost-benefit analyses, sociopathic diagnoses, and even Marxist explanations do not measure. This book grapples with "outliers" in the belief that those ranges where logic goes dark are not *less* true to form, but *more*: more compressed, more unchecked, more committed. And I have come to suspect that our passers doubled down on the model-minority promise not because they had been the less deserving among us, but because they had been among the most. Take this 2012 Pew Research Report on the "role of effort in getting ahead," and mull with me a moment that what it describes is not an extremity but core to the success frame:

> Asian Americans, compared to the general American population, are more likely to believe that individuals can get ahead and make it if they are willing to work

hard (69 percent versus 58 percent). Moreover, *fewer Asian Americans believe that hard work and determination are* no *guarantee of success* (40 percent versus 27 percent) [*sic*][72]

That there norm is an already elevated commitment among Asian Americans to the fantasy that following the rules with diligence and determination will lock in the good life: *For the model minority, cruel optimism is more optimistic, and thus more cruel.* Add to this the knowledge of where Jennifer and Garrett had ranked along that spectrum of rule-followers—she of the conservatory-caliber music and Olympic-caliber sports; he of the exclusive prep school, nearly perfect SAT—and it would follow if they ranked also among the truest of those believers. Indeed, Jennifer's "stunned" surprise at receiving no recognition at the end of middle school,[73] along with Garrett's "astonishment and dismay" at landing none of the Ivys,[74] speak not to dashed hope but to confounded worldview.

cost-cost analysis

How might it be for *these* two to admit publicly to their failures? Lee and Zhou were struck by Garrett's unwillingness to show his hand even for the small spell and safe space of his time with them. But to hold their request for truth harmless is to misappraise its cost fundamentally. Recall the existential magnitude of deceit: On behalf of her aunt who had passed permanently into white society, Adrian Piper figures that "it seems to require so much severing and forgetting, so much disowning and distancing, *not simply from one's shared past*, but *from one's former self*."[75] But where it's understood that "if you're not perfect, then you have Asian Failed,"[76] *passing* means passing for perfect, and it is again *not*-passing that would exact those existential tolls. Berlant has been helping us appreciate "how costly it might be to stretch or open patterns of living beyond those facilitated by available genres and forms of institutional scaffolding".[77] For Garrett to verbalize his failure, even for an audience of strangers, would have meant hearing himself announce the death of someone he wasn't ready to mourn—intolerable even if only for a moment. Jennifer confided her academic straits to no besties or family for the six years of her double life—discretion better to secure the lie, surely, but this exceeds the pragmatic. Consider the life-jeopardizing secrets that other intimates keep: a friend's infidelities, a son's crimes. Deception so total as hers hints at compulsion, where the lie itself has priority above all other emotional needs.

Such compulsion has context. The word "perfect" (variations of which describe Jennifer no less than eight times in Grimaldi's book) is model-minority code for a lot:

> I kept a lot of [problems from my mom . . .] because my family is prestigious and want you to [. . .] be on top . . . they don't want you to mess up, they want you to be perfect . . . It's scary because they expect a lot and when you can't they keep pushing you and you have a problem with it you can't even go to them because they might find out what your problem is.[78]

Per Garrett's professional parents, to fail out of the success frame is to fall out of their social class: "a bachelor's degree alone was 'the contemporary equivalent of a high school diploma.'"[79] Without even a BA to his name, he must rate among the untouchables—or surely would, were his and his family's peers to know. Meanwhile, Jennifer testified in court that the truth of her failures "would shame my parents and they would be ostracized by their friends."[80] For both, their senses of worth, identity, *and* family had been tightly pegged to achievement and guaranteed recognition. Instead of shutting that value system down, the universe's breach of success-frame as contract seems to have forced it into an illogical loop:

NONE WHO FOLLOW THE FORMULA FAIL.

NONE WHO FAIL ARE MY PARENTS' CHILD.

MY PARENTS' CHILD FOLLOWS THE FORMULA.

What has happened to them is inconceivable, inadmissible, on this Möbius strip. And so, Garrett continued unabated to "[express] his staunch belief in the success frame while underscoring how his educational background squarely fit it."[81] Likewise, on the stand, Jennifer's statement, "I was the school's pet, not . . . just the teacher's pet" may have been defiant or plaintive, but its pride is unmistakable.[82] That Lee and Zhou explain Garrett, then, as having falsified an interview "to look better" unfortunately means that they have mistaken his genre: taken him for an operator or a scammer, a bold American entrepreneur of the self.[83] But the success frame is not a story about rational, economic choices; it is a genre in Berlant's sense, "a structure of conventional expectation that people rely on to provide . . . affective intensities and assurances"[84]—even when those conventions allow so little of the self to flourish, discount so much life as failure. His story, like Jennifer's, is cruel optimism not of the too-possible but of the impossible kind.

felt options, lack of

During Jennifer's trial, prosecutors asked her why, if life at home with her parents had been so miserable, she hadn't simply moved out? Why have them killed instead? Her response was not widely believed: "I didn't want to abandon my family. I didn't want them to abandon me."[85] That she cared about their feelings and that she didn't want to lose them were claims too counterintuitive for mainstream taste in murder mysteries. In genre fiction, the kind of homicide story that sells comes down to this: "All the motives for murder are covered by four Ls: Love, Lust, Lucre and Loathing."[86] And so, in the eyes of prosecution and press, Jennifer had clearly acted out of love and lust for her boyfriend, greed for her inheritance, and hatred for her parents. Any remainder—humanity too complicated, emotions too incongruous to contemplate—was handily dispatched as abnormal psychology. (So, nothing here that we normals need worry our pretty little heads about.) In fact, when Grimaldi solicited "well-known American therapist" Barbara Greenberg's opinion for his book, the Connecticut psychologist felt confident in pronouncing Jennifer "a sociopath, someone who lies incessantly to get his or her way and does so with . . . little regard or respect for the rights and feelings of others." The good doctor uses "sociopathy" and "anti-social personality disorder" interchangeably and freely in her assessment of this young woman she has never met, but "says she ran the symptoms Jennifer displayed through a diagnostic test from the *Diagnostic and Statistical Manual of Mental Disorders* (*DSM*), which offers standard criteria for the classification of mental disorders." And, "When asked how Jennifer might rank on a scale of one to ten in terms of severity of [ASPD]," Greenberg answered "emphatically" that "[Jennifer would] be a ten."[87] In its handbook of medical ethics, the American Psychiatric Association does declare it unethical for practitioners to offer diagnoses of "an individual who is in the light of public attention" but whom they have not personally examined. Known as the Goldwater Rule and revived in public discourse about the Trump campaign, this interdict finds remote diagnoses irresponsible even where the mental health of a voluntarily public figure is a question of national welfare—never mind in the case of a young woman in prison, refusing interviews.[88] But let's leave that aside. Fairfield County, where Greenberg's practice is located, has seen a boom in Asian American residents in the past decade; the population in Stamford stands at a respectable 8.44 percent in 2019, while the second-place spot in the county goes to Danbury at 6.09 percent. Still, this is a far cry from Toronto, Canada, where the Asian Canadian population clocks in at 32 percent, much less from Jennifer's high school, where "roughly 60 percent" of her classmates were Asian.[89] And, as we have seen (in chapter two), model-minority pressures operate at a different order of magnitude in high schools where being Asian is the norm than where they are maybe 8 percent of the student body. Greenberg is egregiously out of her depth.

Skeptics of the *DSM* are a varied lot, including practicing therapists as well as the humanist likes of me. Deep internal criticism holds that the tool is fundamentally, epistemologically flawed: it produces reliability (consistency of diagnoses across raters) without validity (demonstrated correspondence between claim and reality). Infamous examples of this include the rampant diagnoses of "hysteria" in Victorian-era women or the designation of "homosexuality" as a disorder; both terms were entries in *DSM-I* and *DSM-II*, until it was agreed that as "diseases" they did not exist.[90] Populated by vote among a panel of reputed experts, the manual is a device created via agreement to enforce more agreement*—yet upon this tautology are built the compulsory apparatuses of insurance reimbursement, research funding, and even publication in journals with peer review.[91] Meanwhile, from the outside, we ethnic studies types certainly have questions for a document that purports to label anyone, whatever their personal or geopolitical history, by a flat set of symptoms. For one, culturally uncalibrated instruments take bad readings—as we have seen. "Sociopaths are often goal-oriented (i.e., lying is focused and is done *to get one's way*),"[92] says Green-

---

* See epidemiologist and former clinician Aileen Duldulao's essay in the *Asian American Literary Review*'s special issue on mental health, for a quick but penetrating critique of the *DSM* in use: "As the gold standard for the classification of mental disorders, the [*DSM-V*] presents the criteria for diagnosis as being objective and even value-free, but diagnosis is in actuality highly subjective. While diagnoses of physical health conditions can arguably be based primarily if not solely on empirical testing of biomarkers and through behavioral observations, this is not necessarily true of all mental health conditions. Major depressive disorder, dysthymia, anxiety, bipolar disorder, cyclothymia, and obsessive-compulsive disorder—these are all clinical manifestations of mental health conditions for which there is no biological test. One cannot be tested for mental health conditions the way one can be tested for cancer, malaria, or even strep throat, even though psychiatric intervention relies heavily on pharmaceuticals that impact neurobiology." "Proof," *Open in Emergency: A Special Issue on Asian American Mental Health, Asian American Literary Review* 7, no. 2 (Fall/Winter 2016): 68.

berg to explain Jennifer, and like our researchers on disclosure she has mistaken Tiger cubs' ways as their own. But more worrisome than the quality-control quibbles of cultural bias is the very output the *DSM* is bent on. Whatever positions a body has assumed under the crush and heat of inequality or exploitation, run them through this diagnostic and it will spit out a reading of individual pathologies, poor posture. For instance, "many minority children, especially African-American kids, are misdiagnosed with conditions such as [Attention Deficit Disorder] or oppositional defiant disorder, which are suggestive of defiant emotional problems resulting from poor or neglectful environments."[93] Checklists such as favored by the *DSM* draw the eye to observable, individually wrapped symptoms—requiring no effort be made to see the whole of a person, much less the arc of her life in context. Though designed for efficiencies of diagnosis, the *DSM* also abets efficiencies of treatment: Untrammeled by empathy in analysis, disorders diagnosed may be summarily dosed, or the disordered sentenced without compunction.

Grimaldi buys that Jennifer is a sociopath, adopting this diagnosis for his own narrative, but Greenberg's wasn't the only consult he obtained. Fenced off in his Afterword is an account the reporter must not have known how to integrate, so jarringly at odds is it with the previous—and, in fact, so disconcertingly close to my own. A psychotherapist in Toronto, Betty Kershner based her essay on Jennifer (which Grimaldi does seem to have published in full) on the court documents he provided her—presumably, the same files he shared with Greenberg. This second opinion is, thus, no less remote, but it proceeds with careful consideration, ethical in both form and content: Kershner prefaces her remarks by disclosing the limits of her knowledge and authority—acts of due diligence absent from Greenberg's casual annihilation—and qualifies all that follows accordingly: "We do not know if they or their families were [X]"; "Children in such families can feel [Y]."[94] She also refrains from any *DSM* diagnosis whatsoever, even in speculation. In interview, Kershner spoke of her wariness around symptom labeling, and her preference for the more intensive modes of analysis rooted in personal histories and psychoanalysis.[95] Moreover, her fourteen-page essay is a concerted effort not to excuse the crime but to explain it, such that we may make out human motivations behind the orange jumpsuit and headlines. (Such an exercise in empathy seems to me the only justifiable reach here for psychological authority. Can I imagine other scenarios in which principle dictates that healers or teachers speak from their expertise to denounce the powerful and dangerous in absentia? Most certainly. But whatever Jennifer is, she has never been powerful. There is nothing heroic about vilifying her name.)

What, then, does Kershner heed in Jennifer's explanations that she has seen enough of love and pain to hold possible? For one thing: why it is that moving out was not, for this trophy child, the obvious solution it might seem. Whereas those limited to the four L's can only wonder whether Jennifer was too enamored of the "creature comforts of . . . middle-class existence" in her parents' house to shack up with Daniel, Kershner suggests the following instead:

> [S]omeone with this type of upbringing would most likely have incorporated the values of her family, and Jennifer's sense of personal esteem likely by now was dependent on public success, presenting a "correct" image to the outside world. She would not be likely to settle for living in a place that she would consider substandard, or in a public relationship that lacked social status. Status was non-negotiable. . . . If she moved out . . . it would become a public shame.[96]

It's intimate-public knowledge that within Asian immigrant communities, sexual indiscretion is the stuff of social disaster, spelling ruin not only to a girl's reputation but to her parents' as well. Even among success-framed children, girls are subjected to "greater parental controls over their movements, bodies, and sexualities than their brothers."[97] The same families that keep a scoreboard of their progenies' academics trade insider information about daughterly virtue: "my aunts will be talking with my mom and they would be like . . . 'Oh, I heard about this girl. Such a promising future and then now she is pregnant, she's living at home. Like, she is outcast.'" From interviews like the above with immigrants' daughters, research psychologist Janna Kim concluded that "gossip, which was passed among parents and sometimes spread through the larger community, implicitly reinforced the notion that sexuality was a morally reprehensible activity for daughters and a threat to a family's honor."[98] To live openly with her boyfriend, Jennifer would have had to be willing to torpedo her family's name, and bear with the consequences.

So there is that. But let's also remember the kind of "status" at stake for the Pans, whose competitive parenting had for years basked at the higher heights of Jennifer's achievements. From this elevation, the plummet of disgrace is itself catastrophic. What the success frame constructs, in other words, is a tiny dais on which families jockey to stage perfection under the constant glare of spotlight—then, below that, such excommunication as is reserved for the feared, the rejected, the too-nearly self. To feel how impossible even small truths are, then, think of failure as a communal phobia, wired with fear/revulsion like that for the racial or sexual Other. Tellingly, Kershner words Jennifer's ambition as being able to "'come out' as a different kind of person" from "the vision of the daughter her parents had wanted," were they gone.[99] To borrow from a study on queer passing:

> [R]espondents feared losing close relationships with family members, friends or colleagues if it was discovered that they were lesbian or gay.
>
> [Some] chose to pass with certain people . . . out of respect for the values or beliefs of their interactants or not wanting to disrupt the lives of those close to them.

As one lesbian stated, "I'd feel bad if I made my parents miserable."[100]

Deception, then, can come of caring rather than sociopathy. Can murder? In a fantasy built by cruel optimism, plausibly.

> On one level, killing her parents was the ultimate way to protect them from the shame of her failure: they would never know how far down she had gone and the world would never know that the family was not a smooth-functioning unit of hard-working high achievers. . . . They would die with some remaining shred of belief in her and would not have to face the shame of social exposure.[101]

Whatever else it was, arranging for her parents to die inside the dream they had insisted on was also a workaround, hatched by someone not practiced at adaptation.

Insofar as coming out to loved ones takes some willingness to test and risk those bonds, this is not what impostors do. Their dutiful adherence to the appearances of the success frame asks of filial piety no quarter. Unlike those whose forms of rebellion—though ever so modest—test the sanctity of the frame (with social science Ph.D.s or careers in nonprofit work, say), Jennifer had embraced her father's ambitions for piano, ice-skating, and pharmacology as her own. Per Sara Ahmed, producing a subject "happy" with her lot "is about the narrowing of horizons, about [her] giving up an interest in what lies beyond the familiar"[102] and, better than most, this is what Jennifer had done. So rather than put distance between her family's values and her selfhood or make them learn to adjust their prerequisites for love, she kept her parents' optimism afloat on borrowed time, paying the cruel dues alone. On a path that would eventually fulfill none of their model-minority expectations, she seems to have been able neither to plan for any other future, nor to relish her present as if she truly gave no thought to tomorrow. Yet, the disappointment or dis-ownment that her deception had deferred would be all the more devastating—to everyone involved—when, finally, it arrived. So maybe five years in, that existence—days spent on meaningless work, moving toward a future she dreaded—had begun to feel not so very different from the prospect of actually enrolling in a pharmacology program of her father's choosing. Maybe Jennifer had grown tired of her daily observances of the success frame and despaired of ever being able to stop. Had she ended this in suicide, no one would have called her a sociopath; she would have been handily absorbed into a genre that rattles off "attempted suicide, cutting, and drinking [as] not uncommon among Asian Americans—girls in particular—because of stress."[103] The public would have blamed her Tiger parents readily, losing them their status along with their daughter. But that the same anger, fear, and desperation can turn to homicide instead, and mean the same thing, some of us will not contemplate.

So let me help. The evidence is clear that Jennifer hired two petty criminals to stage a home invasion and kill Bich and Hann. Signals were arranged; money changed hands. And you would think that, given her many years of experience inventing plausible lies and setting up alibis, Jennifer would have had a formidable cover-up. Not really. Though he had helped arrange this fiction of a robbery by strangers, when her coconspirator and (by then) ex-boyfriend Daniel spoke to police the very first time, he chat-ted amiably and without apparent prompting about Jennifer's troubled relationship with her parents. They seem not to have rehearsed this part: how to perform the lie. It seemed to take little more than simple police inquiries for details of the whole bumbling plot to come tumbling out. Jennifer was brilliant at a number of things, but crime was not one of them; she was a resourceful and skillful liar and a convincing actress, but appar-ently only at the role she had already been assigned since child-hood, which everyone assumed was hers anyway.

That is, Jennifer did neither crime nor violence well, neither having been the focus. That her parents' death would have benefited her in knowable and even material ways is part of the story; it is not the main plot. To orchestrate the murders as she did, Jennifer had to script a kind of conclusion to her fictional life: cast actors for the roles of burglar and executioner, then direct the time and place for the various parts of the action, wherein the terrified victims die offstage, and she, playing the part of the innocent third victim, is spared. This production is a grand finale, and as such a kind of moment of truth—not in terms of its facticity but as a performance of rarefied fantasy. These are the types of moments in which supervillains are given to monologue, the vengeful to power trips. In those final moments, Jennifer "could have told her parents off with anger and impunity"—yanking off her "happy mask" in triumph or listing her grievances and demanding an apology. Insofar as any of those choices would have clinched the genre of her story, so does the choice she made instead: "Jennifer has no final words for her parents," indulging in no compromises of the fourth wall. The import of this Kershner explains as follows:

> This was an opportunity that I do not think Jennifer would have passed up if revenge had been her primary motive. I believe Jennifer really wanted her parents to die thinking well of her. She wanted to preserve what she could for them of the illusion that she was a good daughter and that they were a good family together.[104]

To put oneself out of misery can have to do with protectiveness and preservation, holding intact not life itself but a vision of life that bears the living. As misleading as it would be to define such suicide as malice against the self, there are homicides in which the same applies: I think of Sethe and Beloved, No Name Woman and the baby she carried with her to the well. How much easier to cast these away from us as evil and sociopathy; how much more it demands of us to wade through them as deeds thick with love and tragedy—where wits end and what is interminable or irresolvable goes to die. It is the nature of a limit case to "[give] the lie . . . to easy theoretical positions and to political polemics,"[105] and so Jennifer should here. What convenient fictions have we been guilty of, who would have the world believe that raising trophy children is a bloodless sport, or manufacturing model minorities a victimless crime?

chapter four

Bad Boys

To my right at this shin-high, scuffed table sits Robert Chan. In the seat designated for inmates, he faces the guards who watch over this visiting room, and we talk at a ninety-degree angle. Sometimes expressions are literal: this is a table too low for things to pass under it. But it is also too low to serve well as writing surface or food setting; the spatial rules of this place are an ergonomics of dis-ease. In time-lapse, a video of the room would have shown a flow of prisoners and their loved ones rotating through the tables around two still figures—one with hands folded across his knees, the other hunched over a lined notepad, pencil scribbling—as morning light shifted into midafternoon.

I am here to find out if the crime Robert committed as a senior in high school has anything to teach us about model-minority overachievement, desperation, and deception. It's a case the press gave a name: the Honor Roll Murder, because the victim along with three of the five convicted were Asian American boys on college tracks at their respective schools. It's a story that inspired Justin Lin to make *Better Luck Tomorrow* (2002), still arguably the most iconic of Asian American films.[1] In both versions, the shocking death is preceded by a slow build of criminal activity: from decidedly nerdy cheating rings to illegal substances, all under the virtuous cover of Academic Decathlon. Together or separately, these two accounts still draw considerable energy in the collective imagination: the former a haunting, in the Orange County spaces where it happened; the latter a legend, as if a cultural high point at which *our team won*. Measuring the distance between the murder and its tellings, then, is part of the work of this chapter. How could a communal nightmare become source material for vicarious triumph?

I have been saving for last the cases of two separate Asian men arrested for using bomb threats to cancel two separate graduation ceremonies—at which their families would have listened for their names in vain. Quickly nabbed by the police, these passers instantly became criminals as well as laughingstocks, even though violence seemed more the by-product of their undertakings than the mission. "Bad Boys" folds stories of a legendary murder into a book about college impostors because they are equal-and-opposite ways of passing for perfect. Where the impostors broke laws in order to live by the rules of the success frame, the honor students used the success frame as cover to break laws. Yet, they're not the inversions their receptions might imply. Seen as responses to the success frame, the hapless bombings and the senseless murder may actually "mean" much the same thing. What sets them apart is instead how differently a model-minority imagination invests in them: as contenders or losers in contests of masculinity or neoliberalism. Sorting cases of an extinguished life and of thwarted commencement ceremonies into one set, this chapter clearly does not rely on the usual warrants: Gradations of violent crime are less germane here than the *longue durée* of narrowing options. To suppose someone a passer—whether in the strict sense of college impostors or the loose sense of everyday performances of model-minority identity—is to hypothesize that what defines them is not their choice of weapon but the codes of honor they inexorably followed to an unwinnable showdown. That is, this final stretch began with an inkling: that though theirs seem such different ways to go bad, these black sheep of the model minority are casualties of the same system. Passing traps the passer, and it can be murder to get out.*

the nuclear option

Audley Yung started UC Riverside in 2002 as a biological sciences major, soon changing that to "undeclared in the College of Natural and Agricultural Sciences." There is record of his having taken summer school classes through 2006 but of no regular enrollment after 2003.[2] He kept his tidy, off-campus apartment, though, and stayed involved in student life. As late as Spring quarter 2007, he made friends "via a Facebook page for UCR students interested in photography"; professing a "passion for fashion photography," he did photo shoots for student functions, including "a dance for a Vietnamese student association, . . . and a formal for [his] fraternity." He also called his mother every night, "just to ask how she was doing." I suppose if someone had known how to look, trouble signs plain as day might have prompted a conversation, a dispensation, allowing this young man to love his mother differently. But that dispensation not forthcoming, this "good son who never wanted her to worry, she said,"[3] eventually gave his mom a graduation date he said was his.

---

* As this chapter's title suggests, masculinity and violent crime rank high among its concerns. In public imagination, though, Asian American male violence often free-associates to Seung-Hui Cho (2007) or Elliot Rodger (2014), so it's important to be clear that they are not who we mean. That default leap is a reactionary one. Certainly, there are ways to frame research questions such that a hoax bomber and a school shooter must be dealt with equally, but meeting at the intersection of race, gender, and bloodshed alone does not make the vengeful-loner frame compulsory here. To be clear, placing "bad boys" in the same impostor category as Sara or Azia does not mean ignoring gendered aspects of their racialization or violent aspects of their masculinity. But it is to insist that Asian males need not automatically answer to being Seung-Hui Cho.

Eight hours down the spine of California from Richmond is a long drive alone, so one imagines that Audley tried dissuasion first. *Ma, graduations are dumb anyway, and it's not safe all that way by yourself.* It's only ever the two of them in the press: her total commitment to celebrating his achievement matched by his total commitment to sparing her his failure. So it was that, on Friday, June 15, 2007, Audley Yung "set a palm tree ablaze, left some Molotov cocktails in plain sight and sent threatening notes to UCR officials, warning of trouble if" (not one but) "six weekend graduation ceremonies went forward."[4]

In the affidavit for Audley's arrest, the police detective who took his confession recorded motive with an elegiac tone I appreciate: Ceremonies canceled, "his Mother would return home and everything would be as it once was."[5] This is cited in a local article, which itself runs more poignant than newspapers are given to. A journalist expecting shut doors and waves of "no comment" may well have been moved by the mother's apparent guilelessness, as in her anguish, she instead "encouraged a reporter to walk around her son's apartment" and brought out proof after proof of his good character. They seem to have sat at some length, and it is the kindest coverage Audley receives: "'Don't worry, I'm OK, fine,' he would always say. The mother said she wished she knew her son 'more deep,' putting her hand to her chest."[6]

Remaining press coverage on Audley is scant, however, and perfunctory: a spotty four pages of Google results compared to the over thirteen for Azia, though they were exposed within weeks of each other. Stanford or Harvard may be clickbait, but not UCR. The success frame applies also to being newsworthy, remember: Without elite hashtags, a passer hardly qualifies as impressive or tragic, even to those who know a desperate racial performance when they see one. Phil Yu's AngryAsianMan.com is a longtime news aggregator and opinion leader, and, by his sights, Audley fit a pattern where college kids "drop out, but don't really tell the folks back home, for fear of disappointment. . . . And the checks keep coming, I guess. Then, come graduation time, parents are expecting to see their kid in a cap and gown walking across that stage. Sooner or later, the truth comes out, and there's big trouble." Moreover, he's seen this *"several times amongst friends and acquaintances"* and thinks it could be "an Asian thing." That shared feeling is quickly revoked, though, an intimacy rejected: "But dude, none of those kids tried to blow up the school."[7] Despite citing the local article, Yu pulls no punches about calling Audley an idiot, in four separate ways.[8] An intimate public is not always an understanding one, granted; commenters could be mean to Sara and Azia, too. But the extra jabs for good measure suggest an active investment in stamping this guy a loser—in a contest judged not on personality or talent, friends or looks or athleticism, but intelligence. An academic flop at a non-name-brand school, Audley draws precious little empathy—empathy being a resource distributed not according to degrees of need or even resemblance, but along indexes of value. By the success frame's actuarial tables, this life is not worth much.

Having served his time, Audley is a professional photographer now, I'm happy to report, though he could not be reached for interview, and who can blame him. Still, so little of his story inhabits the public domain—indications are that his mother is an immigrant, and their family not well off, but even this much is unverified—that reconstructing causality is hopelessly beyond reach. Even less is known of Amit Kumar Sinha, who rated only two articles in the *Orange County Weekly*[9] and a cameo in Audley's coverage for the *Los Angeles Times*, despite having also called in a bomb threat (and set a campus trash can ablaze) in order to halt a 2005 commencement ceremony. Police would find him among UC Irvine medical school's graduating class, trying in rented regalia to blend in. In the stands, family awaited his hooding for a program to which Amit had never applied. How or where he spent five years of deception, much less what precipitated them, no reporter bothered to ask. Even from barest facts, though, the design flaw in passing is clear. Remarks a sarcastic *OC Weekly* staffer,

[L]et's face it, we've all been in his shoes. I mean, who among us hasn't lied to our parents about attending UC Irvine's School of Medicine . . . accepting Mom and Dad's financial assistance (it takes about $50,000 a year for a UCI med student to live and study) for years and years and then, on the day of the medical school graduation, panicking that the folks . . . will find out the awful truth—who would blame you for doing what any thinking person would do: calling in a bomb threat.[10]

That the success frame is a human investment scheme—"a future orientation, [subject to the child's] toeing the line in the present for the incipient rewards of a high-paying job, respectable career, and solid family life"[11]—is never so obvious as when it doesn't pan out. Gone bust, passing for model minority contorts into a kind of Ponzi scheme one runs on oneself: spending one's future in the present, until time runs out.

That Audley and Amit both opted for bomb threats has connotations—these are publicly disruptive means, turning personal disasters into mass chaos. In contrast, Jennifer Pan's desperate measure lashed outward but stayed personal, which loosely tracks with gender patterns the United States is nightmarishly familiar with: learned masculinity's sense of entitlement to turn personal grievances into public ones, for all the world to bear.[12] It must be said, though, that neither man intended nor did bodily harm to anyone: Their meager devices were fashioned for the *appearance* of danger; violence was not their design.[13] So violence does not make the bomber—but neither do hoaxes make the impostor.

Eldo Kim's ploy to defer his final exam for "Politics of American Education" (no less) earned him nearly fifteen pages of search results and international coverage. But Eldo was no interloper. A sophomore intending to major in psychology and sociology, his was the signature combination of artistic and intellectual, humanitarian and athletic accomplishments befitting a Harvard undergrad.

In December 2013, however, he was facing the third anniversary of his father's death, in a school culture widely said to be defined by overachievers "scared to fail or do poorly, even a B." The previous night, he'd mildly inquired over dorm Listserv whether anyone could answer "several quick questions about the course";[14] a half hour before the scheduled exam the next morning, he emailed an almost poetic riddle to the administration:

> Shrapnel bombs placed in:
> Science center
> Sever hall
> Emerson hall
> Thayer hall
>
> 2/4. Guess correctly.
>
> Be quick for they will go off soon.[15]

The threat being empty, he was allowed to avoid trial, with all charges dropped provided he complete restitution and community service—an extraordinary resolution.[16] Without suggesting that media or court be less "forgiving, accepting, and even deferential" of Eldo's crime,[17] I insist we understand what was waived and why. While no incendiary devices were involved in Eldo's stunt, what should separate it from Amit's or Audley's is not the presence or absence of objects afire; what's salient is what each stood to gain, and others to lose. Our two impostors disrupted the logistically massive, public-facing business of commencement, yet, in classic passer fashion, reaped no material advantage. Affected graduates lost their pomp and circumstance, but forfeited neither grades nor diplomas. Had Eldo not been caught, though, he'd have profited from extra study time and an edge over any classmates distracted or upset by the upheaval. Though extreme, his bomb hoax is more akin to bribing proctors for extra accommodations than studying for tests one will never take, or renting robes for a graduation not one's own. This is not the gamble of someone weighing costs and benefits clearly, but it is also not the all-in of someone who sees no other play.

Above all, the distinction between Eldo and our impostors is what they stood to lose: for a strict passer, exposure spells wipeout. With their houses of cards about to collapse, Audley and Amit needed earthquakes to disguise the rubble of personal disaster. What they sought to avoid was (of their own slow making but) catastrophic. What our Harvard sophomore sought to avoid was many clicks from that. For one, according to the Dean of Undergraduate Education in 2013, "The median grade in Harvard College is . . . an A-. The most frequently awarded grade . . . is actually a straight A."[18] This suggests a considerable buffer against catastrophe—unless, granted, anything less than perfect is anathema to the self. Being a creature of the success frame makes one susceptible to "identity contingency": I'm not alone in saying that "to 'fail' . . . may have been difficult for Kim to accept . . . because it would not confirm his racialized identity of being . . . 'model minority'," and that, moreover, "being a Harvard student and . . . racialized as 'smart' may have influenced Kim's judgment when he was weighing the proverbial *costs* and *benefits* of . . . what he most likely rationalized as a victimless crime."[19] No matter how well one measures up to the success frame, its nature is to taunt that annihilation lies one misstep away.

In such a moment, a student certainly might become a passer in the strict sense: tell a lie about a final he didn't take, say, then stack ever more on that teetering foundation, until he had no moves left. But, on that morning in December, with the stakes still low, Eldo charted instead a shortcut: taking a sharp right through felonies to bypass the competition. And then . . . officials let him reenter the race. The public apology he wrote as condition of pretrial diversion gave his status as "a student at the College, currently on leave."[20] Whether he ever returns, his story showcases the high redemption value of the success frame. Meet its measure and publics large and intimate agree you're in the winning—so the greatest crime would be to waste you: "If only Eldo had directed the energy it took to concoct this ridiculous scheme into some actual studying. Now he's looking at five years in prison, three years of suspended release, and a $250,000 fine."[21] Miss its marks, and your loss is your own—measured only by the money wasted on you.

In light of the compassion gap splitting public appraisals of the college impostors from the Harvard undergrad, it's worth remembering that they were all passing for the same thing: a standard of excellence that never needs help, never admits defeat. Here, success-frame personhood meets masculinity, and high achievement becomes inseparable from what it is to be a man. Model-minority masculinity hinges on achievement and embeds acute fear of "disappointing [one's] supporters by not returning their investment."[22] This is the backdrop against which we read a murder case as another story of passing, and the convicted as other model minorities.

breaking news

By the time the *Orange County Register* reported Stuart Tay missing, police had already identified those involved in his killing and would move in the next day. I begin with that paper's chronology of the murder and its legal aftermath because, between the lines, it also captures the standoff between the public clamor to know this case and the insufficiency of every fact as explanation.

- Dec. 31, 1992: Stuart Tay, an honor student at Foothill High School, leaves his home in Orange at 4 p.m., telling his sister he must run an errand.
- Jan. 1, 1993: Nearly 11 hours later, Tay's mother calls Orange police to report her son missing. Compton police report finding Tay's car—stripped—at about 10 p.m. There is no sign of Tay.
- Jan. 2: Orange police learn from a friend of Tay's that Tay had mentioned buying a gun from Robert Chan,

a fellow student. The two were to meet at 4 p.m. on Dec. 31.

- Jan. 4: Police arrest Robert Chan, Mun Bong Kang, Abraham Acosta, Kirn Young Kim and Charles Choe, all students at Sunny Hills. The Tay family hired a private investigator to probe Tay's disappearance. The investigator's information is turned over to police, who use it to make the arrests. Chan refuses to talk, but the others tell police a grim tale of New Year's Eve, when they beat Tay in Acosta's garage. Then they buried his body in a shallow grave nearby.
- March 29: Chan is granted a separate trial by Superior Court Judge Kathleen O'Leary.
- July 30: Choe admits his part in the killing and is sentenced to eight years in the custody of the California Youth Authority. He agrees to testify against Chan and the other defendants.
- April 4, 1994: Chan's trial begins.
- April 7: Choe testifies that Chan was the prime mover in the Tay slaying.
- April 25: Francis Crinella, a defense psychologist, testifies that Chan is a paranoid schizophrenic who feared that Tay had wired his house with explosives Tay could detonate at any time.
- April 27: Chan echoes Crinella's testimony about his fear of Tay and admits that he helped four others beat Tay to death and bury his body.
- May 3: A jury deliberates less than three hours and convicts Chan of first-degree murder with special circumstances. Chan faces life in prison without the possibility of parole. Kang pleads guilty to first-degree murder before his trial begins.
- Aug. 8: Chan is sentenced to life in prison without parole.[23]

Over the months of breathless coverage, there were two things no one seemed to tire of rehearsing: the academic profiles of those involved, for one, and the brutality of the murder, for the other. The *Register* ran, for instance, a three-part series on Stuart's life, starting with his Chinese Singaporean parents' "immigrant success story," then tracing the mystifying turn wherein this talented son of a successful obstetrician-gynecologist had been plotting to rob a computer-parts dealer, with a group of strangers he'd approached using an alias. The deception exposed, his killing was plotted rapidly but came slowly, as after twenty agonizing minutes of blows to head and body, with bat then sledgehammer, Stuart died choking on his own vomit, his mouth taped closed over rubbing alcohol poured down his throat.

Alongside each segment, the series provided sidebars or charts with extensive data points about the key figures, like so:

Robert Chien-nan Chan

Age: 18

Birthplace: Taiwan

Home: A seven-room, $264,000, ranch-style house with a pool owned by his parents on a cul-de-sac on a quiet street in Fullerton

Academic background: A senior at Sunny Hills High School, he was enrolled in the rigorous International Baccalaureate Program and maintained the second-highest grade-point average on campus. His score of 1,480 on the Scholastic Aptitude Test put him in the top 1 percent of college-bound seniors

Extracurricular activities: Member of Academic Decathlon team, president of German club, two-year player on football team

Favorite book: *The Joy-Luck Club* by Amy Tan

Hobbies: Listening to music, drawing flowers, weight lifting, eating out

College of choice: Princeton University
Career goal: Pediatrician
Police record: Chief suspect in October beating of Sunny Hills
    High School student who reportedly had bad-mouthed the
    Wah Ching, the Chinese criminal society to which Chan
    told some friends he belonged.[24]

Specially tailored fields, these are populated (though no sources
are cited) with answers suitable for a college essay—aside from
that last one. Robert, too, personified the formula for newsworthiness: routine typification that defies expectations.*

His codefendants included two other honor students: Charles,
a senior, was listed with the following as "Interests": "Choe was
planning for college and a career. When his mother visited him
at Juvenile Hall, she quoted him as saying, 'Mama, I can't go to
college, I can't have a job, my life is messed up.'" Having turned
state's witness, he came to play a disparate role in court and media
from the others. Sixteen-year-old Kirn was a junior in IB, son of
a physician, and described as "studious and interested in computers and computer games. Kim also practiced tae kwan do [*sic*], a
form of martial arts, and started a tae kwan do club at school."[25]
An honor student who had not pled guilty, Kirn faced intense
media scrutiny, like Robert's, and was tried as an adult. Mun and
Abraham, having had no honor-student/model-minority luster,
were more peripheral to press coverage and are not considered
passers here.

Such was in essence the story as it made rounds through the
Associated Press, to *Time* and the likes of the *South China Morning Post*.[26] Replete with details, yet psychologically opaque, it's
the sort of cipher that invites filling in. Little of that conster-
nation or conjecture—within families at dinner or coffee table,
between friends at lunch or on landline—survives for our refer-

---

* See chapter one.

ence, however, aside from the film it's generally understood to
have inspired.

artistic license

While symmetries between *BLT* and the Honor Roll Murder are
too many and too obvious to miss, the film does not cling to the
knowns of the case. Justin Lin's stance has long been: "I made a
conscious decision not to base it on that, or any other, real event,"
stating he'd only followed the developments "through newspapers
and television, like everyone else. . . . Also, as an artist I wanted
to explore and deal with issues and themes that are independent
of true people and events." This answer struck some close to the
epicenter of the crime as disingenuous, and the director's unat-
tributed, freehand approach as reprehensible, exploitative;[27] in
hindsight, it seems fair to say that more diplomacy could have
done everyone some good. Yet Lin's fictionalization of the case—
following its million-dollar questions to whatever seemed to him
their most culturally plausible answers—makes him no maverick.
Author Vanessa Hua was likewise express that, though inspired
by Azia along with Audley/Amit, "Accepted" is a work of fiction,
and her source material goes equally uncited.[28] That is, taking a
stranger's personal tragedy as prompt is . . . the sort of thing writers do, pursuing some epiphany of public magnitude. And it is
the sort of thing academics may do, in public interest's name. In
either context, license is not so much granted as hopefully earned,
by measure of zeitgeist or insight.

The ardor among Asian Americans for Lin's shoestring passion project wasn't universal, but much certainly coalesced along
these lines: "*Better Luck Tomorrow* doesn't break down the 'model
minority' stereotype of Asian Americans as straight-A offspring
of pious immigrants; it blows it to smithereens with a morally
ambiguous tale of sex, drugs and violent death."[29] Whether or
not the film got any actual person's motivations right—not its
priority, as a fictionalization—it tapped a vein of defiance among

then-young Asian Americans: a generation not only hounded by Long Duk Dong stereotypes but raised to pioneer the success frame. That even a thumbnail sketch of the model minority is specific to immigrants' kids is not by chance. With the influx of immigrants and refugees from China, Korea, the Philippines, South and Southeast Asia from 1965 to 1980, by "1990, some 63.1 percent [of Asian Americans] were born in a country other than the United States, compared with 36 percent of Hispanics and 3.3 percent of whites."[30] Asian Americans reaching college age in the eighties and nineties had to have been one-and-a-half- or second-generation by an even greater majority. It's also in the eighties that elite universities began to notice the Asian uptick in their student bodies . . . and to resist it.

> At Harvard, for example, Asian-Americans [in 1975] made up barely three percent of the freshman class. The figure [in 1985 is] ten percent—five times their share of the population. . . . The Berkeley student body is now 22 percent Asian-American, UCLA's is 21 percent, and MIT's 19 percent. The Julliard School of Music in New York is currently 30 percent Asian and Asian-American. American medical schools had only 571 Asian-American students in 1970, but in 1980 they had 1,924, and last year 3,763, or 5.6 percent of total enrollment.[31]

Lawsuits as early as 1983 charged that schools had reconfigured admissions criteria to disadvantage Asian American applicants; they successfully extracted apologies from Brown, Stanford, and Berkeley.[32]

I invoke these contests of entitlements not to arbitrate between them but to show that the success frame was already well in effect in Justin Lin and Robert Chan's youth—its following smaller, sure, but its push-pull factors of racialization and racism, internalization and identity? As good as today's newsfeed. The excerpts above and below come from the *New Republic*, with a celebration of "The Triumph of Asian-Americans" as "America's greatest success story." That 1985 essay covers the key components of model-minority discourse: "an ethic of 'personal responsibility'" emphasizing "education, family, parenting, and strong cultural values."[33] These are (per Helen Jun in a reading of *BLT* we'll see more of) not coincidentally the same qualities touted by neoliberalism—that philosophy patented by American economists in the 1970s, which, packaged as an operating system, began to take over global politics and economies like a virus. The *New Republic* was one of its key mouthpieces.

- [Harvard] . . . offers two explanations for [the lower admission rates for Asian Americans]. First, . . . "family pressure makes more marginal students apply." In other words, many Asian students apply regardless of their qualifications, because of the university's prestige. And second, [a] "terribly high proportion of the Asian students . . . [is] heading toward the sciences." In the interests of diversity, then, more of them must be left out.
- [A] great many . . . Asian-American applicants have little on their records except scientific excellence. . . . Since the values of Asian-American applicants differ from the universities' own, many of those applicants appear narrowly focused and dull.
- But there are good reasons for this. . . . [Scientific] careers allow Asian-Americans to avoid the sort of large, hierarchical organization where their unfamiliarity with America, and management's resistance to putting them into highly visible positions, could hinder their advancement.
- Social scientists wonder . . . how Asian-Americans have managed to avoid the "second-class citizenship" that has trapped so many blacks and Hispanics. There is no single answer, but all the various explanations of the Asian-

Americans' success do tend to fall into one category: self-sufficiency.

And to complete the circle:

- The first element of this self-sufficiency is family. . . . "They're like the Jews in that they have the whole family and the whole community pushing them to make the best of themselves."[34]

This is the success frame in beta mode: with limited release and fewer features, but unmistakably the same product.

Like Robert, Lin was born in Taiwan and grew up in Orange County, attending a high school about eight miles from Sunny Hills (SHHS). He started at UC San Diego in 1990,[35] transferring to UCLA in junior year to study Film and Television. His dad was once an airline pilot but, in the United States, worked 364 days of the year in the family's fish-and-chips shop, fielding the same brand of racist bullying Lin faced at school. An interview in *Wired*[36] cites basketball—the court and the culture—as Lin's playbook to American-style masculinity, and it's not hard to fathom that some of these experiences found their way into his film about Asian boys in OC. His protagonist Ben plays basketball, while racially beleaguered masculinity is a subtext to quite possibly the entire plot. That plot in summary:

Ben . . . spend[s his] days worrying about SAT scores and perfecting [his] free throws and checking out girls; [he and volatile best friend Virgil] also scam stores out of computer equipment through a buy-and-return scheme, with the help of Virgil's cousin Han. . . . Along with the school's manipulative valedictorian, Daric . . . , the teens get involved with a cheat-sheet ring and dip into drug dealing . . .[37]

Things spin out for good when a private school senior enlists their help to burglarize his own home. Steve has everything—the Ivy League acceptance letter, the girl, even the secure masculinity—but his bewildering scheme ends in a deadly maelstrom of the group's jealousy, resentment, and panic.

Having seen the film "with a young Asian-American audience," an *LA Weekly* reviewer noted that for the first hour, they "howled at its social comedy," details that he, a white guy, "didn't even know were jokes."[38] For its intimate public, *BLT* is a call-and-response of shared anxieties and fixations, habits and assumptions. Appreciative viewers "took delight in the highly taken-for-granted context" that spoke "to a certain Asian diasporic audience and community" to which they felt they "belonged"; they called Ben's voiceover "lovely, full of knowing lines about double identities, parental expectations, and getting boxed into an identity you didn't quite choose. ('I guess it just felt good to do things that I couldn't put on my college application.')"[39] In Ju Yon Kim's words, when it comes to racial performance, "homework becomes you," because it's a life's rituals that make a type.[40] So the movie gratifies success-frame viewers with scenes of SAT-vocabulary drills—and mortifies them with run-ins with stereotype. Being mistaken for a "math club" while out partying, say, "tugs at a distinctly rebellious thread, born of frustration, [at] a world that tends to see you only one way."[41] It's cognitive dissonance to be mocked for one's excellence, and it will eat at you. So what a visual pleasure these "screen doppelgangers" be, kicking ass and getting A's.[42] That is, what *BLT* celebrates is not actually "resisting the 'model minority' myth" qua burning it down. No, for publics "who alternately embrace and resent their identification as Asian," this is a fantasy about being it all.[43] Headier still to contemplate? That the success frame can be a secret identity: a pair of glasses behind which no one suspects you of fighting extraordinary crimes . . . or of committing them.

You see, what *BLT* nails is that dissonance and its extraordinary satisfaction: "My friends and I thought it was exciting to see Ben and his team steal and lie and scheme and defy what society expected of them, their straight [A's] serving as alibis, and their school clubs covering for them."[44] The shoplifting these boys do is importantly not basic grab-and-go. Their MO is first to target a big-box store by acquiring a set of its rotating return stickers, then charge hundreds of dollars of tech merchandise, exit, come back to pluck identical items off the shelf, affix said stickers to each, and return the second set at the register with the original receipt. This entails two successful, face-to-face performances as customers with good credit, who are due service if the corporation wishes their continued patronage—even if they are maybe seventeen years old.[45] What we see in action is a pirated use of "stereotype promise," which social scientists identify as the benefits of "being viewed through the lens of a positive stereotype." In the orthodox version, "students who are viewed favourably by their teachers would likely perform in such a way that confirms the positive stereotype and show positive academic outcomes *as a result*."[46] All of this is supposed to take place unconsciously, on the level of implicit bias: People associate Asian phenotypes with certain ideas, and students conform to expectations without particular awareness of doing so. That is, this boost is understood as something Asian Americans may passively receive—not something they may knowingly activate. So defined, stereotype promise abides by the ideologically obligatory thesis that model-minority identity is externally imposed: an opiate of the people even if, like religion, the myth have real effects.

That is part of the story; not all of it. So defined, stereotype promise cannot account for this: "Our straight A's were our alibis, our passports to freedom. Going to a study group would get us out of the house until 4:00 in the morning. As long as our grades were there, we were trusted."[47] That bit of the voiceover is one of those "knowing lines," a trade secret uttered aloud and hailed by others in the guild. On both sides of that screen we have possessive investment in model-minority identity: in the film, not some earnest trailing after someone else's good opinion, but a heist-like use of resources; in the audience, no scandalized gasp of disillusionment, but an appreciative recognition of mastery.

The kind of possessive investment I mean, though, is version 2.0. In his original coinage, race scholar George Lipsitz attaches "possessive investment in whiteness" to fairly literal kinds of resource-hoarding for economic and political dominance:

> From the start, European settlers in North America established structures encouraging possessive investment in whiteness. The colonial and early-national legal systems authorized attacks on Native Americans and encouraged the appropriation of their lands. They legitimated racialized chattel slavery, restricted naturalized citizenship to "white" immigrants, and provided pretexts for exploiting labor, seizing property, and denying the franchise to Asian Americans, Mexican Americans, Native Americans, and African Americans.[48]

He traces this legacy of inequality down into the "covert but no less systematic" mechanisms of present-day capitalism and democracy,[49] in a model that emphasizes material interests over personal attitudes: Those with power "invest" in the infrastructure that generates their ongoing advantage, whatever their feelings about racial others. White heritage in the United States is a social system about amassing what there is to "possess."

For social justice, then, the battlefront has been at the base of these infrastructures, whether to dismantle them or to adjust their distribution. Studying civil rights movements, however, some argue that ground gained especially post–World War II has implications for our understanding of possessive investment itself. Per legal scholar Tom Romero II, "national legislation, from the Civil Rights Act of 1964 to the War on Poverty" has "created the conditions by which a fundamentally new possessive investment in color emerged," "one where a person's non-whiteness had political and legal value." That is, "legislation in the 1960s created incentives for individuals of many of the nation's subordinate, but inconsistently racialized groups, to identify as 'people of color.'"[50] For instance, despite lawsuits throughout the 1900s in which South Asians (like other Asians in the United States) sought legal classification as "free white persons" in order to gain the rights of citizenship, when the 1970 Census unexpectedly listed them as white, "An umbrella group of Asian Indian organizations then launched a campaign for reclassification as minorities in order to become eligible for affirmative action programs and to benefit from civil rights initiatives."[51] Accorded "cash value," nonwhite identities can also supply possessive investment by Lipsitz's specs, however high or low their valuation.

Romero's use of possessive investment, though, includes an "added . . . moral and emotional dimension" that he admits is not faithful to Lipsitz's formulation. The original focus on social systems pays little mind to people's "sincere and highly personal investment" in racial identity and its practice[52]—but it would do well to. Because not all assets are tangible. As Nike or Apple well know, there is equity in reputation, and a brand is property in moral and emotional form. Companies go to great lengths to build and maintain this cornerstone of competitive advantage because they know: "For customers, brands can simplify choice, promise a particular quality level, reduce risk, and/or engender trust."[53] Included in the value of "whiteness as property" is historically subsidized access to better schools in better neighborhoods, yes—but also presumptions of innocence and belonging. As a cultural product, model-minority identity likewise smooths access to quite a bit of infrastructure *and* includes the benefits of a strong brand. To be presumed smart, hard-working, rule-abiding *good kids*[54] are tremendous benefits of the doubt.* These reputa-

---

* Unlike whiteness, however, the model minority "brand" is revocable, subject to flipping its bearer from paragon to pariah with stunning suddenness. "Belonging"

tional credits are surely helpful for those playing it straight; the self-fulfilling prophecy of stereotype promise is real. But for those on the make, they're priceless. A researcher working with Korean American teens found that when participants were asked about the ways they responded to model-minority discourse, "the most common answer was to take advantage of it": "I think [it] helped me get away with a lot. I copy a lot of homework but I never get caught."[55] Brands forge shortcuts in consumers' choices about where to put their time and money; they are handiest precisely when they can cover for what is not strictly true.

In Ben's words, "As long as our grades were there, we were trusted." Absent those grades, though? No trust, and no *BLT.* Asian America's still-favorite movie[56] is not the story of habitual C-students who reject the success frame, nor of impostors who stake everything but don't make the cut.* Either alternative might have "resisted" the model-minority myth by refuting it, but again, Lin's movie is not about hurting the brand. It's actually about burnishing it, and leaning into the fantasy that "even the gang members: they'll do crimes, however, the kids that are in gangs get straight A's in school."[57] That claim comes from an interview sociologists

---

is not one of its core attributes. Dating from the mid-1800s, "Yellow Peril" discourse cast Chinese, Japanese, and South Asian migrants as "inassimilable aliens" who threatened the U.S. body politic with "economic competition, disease, and immorality" (Erika Lee, "The 'Yellow Peril' and Asian Exclusion," 537). And while later racial politics saw fit to recast Asians for new expediencies (see Madeline Hsu's *The Good Immigrants*), the early connotations remain locked and loaded: the difference between expedience and threat as slight as the breath between achievement and *over*achievement. Asian American racialization rests on this hair trigger, even if it be not sprung for years on end. But there is plenty of scholarship on that dialectic (see, for instance, Anjana Mudambi's "South Asian American Discourses"), and, moreover, Asian American studies tends to inflect the Yellow Peril as reality to obscure the model minority as myth. I don't dwell on Yellow Peril rebuttals here because my intent is to compensate and rebalance the discussion.

* An impostor's relationship to "reputational interest" is so "intrinsically bound up with identity and personhood" that no future can be conceived without it (Cheryl Harris, "Whiteness as Property," 1730, 1734). Chapters two and three see this out: that to pass as do Audley or Amit is to shore up the brand, even at the cost of the self.

conducted with an Orange County Chinese immigrant's kid—
wholly unrelated to the film—but their subject would have been
twenty-two or twenty-five years old when *BLT* came out, and
twelve or fifteen when the Honor Roll Murder was front-page
news. Do studious Asian gangbangers truly abound? It's hard to
say; the research is scant and inconclusive.[58] What's clear is the
romance this notion holds: "Don't underestimate overachievers," a
reviewer crows[59] (implication being *just in case*).

As for Ben's double life—Academic Decathletes selling drugs and
buying prostitutes—it consummates with peak irony: "The morning after I lost my virginity, we won the national title."[60] And that
is the last indispensable point about *BLT* as fantasy: it operates as
tonic for wounded masculinity. For his script, Lin clearly drew
from real life. He echoes early hypotheses police floated about
rivalry between Robert and Stuart over the young woman who
linked them: Stuart's then-girlfriend, she had dated Robert briefly
the previous year.* And, presumably, Lin drew from formative
years in his own corner of OC suburbia, formerly-white bastions
shifting in the 1980s and 1990s to house a visibly Asian minority,
and full of racial tension as a result.[61] Accordingly, perhaps, the
film's most "frequent" reading has been as "a crime-drama that
seeks to intervene against the emasculation of Asian American
men in Hollywood by portraying them as hypermasculine 'bad
boys.'"[62] This is not surprising; aggrieved (straight) masculinity
has been the way we talk about Asian men in the West since the
launch of Asian American identity politics in the 1960s, into the
present day.† In Lin's film, its injuries take two forms: disrespect
by white men and rejection by (Asian) women. For each, the film

---

* Neither prosecution nor defense upheld jealousy as the motive, and Robert
affirmed in interview that he discovered the relationship only afterward.

† See, for starters, Frank Chin, Jeffery Chan, Lawson Inada, and Shawn Wong's
Aiiieeeee! An Anthology of Asian-American Writers (1974), David Eng's *Racial Castration: Managing Masculinity in Asian America* (2001), and discourse around the
figures of Fu Manchu, Long Duk Dong, Seung-Hui Cho, and Elliot Rodger.

offers a salve in which viewers can share. At a house party, the boys are accosted by a white jock who mocks them as a bible study group and tennis-playing Daric as not worthy of his letterman's jacket: "you got to play a real sport to wear that."[63] In the fistfight that follows, Daric shoves a gun in the bully's face and scores his panicked apology. The boys take turns kicking and punching their nemesis, then take off. Though the scene immediately thereafter knocks the shine off their newfound machismo—a carload of tougher, browner boys with bigger guns pulls up next to them, and suddenly Ben's crew are the shark smug from swallowing a guppy, only to be devoured by a whale—their victory against the white classmate stands. They are never called to account and, instead, bask in new respect on campus.

Because *BLT* has but one love interest, Stephanie makes an exceptional index of male status. At the top of the plot arc, the cute Asian cheerleader is so far out of league for Asian-male Decathletes Ben *and* Daric that her very existence is, ostensibly, emasculating. Meanwhile, as Steve's steady girlfriend, she signals his station as "the ideal Asian American man; he is wealthy, accomplished, academically brilliant (having been accepted to numerous Ivy League schools), [and] conventionally attractive." So secure is Steve, he can afford to take Steph for granted, outsourcing her to Ben to escort her to a dance while cheating on her with a white classmate. As the movie unfolds, Ben progresses from assigned lab partner, to friend, to Stephanie's new man. Sexual rejection being the one "problem" our protagonist clearly solves, emasculation presents as the engine of his character development, and even the submerged motive for the murder: "Ultimately, Ben is compelled to . . . [beat] Steve . . . to death out of jealousy."[64] That is, in fact, how Daric sells Ben on double-crossing Steve: "He thinks you're fuckin' dickless. . . . [W]hy else would he let you take his girlfriend to the formal?"[65] But it's actually Daric's own humiliation he channels in that pitch: Early on, he'd bet the boys $100 that he and Stephanie were going on a date, only to have them witness her arrive at mini-golf with Steve in tow and a girl for Daric. Much later, Steve rubs Daric's face in the memory, revealing he'd been in on the public emasculating, too.

> [*Steve, to Daric and Ben*] So, this is like the "I love Stephanie" fan club. You know, Daric, you're a pretty cool guy. I can't believe Steph thought you were a stalker or something. Yo, what'd you think of her friend?
> [*Daric*] What friend?
> [*Steve*] The one she brought to mini-golf.
> [*Daric*] All right.
> [*Steve*] Yeah. Isn't Steph the best?[66]

The gibe seals Daric's determination to punish Steve but good, and the fatal attack is the very next scene.*

Brief pissing contests like that litter the dialogue of *BLT*, obvious points in the masculinity plotline. Less obvious is the parallel arena, where bouts are staged over not a sex object, but a success frame. Rewind that same conversation above for less than a minute of film and you get this:

> [*Steve*] Hey, Daric, where you going to go to college next year, man?
> [*Daric*] I just turned in my apps last month. What about you?
> [*Steve*] Ah, it'll be an Ivy League for sure. I don't know which yet.
> [*Ben*] You already got in?

---

* The film makes a key departure, though, by rendering Steve's death as an accident: the beating itself was intended but careened into murder. Also noteworthy is that our protagonist had objected to the entire scheme and taken as distant a role as possible when the group voted to carry it out. Ben's "crime of passion"— out of panic and then sudden rage, striking the blows from which there was no return—is thereby made more tolerable by extenuating circumstances.

[*Steve*] Yeah, of course. . . .

[*Steph, leaving*] Excuse me, guys. Too much testosterone.[67]

While Steve exerts dominance in both arenas, these are not inter-changeable contests. The first is a game for scavengers, one that play-ers lose and losers play, and to be the prize is also to be conquered. To so much as spar in the second, though, one need already to have qualified, in round after round of competition. That exchange has the dog-whistle quality of inside jokes: each casually worded line a strike or feint or parry, crackling with possessive investment. Stephanie hears it just fine, and although Lin has her leave as if women do not compete, the Asian American women in his audi-ence hear it, too. The critic who called Lin's characters her "dop-pelgangers" recognized in them her own "age, ethnic background, socioeconomic status, family values, and academic drive."[68] If *BLT* nailed a zeitgeist, it wasn't by objectifying half its audience. What thrilled its intimate viewing public were Subtle Asian (American) Traits[69]—instantly recognizable and bonding—and in their child-hoods only beginning to emerge as a meme.[70] In other words, reading masculinity by rote, we miss when the script changes.* In model-minority life, "nerd" is a humblebrag—connoting belong-ing or even deference/gloating—and gender-neutral. I'd wager the film's staying power doesn't lie in its masculinity quest-narrative, because that's not what it got right about the Honor Roll Murder.

plot twist

My first letter to Robert explained that I saw his story as "the unsolved mystery of the Stuart Tay murder—not the who, but

---

* It's to these types of changes that psychologists Alexander Lu and Y. Joel Wong ("Stressful Experiences") refer in identifying two major categories of "masculin-ity-related stress" for Asian American men. They assert that, since conventional American forms of masculine competition (like sports, dating) put Asian men at a disadvantage, Asians may invest more of their sense of self and manhood in forms tailored to them by model-minority racialization (i.e., academic/career achievement).

the how and why of you and your particular set of friends going down that path." In early exchanges with him and with Kirn, I conveyed that what mattered to me weren't the fine points of the crime. Kirn, who'd served twenty years of his life sentence and was paroled in 2013, would be unable to discuss the case per se at all. With a petition to commute his murder sentence then pending in the courts, he had no reason to talk to me, and something meaningful not to jeopardize. Nonetheless, he answered an abbreviated list of questions over some Szechuan food one evening, and though slight in quantity, his accounts of himself at sixteen make a difference for which I'm grateful.

To meet Robert, I drove to the high desert—a term I'd never given much thought to, until that morning's trek along the gravelly perimeter of a prison. As I leaned into a January wind nearly able to hold me up, it clicked that this vast flatness fringed by mountains and scoured dry by air? That must be what they call it. There are guard towers and barbed wire but no trees or grass or wildflowers. Part of the punishment, I think, must be to see nothing beautiful if the powers-that-be can help it. In the months after that interview, Robert answered follow-up questions for me by mail. In clunky Courier font but memoir-worthy detail, he channeled a wry, cocky kid he'd stopped being one day, nearly thirty years ago.* These twenty-one letters are a very different writing assignment than the essay he submitted for the Elie Wiesel Foundation's Prize in Ethics contest.[71] But if both are petitions in the court of public opinion, the letters are the harder prompt: to commute the monster sentence not of a man reformed but of one about to do the irrevocable.

Through Robert, I was able to reach his sister and high school teacher, for takes importantly different from his own. But these interview notes being fragments—keywords and key phrases, like

---

* In the first of these, he signs off three single-spaced pages of memory-regression with, "As we used to say at Sunny Hills, / Later, / Robert," and it feels cruel what I've asked him to do.

so many data points—I would not have liked to see this chapter without the letters, or the shoebox labeled "Robert Chan" that Dr. Lampman retrieved from storage. Robert's favorite teacher is a trained historian, as luck would have it, and he kept things that the courts and the internet didn't. In fact, there'd been a moment in fall 2019 when it seemed this book might be a chapter shorter: All court records from every trial related to Stuart Tay had been destroyed, the county clerk informed me . . . the preceding July.* But, as luck would have it, the purge spared two folders from Kirn's parole hearings, held over by his active petition—just enough to determine that the machinations of prosecution and defense were not where the answers to my questions lay. This last section excavates none of those trials per se; just the ruins of two high school careers, with help from the men who emerged from the ashes.

I'd been so immersed in researching high schoolers from 1993 that I started, embarrassed, when a man in his forties greeted me at the visiting table. Now seated, in a chambray shirt and dark blue pants, wearing glasses and his hair tied back, his body language isn't stiff but quiet . . . maybe careful not to startle me again. Robert is obliging about my list of questions, even though at this interview it's probably more important to him that we get around to his present than dwell on his past. "The usual" Ivies, he says, "plus Duke, Stanford, Cal, UCI"—rattling off the places he'd applied with notable ease, for someone who'd not needed that information in a very long time.[72] Along with his junior-year transcript (A's down the line), and extracurriculars (beribboned in Academic Decathlon, rounded out with team sports and a regimen of volunteerism), universities would have seen Robert from Patrick Lampman's eyes:

> [A] most able student *committed* to taking the rigorous
> full diploma track in the . . . International Baccalaureate

---

* Shades of Frank Chin, I felt then, knocking at John Okada's widow's door.

program. In every course he has been *extremely competi-tive* and sought to ensure his place in the top ranking of his class.

As a student, Robert is without obvious weakness—a fine writer, strong class participation, and dependable collaborator in all extra and co-curricular activities. He *prides himself on being well prepared* and always ready to test and *challenge himself and others* in every context and every issue. . . . [T]he two descriptors most apt for him would be *focused/intense* and *ambitious*. These two high-energy terms, it seems to me, have been most responsible for his achievements in classes.[73]

No doubt some admissions officer somewhere read this as, "Grade-gunning Asian with med-school aspirations," and figured Robert for a type. But yes, and no. Friends knew about him something teachers would be less apt to see: that he excelled despite a "nonchalan[ce] about classwork—doing just what needed to be done."[74] Sure, this suggests brainpower in excess. But with hindsight 20/20, I'd say it's also indicative that Robert did what the success frame said he had to; he was not a true believer.

It wasn't until he started middle school in Fullerton that Robert's parents delivered their first spiel about college: time to get serious, no more screwing up. (His grades had always been high—anything below excellent being met with corporal punishment—but, previously, they'd lived in towns where the bully-to-Asian ratio was not good. He'd fought back and been tagged a troublemaker.) Family messaging about education had been both narrow and fragmentary: No one laid out a narrative about career paths, yet grades were "the only thing [his parents] seemed to care about"; his father did a Ph.D. in mechanical engineering in Connecticut, yet when they enrolled Robert at Sunny Hills, "we didn't really understand what IB was for."[75] Neither did adminis-trators feel the need to justify it, in a school where 83 percent of his class took the SAT, and the success frame enjoyed the status of fact: Robert had "no real interest in being a pediatrician," he said, but "with school counselors, 'doctor' or 'lawyer'" seemed the "only acceptable answers" to give.[76]

"This was a weird-ass school," Robert shrugs. "In other high schools, athletics were the big thing. Here, if you weren't good at academics, you were looked down on." Academic tracks turned into social hierarchies, with IB at the top, honors as second tier, "dabblers" in honors cast a rung below, then, last, "regular people."[77] Among teachers, it was an open secret that IB was "where the school's money and attention was going,"[78] and IB was disproportionately Asian, in an already disproportionately Asian school. The SHHS student body back then may have been 45 percent Asian and 43 percent white, but in IB, teachers and students alike experienced it as over 60 percent Asian, and predominantly* Korean.[79] Not that every Asian student was a high-achiever, but there were "so many, [they ran the] whole gamut . . . pretty-boys to jocks to nerds," and there were IB versions of each[80]—meaning that Sunny Hills in the early 1990s was precursor to San Marino or neighboring Troy in the 2000s, and not at all typical of Orange County high schools.† While the county at large had seen its Asian residents triple in the decade since 1980, to an average 10 percent of the population,[81] SHHS didn't share the racial dynamics of schools where Asian American students were still a numerical

---

* Koreans comprised 57 percent of the Asian population, but Kirn and Lampman alike guessed that figure at 80 percent. A state-sponsored program in South Korea recruited students (often by "parachute") to the well-reputed IB program while Korean immigrants gravitated to its attendance zone, legitimately or not. Said the head of the Korean American Association of Orange County, "Many Koreans consider Sunny Hills 'the best high school in California'" (Jodi Wilgoren, "School Stands Out for Better, for Worse," *Los Angeles Times,* November 27, 1994). The concentration of Korean (Americans) "[drove] the change" in academic culture (Lampman, interview)—with noticeable effects that SHHS translated bulletins into Korean, and Korean parents formed a second PTA. SHHS was, in other words, the hub of an ethnoburb.

† In fact, Lampman explains that the infamy of the Honor Roll Murder drove parents to find an alternative; this was when the IB program at (Azia Kim's alma mater) Troy ascended, and Sunny Hills' IB dimmed.

as well as cultural minority. At Sunny Hills, the bullying arche-type of (white) jocks on (Asian) nerds was not a thing. Instead, racial tensions about the "Asian Invasion" flared in resentment and insults—from non-Asian students and parents alike, a sense that "you didn't just invade; you became the top dog."[82]

It's not safe to assume in such an ecosystem that Asian boys mainly operate from rejection and ridicule.

> Many students said they have individual friends of varied races, but that cliques form along color lines. At break, lunch and after school, *Koreans dominate the center of the quad,** whites mingle on the fringes of the leafy court-yard and Latinos—8.5% of the student body—gather elsewhere on campus.[83]

Moreover, in this Orange County suburb, Asian students were often the children of professionals and typecast as "all academ-ics *and* money"—materialism being the other pillar of SHHS popularity.[84] Tracing the historical and social demographic fac-tors that brought this uncommon student body together is not our business here, but suffice to say that what teens make of their social order derives from immediate surroundings—and it's been shown in schools where Asians dominate academics like a caste that model-minority identity gets naturalized: Those students enjoy a privilege, not "to be considered normal" but "to be con-sidered *exceptional.*"[85] Robert might well have assimilated here, to an in-crowd of smart Asian immigrants' kids. After all, it seems like at this school, finally, he would have blended in—such a nice far cry was it from rural Connecticut. But by fifth grade, the Connecticut white boys had stopped ganging up on the "chink"

---

* Note that in this racial map, "Korean" isn't a literal description. Here as elsewhere, in press coverage and interviews, its use varies: often as-prescribed, to differentiate this ethnicity from Chinese or others; but sometimes off-label, to mean Asian-at-Sunny-Hills more broadly, the way Kleenex stands for facial tissue because it so dominates market share.

and started inviting "Robert" to birthday parties, summer camps. While, if Robert's hand-me-down pants and his parents' "poor-people habits" didn't stand out there, they did in Fullerton. Robert took an outsider stance at Sunny Hills, but the insiders weren't the usual suspects.[86]

Among my follow-up questions was how he'd spent weekends as a kid, and had Robert answered with math drills and piano lessons I'd have had my biases confirmed. Instead, I'd stumbled upon this:

> [From fourth grade through sixth], weekends were spent . . . with the other neighborhood kids, who were all children of poor immigrants—Puerto Ricans, Indians, Chinese, Korean—who lived in the old brick tenement housing project [near UConn]. . . . We ran through the forests and collected acorns and pine cones, and hoped to maybe find some shed deer antlers too (never did). By the shallows of the creeks we sometimes caught crayfish and were always on the lookout for a lucky discovery of a fossil rock. We dared each other to ride our beat-up used bikes all the way down the stretch of residential road that lurched beyond the tenements into the forest . . .[87]

Turns out, his childhood had been snatches of *Stand by Me* (directed by Rob Reiner), starring boys and girls in shades of brown. That movie ends with the narrator confiding, "I never had any friends later on like the ones I had when I was twelve. Jesus, does anyone?" I think maybe his little band was Robert's touchstone—the thing he looked for ever-after, the thing that told him what Sunny Hills was missing.

If typical high school popularity contests are toxic, at SHHS they were only differently so: "Honors students try to one-up each other on how much work they have or how little sleep they've gotten and brag about addictions to No Doz and Vivarin." Such was the culture that one South Asian junior felt "classmates 'look the other way' when they hear she is not in honors math."[88] In schools where this is enough of a phenomenon to get a name, it's called "academic bullying," and Asian American students are the aggressors.[89] Robert knew people used academics to exclude, and he was not about to let that happen to him—but neither did that mean he put stock in what he called the "snob-ocracy."[90] He thought it bullshit, such "worship" of grades that to him came "without even trying," but he would play to win. The crown jewel of Robert's high school résumé was a contest in his junior year, sponsored by the *LA Times in Education*. The nine-day, all-expenses-paid trip to Singapore was a coveted prize at SHHS, though not one that Robert particularly wanted. He applied for the one remaining spot on the existing school team at a good friend's request, though—and was rejected. Word was, someone on the team called him a moron. So, he formed his own: recruited that friend and four kids from the honors track then bested over 530 other teams to become one of five to go.[91] "This accomplishment was special to me," he wrote to Lampman, "in light of the circumstances involved": that is, the "humiliat[ion]" of his "doubters." If the *BLT* exchange between Steve, Daric, and Ben was sparring, this was MMA: "I pursued success with a fierce determination to blow away their falsely based notions of superiority. . . . I felt a sense of pride not only for mere victory, but also for establishing respect in the face of scorn."[92]

In prison, Robert came to see education differently: he is surrounded by those whom public education has failed, men from families stuck in the cycle of poverty. But, what he saw of it at SHHS, he called a "false value system," inducting boys and girls alike into careers that meant nothing to them, which yet they policed each other into pursuing. He recalls a classmate who declared dreams of becoming an architect and was met with jeers of "Why? They don't make as much money." To set medical or law school trajectories was to stake oneself at the highest levels of competition; anything else was to concede defeat. Not that every high achiever was so mercenary, of course; success-frame

subjects may "genuinely [have felt] the pull of fields like medicine, engineering, business, and the like," because of "real filial
piety at work."[93] As part of Kirn's work today as a prison-reform
educator, he rails against the toxicity of Asian American investment in model-minority standards—perhaps because his sixteen-
year-old self lived them so diligently: "[IB/]AP student, National
Honor Society, son of a doctor with plans to follow in his foot-
steps to medical school, computer nerd, avid martial artist, piano
player . . ."[94] In interview, Kirn was remarkable for how much
he remembered about SHHS: It was then third in the state, he
told me, in National Merit Scholars, after Harvard-Westlake and
then Palos Verdes' Peninsula High—but the latter had like thirty-
five hundred students to Sunny Hills' maybe sixteen hundred,
yet Peninsula managed only a few more National Merit Scholars
to its name.[95] I'm heartbroken for that kid who, in the police station before formal charges were filed against him, asked for his
backpack so as to do his homework.* Robert, however, applied
to the Ivies because that's what one did and, as Lampman rightly
said, he was extremely competitive. But meantime he plotted his
escape, unwilling to picture himself doing another four years of
Sunny Hills at college, much less a lifetime of it thereafter. Sitting
in jail after *his* arrest, Robert figured wryly, "Well, at least I don't
have to do homework anymore."[96]

Surprising enough that two such different takes on school life
should converge in the same violent crime. Striking, too, is that

---

* How this act comes across differs starkly within the intimate public versus
outside of it. The moment "lingers" in the memory of an Asian American woman,
and she refers to it poignantly while reflecting on *BLT* twenty-five years later (Jao,
"Why . . . *BLT*"). But to a general public apt to racialize, the homework becomes
indicative of Yellow Peril—disturbingly unfeeling, inhuman: "Lt. Tim Browne, a
spokesman for the Orange Police Department, says he watched the boys as they
sat . . . waiting to be booked on suspicion of murder. He says he tried to read their
faces, looking for some sign of emotion. 'There wasn't any,' he says. No remorse, no
anguish, not even any fear. One of the boys sat, manacled to his chair, doing his calculus homework" (Cheryl Lavin, "Young, Well-To-Do, Intelligent—and Charged
with a Brutal Murder," *Chicago Tribune*, February 1, 1993, available at https://www
.chicagotribune.com/news/ct-xpm-1993-02-01-9303174606-story.html).

Robert has a sibling—who shared his distaste for that success-frame gauntlet yet made it through with entirely different choices than his. One not given to dramatic language, Grace* said over tea that she'd "reacted very strongly to" the "narrow-minded approach" of that academic culture and opted in her senior year not to finish the IB curriculum. She got into a brand-name university regardless, and there (though it was not the art school path she'd contemplated) she recalls one freshman-comp essay clearly: Asked to relate when she had defied a stereotype, she wrote of choosing not to go into medicine.[97] She's now a professional in another field, having managed (despite everything) the quiet upward mobility that gives neither press nor police any business. Like Azia's sister and Jennifer's brother, Robert's sister† landed well within standard deviations of model-minority life, and, for that reason, they are important reminders: This is a book about outliers. Its warnings aren't simple cause-and-effect claims, or even over/under predictions about whether to bet on the success frame. It is a reckoning, of what it takes to compress children into diamonds—of what is lost, even should the outcome be net gain.

breaking bad

Some basic facts got misreported, as if once in public domain, they took on lives of their own. Robert's destiny for Princeton, for one, was cited so often it became canon—but in actuality his application there was denied. Some things were skewed by the movie. Of the five boys convicted, only two were really friends: Charles and Robert had been close since eighth grade; the others, Robert had met mere months ago or recruited for the job Stuart wanted done.

There's no getting around it, though: Of the choices that led to ruin, Robert's were pivotal. He and Stuart, like a tragic duo,

---

* A pseudonym.

† Intriguingly, all of the siblings were the younger of two.

were drawn into each other's orbit by things each was pretending to be. In Kirn's words, they were the "same person."[98] To school friends, Stuart "boasted of being involved in illicit computer hacking and counterfeiting,"[99] and he initially presented Robert with schemes for the latter. Although these came to nothing, the two did not stop:

> *Stuart and I [then]* . . . *planned* to rob a computer parts dealer whom he knew, but that plan fell into an exchange of threats when *we disagreed* on how the robbery was supposed to go. After I found out that Stuart had been using a fake name with me, *I told the other youths* (who were also part of the robbery plan) *and convinced them* that Stuart couldn't be trusted and needed to be killed.[100]

Paranoid schizophrenia was not a factor; that was just Robert's defense,[101] and not a great one. But good luck explaining why an ostensibly middle-class kid would otherwise choose such shady dealings, risk so gleaming a future. By general consensus, that could be nothing but crazy.

What was it about MDs or JDs that Robert was allergic to? Nothing inherent—any more than the status trappings that thralled his peers and their parents are intrinsic to law or medicine. It was maybe the consensus itself that bored him: everyone from school to home so cocksure that following rules and working hard would guarantee success and that by "success" one meant money, because from money would follow "financial security . . . nice things . . . and prestige." "Never," he writes, "did they talk about the other things that can come from work, like a sense of accomplishment for a job well done; fulfillment in doing something meaningful that one believes in; pride in one's craftsmanship; a lasting legacy for society, to make the world a better place." For a guy who'd liked best his high school art class and his elementary school woodshop, this ill fit could have fueled idealism; it bred cynicism instead. Alternative ways he could make a

living, he figured: as either a personal trainer or a career criminal. Equally ludicrous, maybe, these alternate realities for a likely
valedictorian. But why? Robert's interest in fitness was genuine;
he enjoyed weight lifting and football. And it mattered to *him*,
"the fun or drudgery of the actual work itself." But if, by society's
judgment, the "only difference between jobs . . . was the speed
by which money could be accumulated," which route comes with
more respect?[102]

Robert's invitation to the Wah Ching came through a classmate in German, freshman year. "Rick" was a sophomore with
the swagger of the Triad and a different kind of dominion at
school. From him came Robert's education in New Wave music
and fashion, along with his first "stylish" outfit. What that gift
must have meant to this kid whose clothes marked him as poor.
"I copied [Rick's] clothes, haircut, and stance"—keen for a value
system that could put the snob-ocracy to rout. So, Robert began
to socialize with the gang and take part in some low-level activities: distributing counterfeit bills, selling weed. . . . The money
went to wardrobe and soundtrack for his new persona. In Rick's
junior year, he asked Robert to sit the SAT for him, and a new
line of business was born.[103] Robert never officially joined the
Wah Ching, though—partly because he was admonished against
it by a white female friend whose opinion he valued. She lived
in a trailer park, had family members who'd done time, and
planned to go to art school—a path he "wouldn't have minded"
but couldn't grasp as a way to earn a living.[104]

Also, in his first two years, Robert played on the football
team. There in the (relatively small, socially marginalized) athlete
crowd—mostly white, with a few Blacks and Latinx, and a quarter or more "very Americanized" Asians—he "did feel accepted."
Instead of overachievement and materialism, he saw in this group
a "fun-loving . . . relaxed attitude toward most things."[105] And
to belong *here*, he was willing to put in the work: Teammates
told reporters "he was a mediocre player, but his hard work and
determination earned him the respect of the stars on the team."

Chan "was the only one who worked really hard at football even though he didn't play (on the first string)," said Mark Enrico.

"He was a real nice guy," said former teammate Kevin Lee. "We always called him 'Smiley' because he always had a smile on his face."[106]

From his cell, he writes, "Now that I think about it, in terms of personal disposition and racial composition, the Sunny Hills athlete clique wasn't much different from the kids back . . . in CT." Though, of course, there's no knowing, his feeling is "certain that had my family stayed" there, "that's the kind of teenager I would've become."

> I would've went to the end-of-the-year 6th grade dance with Erica Archambault, went on to high school with the . . . kids [among whom he'd already won his place] and had a better chance of being allowed to play sports the full four years, the difference being that the absence of a large Asian population at school would've meant also the absence of the rabid one-upsmanship that consumes parents of Asian overachievers, translating into less pressure—perhaps?—at home.[107]

That is speculation, yes. What did happen is that his dad refused to sign the consent form for Robert to play in junior and senior years. Mr. Chan called it a "waste of time," "didn't think it was important," and his son could not persuade him otherwise.[108]

Robert recalls his coach disdainfully describing football at less prestigious schools as a "diversion program": a way to keep boys out of gangs. There's something to that,[109] because without football practice every afternoon, Robert found himself with voids in both time and belonging—which he turned to Wah Ching to fill. In junior year, he ramped up his illegal activities: acquired two handguns, smoked occasional meth, and even tried to find his own supplier so that he could sell weed at school without giving the gang a cut. It's as if, not content to be a cog, Robert committed to taking the rigorous track in this alternate status scheme. Unlike his athlete friends, whom he'd valued because they didn't seem to care about the things that obsessed everyone else at school, gang life was for Robert a more thrilling way of achieving the common, ultimate ends:

> [If] all careers served the same purpose at their core . . . to pile up money . . . why wouldn't "gangster" be just as good . . . ? . . . it brought in money at a good rate, . . . came with its own prestige and status . . . , [with] the added benefit of physical security (guns & homeboys).[110]

Failure was not an option, so he was going to beat the SHHS snob-ocracy at its own game—one he found neither mentally nor morally superior to criminal activity. After all, who were his SAT-scam clientele but fellow IB students?*

It sets Robert apart from the other passers in this book that his outlier's journey did not start with failure; yet that is not to say his choices weren't constrained. By Grace's estimation, her parents didn't pressure her much in high school; after Robert's tailspin, there seemed to be either too much risk or no point. Her experience of their mother was of a "free spirit," apt to say, "We don't need to compare to everyone else." Even still, the "encouraged"

---

* Lampman remembered an instance in which thirteen students in his IB class were "booted from the National Honor Society" for copying each other's homework. Amid the scandal, a guidance counselor explained that, "on our campus, which is so competitive, you're going to see some cheating" (Nick Anderson, "Cheating Episode Roils Elite O.C. School," *Los Angeles Times*, April 10, 1997, available at https://www.latimes.com/archives/la-xpm-1997-04-10-mn-47232 -story.html). Studies reinforce this sense that at competitive schools, it comes with the territory: "There's a lot of cheating that goes on in order to do well" (Dhingra, *Hyper Education*, 31). Robert observed that, because academic standing also determined social standing, "people pretended they were good students—it happened a lot. Then grades would be announced," and the truth would out (Chan, interview).

professions were clearly-enough limited to physician, lawyer, maybe engineer, that choosing something else felt like bucking a world of expectation.[111] To her older brother, no such quarter had been offered. Deviation having no place, Robert chose to be deviant over deficient.

He kept up his grades through junior year, though, in no rush to ditch his secret identity. Asked if the honor-student role acted in any way as a cover, Robert responded, "Yes, yes, yes, and yes. Absolutely, of course. [It] made everything easier." It worked at school:

> Teachers, parents, and adults in general never questioned what I did or said. If I had an excuse for why homework was being turned in late, . . . it was believed. Whereas, a . . . non-honors/IB student's excuse better be really good and airtight, or it wouldn't be accepted. . . . Looking back I'm amazed that . . . [neither] I, nor my test-takers . . . ever got busted for the SAT scams.[112]

And it worked on the streets: "When the cops saw cleancut Asian kids driving around, they waved to us with a friendly smile . . . so we started changing into a different set of clothes and combing our hair to look as nerdy as possible whenever transporting illegal goods." In articles and even trial transcripts, there's the odd reference to people chauffeuring Robert around; this was taken for evidence of his power over others.[113] The actuality was still criminal, but teen-size. The car he had access to was his mother's gray Oldsmobile—just the thing for running weed, not to be seen in otherwise.[114] In other words, he was "very much aware" of the model minority as brand, and "exploited it fully":[115] using it for advantage among Asians and non-Asians alike; playing different strains of Asian, and different types of masculinity, as occasion warranted. Does this seem like a good time to trot out Asian American masculinity's favorite villain: media representation? Robert rolled his eyes at the suggestion. That was not his corner of the universe. He learned of the caricature of Asian men as "bookish and emasculated lames," watching the offending movies for the first time, in prison. Masculinity for him had been knuckles and shiners, traded quid pro quo; later, trouncings at Academic Decathlon, or contests of "clothes, cars, and cash."[116]* This was a guy with a chip on his shoulder, yes, but not that chip.

Since Stuart left no record of his early interactions with Robert, his killer's accounts stand alone. I'm sensitive to the imbalance of that and strive here to fill in gaps in the public record, without taking liberties with the victim's memory. That Stuart was the driving force, though, in first seeking out Robert and later charging him with assembling a crew to rob Stuart's desired target— this is uncontested by prosecution and defense. Without indulging in idle detail, I aim to interpolate between those plot points, so that we might understand at least one of these key figures.

Such planning and revising as must have preceded Stuart's first contact is the stuff of Hollywood. Elaborate intrigue, unnecessary obfuscation . . . there was a game afoot. In maybe September 1992, Robert "got a call from some guy, who didn't give his name right away, claiming to know certain things about me—where I lived, a bunch of personal things. Didn't say why he was calling, just kept calling, [and] intimated that he was into illegal stuff." Eventually, a meeting was arranged at a Denny's, for Robert to inspect some counterfeit bills that he and his mysterious caller could partner in circulating. But first, he was instructed to "call this girl to go with you" as a date—that girl being Jennifer Lin. Mystified, Robert expressed that she was unlikely to agree, hav-

---

* A 2012 study suggests he may not be such an outlier in this now: Surveying Asian American male students at research universities, psychologists found that "only 11.4% of participants identified the sexual/romantic inadequacies stereotype" about Asian men; "in contrast, an overwhelming majority (82.9%) identified the intelligence stereotype." (Y. Joel Wong et al., "Asian American Male College Students' Perceptions of People's Stereotypes about Asian American Men," *Psychology of Men and Masculinity* 13, no. 1 [January 2012]: 83).

ing rebuffed him quite recently. "Just try," his caller said, and Jennifer said yes. These were "outlandish requests," Robert felt, but that, at such a disadvantage, he had to comply: Whereas "Martin Chen" seemed to know an awful lot about him, he had no idea who this guy was. Stuart showed up with a second girl posing as his date. After small talk, he asked the ladies to excuse them and showed Robert an (obviously) photocopied bill.[117] If Stuart's intent here had been to put a stop to some dude's calls to his girlfriend, how convoluted and senseless a strategy.* If, however, the idea was to experiment in shadier dealings—without starting at the bottom—then maybe bedazzling his one potential contact to Wah Ching seemed like a plan. Unfortunately, the Robert he tried this on was lost in his own charade and fragile as a bomb.

By the time Stuart made his approach, Robert's nerve for gangster life had badly frayed. He'd gotten into it for the glamour, powered by an entrepreneurial optimism—but had no real experience in the industry. Busy "posing with some real-life dangerous props," the only targets he'd ever even *seen* shot were cans and bottles. Drug runs must have felt like fully-immersive video games, until a bad one brought home that not everyone was cosplaying.[118] He felt his imposture: servicing a hard criminal reputation he now knew he couldn't live up to but didn't know how to peel off. The strain of it surfaced in episodes his defense would later embroider and call psychosis: Where he'd previously chosen his outfits like armor, he didn't shower or change his clothes; where he'd previously vied for top marks, he skipped classes or assignments. Such mild lapses, really, but by model-minority measures, signals of catastrophe. Robert stopped passing for the perfect student, ironically, because gangster life had started to look impossible. And yet, even as he ceased to see a future on either conveyor belt, force of habit carried him forward. He

---

* That Stuart's interactions with Robert may nonetheless have included sexual competitiveness is quite plausible as an undercurrent, but not a primary motivator. This meeting was the last they spoke of Jennifer, and the last Robert spoke *to* her, their terse phone exchange not having been conducive to follow-up questions.

signed up for Academic Decathlon again senior year, though he couldn't actually say why: "When you're so used to doing something, it doesn't go away easily . . . the whole academic thing."[119] And though he had no desire to defend a gang he'd soon decline to join, or beat up the guy rumored to have defamed it, once he was publicly baited, he knew no way to back out. Watching as Rick sicced a crew of maybe eight Wah Ching on someone he'd always liked, Robert realized he'd *been* this guy being jumped, so many times as a kid. That had he stayed to letter in football, he might well be one of those "jackets" the gang was so eager to teach a lesson.[120] That it was also him on the ground.

From Singapore to this beating was seven months of 1992. He'd looked set to spend that summer with a new posse, met on the trip: Asian girls from Chino Hills' Ayala High, they studied and partied, neither too much, and relished the contact high in his company. Through them Robert met his girlfriend, whom he seems to have liked for all the right reasons—but maybe they liked him for the wrong ones, because one of them asked him to find her a junior-prom date . . . from the Wah Ching. This is another future Robert sees curving away from him, in which a carload of guys never shows up to insult some girls in corsages or pull guns on their offended friends. In that future, he goes to the Ayala prom, keeps cruising downtown LA with them on weekend nights, and, come summer, they ragtag it after adventure, the world their forest. Instead, Robert spends the summer with Abraham, scouting spots to grow his own supply of weed, determined anew to become his own kingpin. "But even [that] amounted to nothing, and I felt . . . unable to break into the big leagues no matter what I tried, no matter what dangerous situations I kept putting myself in."[121] And the loneliness gutted him. Here in this feeling that there was simply no pulling out a win, he went for the honorable ending. As one does. The fall after he'd have graduated, SHHS administrators reported "at least two" student suicide attempts by pill.[122] Had Robert sent the 9mm into his temple that quiet afternoon, such a mournful and unsurprised story the public would have told.[123] But three times he tried and three times set the gun down. He registered this as cowardice, and it would further damn him. "I felt trapped . . . with no way out, not even *that* way now." It would also send him into a spiral of shame, hypermasculinity, and overcompensation. He relates his next few months to what he's since heard in prison from other gangsters who couldn't go through with suicide: having "failed," they spun alike into "a lashing out; a hypersensitivity to what others thought of them; a seeking of more and more danger to prove one's mettle . . . ; the use of violence in increasing measure."[124]

It was in such condition that "one day, sometime after the summer had ended, [he'd] felt kinda lonely" and thought of a girl he'd gone on some dates with sophomore year. Though they hadn't spoken since she broke it off, he dialed Jennifer Lin. "And the rest is, well, you know . . ."[125]

This was also about the time that Kirn entered Robert's orbit, not so much looking for trouble as tractable to it, so long as it meant having friends. If we were coding this data, the various terms that populate both boys' histories might add up to an argument—bullied in the lower grades, corporal punishment common, pressured academically, given no allowance, shoplifting early on, hungry for belonging—but I think that would make for a false sense of predictability or determinism. Their alienations at SHHS were not the same. Kirn grew up in the Fullerton community, where many of his parents' friends were classmates from their medical and nursing schools back in Korea, and the rest were members of their Korean American church. Yet he couldn't find footing among their kids, somehow not mainstream enough for the U.S.-born crowd but obviously not a "FOB." His interests (computers, taekwondo) had no high school followings at the time. In sixth grade, it was both white *and* Korean American boys who picked on him, and, at the end of sophomore year, he'd been booted from a small Asian American clique who, despite not being particularly cool themselves, decided to consort with the computer geek no longer.[126] While Robert could chalk up his exclusion from Sunny Hills' inner sanctums to language or ethnic differences (or to values he rejected), for Kirn, it felt personal. So, sure, he'd known of Robert's extracurriculars by reputation and some spending money from SAT scams didn't hurt, but these weren't the draw. Rather, the "worst thing you can be in high school is a complete outcast," so if a group would have him, he'd go along. The psychologist at his trial would testify that "through constant [parental] control, through making decisions for him, through promoting the idea that his parents always knew what is best for him, . . . Kirn has developed . . . into a youngster who is overly compliant and with little idea about how to make decisions for himself."[127] This is plausible; certainly there is research to that effect.[128] Yet, if maladaptive obedience is a liability of what Kirn now calls "Tiger" parenting, it still stands to reason that, were this an entirely different set of boys, he'd have endorsed an entirely different set of norms. Was Kirn a product of the success frame? Given his hegemonically sealed world, no doubt. But it doesn't strictly follow that his sitting lookout, for what he didn't necessarily believe would be murder, was "about" that frame. The desire to fit in is endemic to high school; the kid still doing his calculus homework meant the status quo no harm. That is, he became an outlier by accident.

A telling of the story that truly centered Kirn would not be *BLT.* Thematically, it would share more DNA with *Heathers* (directed by Michael Lehmann):[129] a fable of the dark rule of popularity, though set at the opposite end of the pecking order from Kirn's. Privileging book smarts did not exempt SHHS from the barbarity of pecking, high school style. That this outcast found himself in a very wrong place, at a very wrong time, indicts high school culture generically rather than model-minority culture specifically. And as Robert lives to regret, the other Sunny Hills guys were ultimately there because of him: "It was my fault."[130]

In an essay on how race played out for these honor roll defendants in trial and press, Nary Kim is struck by the discrepancies between the specifics of the murder and its extravagant treatments, especially the zeal for calling Robert its "mastermind":

> [J]ournalists dubbed the killing a "near-perfect crime" and the deputy district attorney proclaimed . . . that Chan "almost got away with" murder. The testimony offered at trial painted the murder as meticulously planned—stressing details like a dress rehearsal, rubber gloves to cover fingerprints, and a faked carjacking to mislead the police. Yet the hasty attempt to bury Tay's body in a too-shallow grave and burn the bats and clothes in a beach barbeque pit exposes a plan that was far from flawlessly devised, executed, or concealed.[131]

She argues that his model-minority attributes limited Robert's viable defenses ("unhampered by the economic struggles or social excuses that . . . criminal defense attorneys" are accustomed to cite for mitigating "sentences for their clients"[132]), while Yellow-Peril tropes explained him readily as a cruel, cold, evil genius.* The brutality of the method fed that perception. Why not do it quickly, with one of the guns he owned? But pulling the trigger on a person was not something he knew how to do. He'd never shot anything alive. Beatdowns, though, were familiar, prosaic. This he could process: a beating with more . . . follow-through. And he had assurances from Abraham that this way would be "quick and easy": one blow to the back of the head and the target would be unconscious; finish with rubbing alcohol; hide remains. How tidy that mental picture. Abraham claimed firsthand experience—he'd helped a friend get rid of an abusive stepfather this way before—but now Robert suspects he was one more teenage boy faking it: three of them puffing up their feathers, for all they were worth.

---

* Academic ability worked against Kirn as well, even probation judges finding it hard to believe that with his intelligence he could be easily led.

The ventures Stuart had for months been pitching to Robert had not been going well, and the two boys not exactly tracking toward friendship. None of his vaunted counterfeiting connections had proved credible, yet the mysterious "Martin" was still angling for the upper hand. He kept Robert guessing with posturings of danger, whether claimed gang connections of his own or something more unnerving, as when Stuart upshifted his proposal from burglary to robbery and Robert wanted out. The former is a property crime; the latter meant acting while the computer-parts dealer was home. To rattle Robert's refusal, Stuart pulled strings like a self-styled Morpheus. That November, OC held its Academic Decathlon scrimmage at Foothill High School. Because sometimes life is like that. Robert knew this as Jennifer's school, but not as Martin's. When he stepped onto the quad for that day's competition, a young man he'd never seen before walked up and handed him an ace of spades card—delivering on Stuart's promise to "show you that I have people everywhere." Alongside the elaborate stagings, though, were the cheap shots. Robert remembers belittling comments, Stuart "making fun of my pants." Coming from a peer in a sixty-thousand-dollar car,* such mockery rankled with class superiority.

Had Stuart let him walk away, Robert thinks now, "I might still have been arrested doing something else" later, maybe just as bad, maybe not. But had Stuart let him walk away, Stuart would have lived.[133] Instead, the intimidation tactics cornered a guy who already felt trapped. Robert didn't intimidate easily, but he'd stomached a lot from this "Martin" character, under the (fading) impression that this "heavyweight connection" might land him the kind of legitimacy to redeem . . . everything.

The last straw was when Martin inadvertently let his wallet pop open and his driver's license peek out enough for

---

* The sticker price of Stuart's 1990 Nissan 300ZX (Froomkin, "New Year's Eve") in today's money.

me to see his name was really Stuart Tay and that he lived in a different city than he'd been claiming and [was still a minor]. This destroyed what little credibility he had left, and . . . my last hope of making a score big enough to over-shadow the shames that had preceded: my putting up with his bullshit and mind-fuck games, his disrespect, and his outright threats—all of which was reminiscent of, but . . . worse than, the bullying I'd suffered as a kid, because at least in grade school I could fight back right away; and then of course, there was my invisible albatross of not being able to pull the trigger, that failure to follow through.

Stuart's timing was the worst.[134]

So, Robert began to script his own bit of theater, rewriting the roles for the guys he'd recruited, giving them new motivations. All of them had felt, when the assignment morphed into robbery, that "we don't want to do this job anymore." But it was Robert who convinced them that "there's only one way to deal with this." So yes, they had a dress rehearsal. No, they hadn't any idea what it would really be like. There was a lot I couldn't ask Robert that day in the visiting room, so much that could follow only as trust built. What he would say about Stuart's death, though, I needed to see once and never again. *It was supposed to be easier than firing a gun.* Instead, the doing was its own punishment. "Quite horri-fying, really," his words quiet. Not like the movies. Swings make contact, again and unbelievably again, both still awake, rage fled, bashing from fear, unable to stop once he started.

discussion/dénouement

There would seem to be so many exits on a route to murder—any number of turnoffs for a rational person harboring the slightest doubt. Tell the authorities. Quit the street life. Go to college. Come clean. Accept punishment. Ask for help. Study harder. Admit you were faking all this time. Yet, these were no more possible for Robert than for Jennifer Pan, though the bleakness of their tunnel vision used different trigger words: for him, winning; for her, perfection. Terms and conditions already scarcely tolerable would be flat-out unlivable as outright failures . . . and each had already tried the death thing. "[C]utting, pills, alcohol" use, suicide,[135] murder—to place these in the same realm of possibility is not to collapse them; from such choices diverge meaningfully different plotlines. But for the honor student or college impostor, such lines stem from the same implacable genre.

That Robert arrived at his impasse *despite excelling* at the success frame is eye-opening. In early chapters, passing for model minority had meant masking imperfections, by either cheating or simply dissembling; our impostors distinguished themselves by taking the latter course beyond some rational point of cost/benefit, having finally fallen short in some way that felt insurmountable. Robert prided himself on besting the academic competition cleanly; it was in crime that he faked an excellence he did not have, past reason and self-preservation. Yet, even there, assuming deficiency as cause would steer us wrong: Quick to protest emasculation, Asian American studies may misrecognize forms of hypermasculinity, whether bloody or bookish. Certainly, hypermasculinity and emasculation draw from the same toxic logic, but a game's habitual winners and losers have drastically distinct lived-experiences, and starkly different senses of self. Likewise, when it comes to explaining deviance, scholarship often resorts to a deficit model—proposing that "Korean kids join gangs," for example, "because no matter what they do or how hard they work they can't fit the model minority stereotype"[136]—supposing failure the only reason to violently reject the success frame. "Scholars also [suggest] that Asian Americans who internalize the misleading model-minority image, even if positive, can be damaged psychologically *if he or she cannot live up to* his or her own and society's expectations"[137]—as though the only harmful thing about that image lay in not measuring up to it. But that Robert found hyperachievement noxious even as he hit its marks calls for fresh theories; that he felt nothing less than a criminal underground would win him his freedom shows the grip of what he fled. This is not to say it was rational; he gravitated to criminal life like a small animal to cooler perches. Like any act of passing, though, it does testify to the grimness of the alternative and the paucity of felt options. In the closed system of the success frame, there are no legal moves for opting out: Everything is ranked; you are your highest combined score; so choose strategically. Anything like real agency is outlaw. So be it. Not under dispute here is that Robert (like all our passers) made his own choices. Yet no multiple-choice question is an expression of free will. As with hegemonic masculinity, a toxic logic frames only toxic options, more or less.

When [economist] Gary Becker published his seminal study, *Human Capital*, in 1964, he hesitated about the title, concerned about its possibly dehumanizing connotations in defining human beings in terms of market value.

Twenty-five years later in 1989, Becker stated in a public lecture, "My, how the world has changed! The name and analysis [of human capital] are now readily accepted by most people not only in all the social sciences, but even in the media." . . . Education, parenting, and job training are [now] all regarded as "investments" in human capital that produce measurable rates of return in both increased productivity and higher wages.[138]

Half a century is long enough that most of us alive today* have little or no sense of microeconomic life before neoliberalism began to rewrite it. Yet, what was abhorrent back when the Rolling Stones and the Beatles topped the Billboards now feels so obvious it strains the mind to think otherwise: *Of course, knowledge and*

* About 75 percent of Americans in 2018 were born in or after 1961. ("Resident Population of the United States by Sex and Age as of July 1, 2018," *Statista*, June 2019, available at https://www.statista.com/statistics/241488/population-of-the-us-by-sex-and-age/)

skills should be cultivated for maximum economic advantage. Does that statement ring with cold, hard truth? Does it feel like natural law, harsh maybe but to be ignored at one's peril? *Sure, it'd be nice if life weren't governed by "market relevance"; be nice to levitate, too, but that is not how the human world works.* This is how a genre feels. Remember, genres organize ongoing relationships between the subject, her historical/material circumstances, and her patterns of interpretation: they organize "conventions about what might be hoped for, explicitly or secretly, and the bargains that can be made with life."[139] In the stories neoliberalism tells, we are atomized units of competition, valuable for what we can contribute to the economy but otherwise deadweight. In those stories, the "worth of a thing is the price of the thing. The worth of a person is the wealth of the person,"[140] and we are entitled to only so much of life and liberty as we can pay. To believe something's price captures its value is to agree that only what can be sold has worth. To live by supply and demand is to be ruled by popularity, however vacuous. To endorse such a system is to accept as moral "the threat of being left behind," because those with "no competitive edge" have "no future," the market seeing no use for them.[141] Yet it's no fairytale that, even in dire crisis, the above need not make sense. In America's response to the Great Depression, the term "human resources" meant neither job fairs nor management training, but an assertion of humanity as worth preserving:

> [W]e are giving opportunity of employment to one-quarter of a million of the unemployed, especially the young men who have dependents, to go into the forestry and flood prevention work. This . . . means feeding, clothing and caring for nearly twice as many men as we have in the regular army. . . . We are clearly enhancing the value of our natural resources and second, we are relieving an appreciable amount of actual distress. . . . [W]e are conserving not only our natural resources but our human resources.[142]

What's left of a liberal democracy that can choose forests over lumber, springs over bottled water, is evidence by analogue that human capital is not inevitable, and its designs on personhood not benign.

Model-minority and neoliberalist ideas had each been kicking around for a while, but they entered the cultural bloodstream at around the same moment and began their spread in tandem. This is not coincidence, Helen Jun points out, because the mainstream campaign that cast Asians as America's "good" people of color drew from a neoliberalist rubric. Said public-messaging granted a historically vilified race nigh-exclusive claims on frugality and hard work* and argued that their "education, family, parenting, and strong cultural values" made them "self-enterprising, self-regulating subjects."[143] This narrative aimed to discredit Black and brown grievances, to stave off systemic change—and did so by defining exemplary Americans as economic units that optimize their own value, incur no upkeep costs, and spell maximum system profit. As racializations go, this sugarcoated one goes down easy (anointing Asian American assets as earned, merited) but is vitiating nonetheless. Success on neoliberalism's terms means societies and selfhoods both more meager—richer, if lucky, but only by one thin measure.

Jun sees *BLT* as capturing the toxicity of what is neoliberal about model-minority life, and I agree: this is where Lin shines. In his lunchtime montage ("clubtime . . . where everyone loaded

---

* From the two famous articles introducing the term "model minority": "At a time when it is being proposed that hundreds of billions be spent to uplift Negroes and other minorities, the nation's 300,000 Chinese-Americans are moving ahead on their own," "winning wealth and respect by dint of its own hard work" ("Success Story of One Minority Group in U.S.," *U.S. News and World Report*, December 26, 1966). And, point of fact, Japanese American college degrees were lauded for being "almost never in liberal arts but in business administration, optometry, engineering, or some other middle-class profession. They obviously saw their education as a means of acquiring a salable skill" (William Petersen, "Success Story, Japanese-American Style," *New York Times*, January 9, 1966, 40).

up on their extracurricular activities for their college app"), she spies a subversive critique:

> The rigorous self-discipline required to constitute oneself as the ideal candidate for the competitive market is . . . characteristic of a larger constituency of students, all similarly engaged in a frenzy of self-cultivation. . . . Such deliberate calculation and empiricist *instrumentalization of every social action* (what neoliberalism calls "rational choice" or even "freedom") is represented not as heroic self-enterprise but as objectifying and cynical self-interest: "As long as I could put it on my college app, it was worth it."[144]

It makes sense should Lin, on his own "art school" path, have a few choice things to say about the success-frame mindset. Could be he, too, saw the hypocrisy of overachievement too naked to be impressed: "whether translating doctor's orders for a Latina mother, collecting cans for the food bank, or organizing an early morning volunteer beach cleanup,"[145] Ben's ostensibly noble pursuits meld into college-app currency, like some amoral alchemy. In any case, it's this all-consuming instrumentalization Lin offers as the impulse behind the boys' deviance: "It started with a pack of baseball cards, and then it snowballed. I guess it just felt good to do things that I couldn't put on my college application."[146] In other words, when human capital would have you manage your every exertion like a line-item, there are no sanctioned ways to keep something of yourself off the books.

Yet, this is such bland insidious harm, I despair of finding words true enough to make the cruelty of resource extraction show. Tell me, *when you are raised in a box, what hurts?* When "possibles are lost before they can be lived, experienced, or imagined,"[147] it's a wonder that any of us know to miss them. Sometimes they manage to ache, our phantom futures, but as neoliberalism takes hold globally, will no one see anymore the horror in being veal? This is what a "culture of competition" plies into its high schoolers now: "Among these young people is [a new] extent to which their total selves [are] oriented toward personal success and the *management of risk*, and their seeming awareness that particular identity characteristics [have] value as *psychological capital*." As daily practice these become a "constant compulsion of the high-achieving students to be, or do something, 'productive.'"[148] That is business jargon, and it should din the ear applied to humanity's future, but if it sounds admirable still, take it from the business schools instead. Mentalities ruled by the "economic evaluation of time" afflict hourly workers, of course, but also lawyers, consultants, even doctors—and on either economic end, studies in organizational behavior find persons "prim[ed] to think of their time as money" to be diminished in their ability to value or enjoy unremunerative pursuits, be it volunteering or not littering, or simply taking time "off."

> [A] commodified view of time caused lawyers to become alienated from the events in their lives (such as coaching their children's sports) because they were chronically thinking about the opportunity costs of their non-work activities such as . . . spending time with friends and family. Moreover, constantly thinking of work primarily in terms of its monetary aspects separated people from the noneconomic meaning of that work; that is, the intrinsic interest in and sense of accomplishment from doing something for itself. Consequently, work might become more stressful because its meaning and purpose would be lost in its close association with an external reinforcer—money.[149]

Where time becomes a tightly regulated commodity, there are options well-rewarded by the point system or there are None of the Above—that is, "wastes" of time. Choice is thereby streamlined into an algorithm of very few variables and not enough questions. We start this ever younger now, and condition young people who "run faster and faster, so that by the time they finish college, they can make the leap into the rat race."[150] And so stress, a by-product of this preprofessionalism, is "[n]o longer reserved for high-school students" but "reaches down to elementary school," such that training fifth graders to manage it becomes a "main emphasis" for administrators in high-performing districts.[151] As one outspoken critic of neoliberalism has so well put it, youth "now [being] nothing more than a preliminary form of adulthood, . . . the quiet desperation of middle age has been imported backward into adolescence. (If Arthur Miller had been at work today, it would have been *Death of a Senior*.)"[152]

Omelas

That here in its last pages, this investigation into passers names as its culprit neoliberalism over Tiger parents may surprise, but we know better than to stop at the most obvious suspects. In the model-minority racket, families and communities are not innocents—but neither do they call the shots. Henchmen, they just do the dirty work . . . though they do it exceptionally well. The success frame, after all, is the template into which neoliberal subjects are now broadly recruited. Those like Florida governor Rick Scott, for example, who see higher education as a "marketized good rather than a public right" and would usher college majors all the more into "'practical' fields [like] engineering and biotechnology rather than the humanities" or measure a program's value by the "earnings of its graduates,"* take pathways pioneered by post-1965 Asian immigrants and their children.[153] The racial paradigm itself is not the problem; it's the solution of the future. The problem is the future.

So, tiger or rat, the cultural trappings of ancestorly rhetoric are so much red herring. *Perfection* and *winning* are mandates

---

* We would recognize as tautological a society that likewise rewarded only religiosity, say, and then pretended it were measuring objective "quality" and universal "value" when it ranked schools on their output of orthodox graduates.

of profit maximization; pious trappings make them harder to shake. Families vary in the degree to which they see themselves as model minority, enforce the success frame, and orchestrate their offspring's ascent or downfall. Hardly, however, do they act alone.* Speaking of Silicon Valley high schools she studied in 2000, which boasted Asian American student populations of over 50 percent, Shalini Shankar observed that academic/social tracks formed not spontaneously but with social engineering: "school faculty and administration foster and help maintain these distinctions . . . by privileging some [students] over others." Not only are students greeted with model-minority expectations from their teachers but these high-pressure, "narrowly conceived ideas of success . . . leave little room for alternative meanings." It struck Shankar that "teachers and administrators routinely offered me unsolicited lists of their top Desi students who were also involved in leadership, sports, and clubs,"[154] which alacrity spoke to their own investments in these profiles in achievement. Lampman witnessed this at SHHS, where "careers depended," and had indeed thrived, "on the excellence of students," so "administration played to the media, fed into pressure culture."[155] "'There's no connection between the school and these crazy incidents,' said George Giokaris, Sunny Hills principal from 1989 to 1993. 'There would have been no way to have ever predicted that these kinds of things would happen.'"[156] Predict the murder? Of course not. Yet, among students was an unsettling sense of generalizability, for *these kinds of things*: "I expected something like this to happen. What happened to Kirn didn't surprise me as much as how much I understood what he did."[157] And even as the school newspaper grappled wall-to-wall with commentary on the five arrests, the very same

---

* Matter of fact, it's much remarked that in *BLT*, parents make no appearance at all. Far from being irrelevant or erased, however, they (brilliantly) need no further personification—being already present "in the way that social mobility is understood by their sons to be acquired through higher education" (Ruthann Lee, "Ambivalence, Desire," 58), and represented by their partners in neoliberal socialization at school, who are in loco parentis.

edition trumpeted "a record number of thirteen seniors have been admitted early to colleges and universities in the country," then listed each by name and destination.[158]

What we can say, looking back across Azia, Jennifer, and Robert's families, is importantly not that they were all off-the-charts, outlier Tiger parents. (Again, had they been, we'd need worry only about kids living that unfortunate extreme.) In terms of severity of measures taken to enforce the success frame—beatings, deprivation, manipulation, control—these families seem to represent a range, with Robert's parents somewhere in the middle. All of them, however, put their stock in the guarantees of being model minority and moved inside (educational, ethnic) echo chambers of that cruel optimism. In such contexts not only do successful "teens participate in school activities, plan multicultural performances, and run for elected offices while remembering the importance of securing admission to the college of their choice" but adults (including researchers) call this "manag[ing] to have a balanced life."[159] What it is, actually, is managing to have a balanced résumé. And so mine is also not an argument about the salvific properties of arts and humanities or even football, because the Midas touch of neoliberalism would gladly list the lot for college credit, weighed like any gold. No, it's the system itself that ails us, having made its values so totalizing that we agree even to this: "Human beings do not have any rights simply because they are citizens of a country—indeed, any tangible benefits (healthcare, welfare, etc.) that an individual receives from the State must be *earned* and not simply granted."[160] That is, while it's not clear what a nation is for, if not its people, even citizenship grants no right to have *needs*—not to claim more resources than one earns, to be unprofitable yet need care, or (I write this amid rally cries to let COVID-19 prune society of its deadweight*) to

---

* "Right now we're hearing two statements being made. One, from the President and his circle: we have to save money even if it costs lives. The other, from the Centers for Disease Control and similar organizations: we have to save lives even if it costs money. Which is more important, money or lives? Money, of course! says

be unproductive and deserve to live. This is pathological in the same sense that the corporation is understood to be pathological: on principle, because it is constructed by law to care only about shareholder gains. While a human creation, its program is written such that given any "resource," profit-extraction is its only mandate. The only good cost is an externalized cost—buried in someone else's soil or flesh to seep and bloom.[161] It's from such corporate philosophizing that humans mean capital, or even raw material; neoliberalism remakes citizenship in that image.

Let me be clear that it may not smart, being this kind of citizen: So long as you expect to be productive, such that the penalties of disposability or worthlessness fall on someone else, this Faustian bargain may feel like fair dealings.[162] But being that kind of *child*? Just as living in an ecosystem of corporations now feels natural, a social contract widely promulgated can come to feel like universal truth: "I felt pressure from [my mom] because she gave up so much. I have to give back to her, so only [lawyer or doctor] jobs that make enough money are acceptable. It's very money-based."[163] You may well endorse those terms; even then, they can eat you alive. Robert's parents had stopped hitting him in middle school, and as long as he brought home top grades, they didn't ask many questions. But grades were also "the only thing" *about him* his parents "seemed to care about." Put this slight another way, and its neoliberalism shows: Model-minority children "struggling to do their best and to please their parents" may despair "that they often do not feel parental concern or understanding for them," their "well-being," or "their situation, but more so for what they produce."[164] This means it is not enough to insist, for the sake of rejecting racist caricatures, that Asian immigrant parents only *come across* as "uncaring" because

---

capital and its spokespersons. Really? people reply, uncertainly. Seems like that's maybe going too far? Even if it's the common wisdom?" (Kim Stanley Robinson, "The Coronavirus Is Rewriting Our Imaginations," *New Yorker*, May 1, 2020, available at https://www.newyorker.com/culture/annals-of-inquiry/the-corona virus-and-our-future) "they are just [better at] practicing contemporary neoliberal logics as expected of all of us." We cannot oppose neoliberalism by agreeing to downplay harm it repackages as "caring"—especially when parents use the same doublespeak. If our families are better at neoliberalism, neoliberalism weighs worse on us. It is Dhingra's thesis that hypereducating immigrants are bent on preparing their children to *outcompete* both white Americans and their ethnic peers. Dhingra notes that Asian American kids in success-frame schools "*compare themselves* with other students in order to measure their worth" and, in fact, seem unable to stop, even to their (self-) harm. Between these two points is a straight line, and we should not be asked not to see it.[165]

While it's not clear what a family is for, if not its children, the model-minority family in which a child must *earn his keep*—by repaying parental "sacrifices" in dividends of wealth and prestige, forever—grants him no claim to resources he didn't generate, no discretion in the spending of his time, no security to differ and still be welcome. No license, even, to the validity of his own longings. The terms of the life Robert had been issued, he extrapolated from its knowns:

> I had no rights to the usual things that matter to a teenager . . . [that] was explicitly stated. I had no right to socially acceptable clothes; no right to an allowance; no right to a job (like, a legit part-time job to earn spending money . . .); no right to go on dates; no right to play sports; no right to any affection or praise from my parents. . . . I was powerless to change the situation about not being allowed to play football because that required parental consent. But with regards to [the rest], . . . I went outside the home and made these things a reality.[166]

It wasn't the being without; it was the doctrine behind it. That he was a being without rights. That what he was given, he owed. That his future was in hock, and thus his present not his own as he worked toward the high net worth that would make him a net positive. That he deserved nothing inherently, not even an explanation. In a time before the model minority, one of our finest early writers gave homage to Japanese family like this: "Simply by existing a child is delight."[167] But not for Robert this feeling; his was the precarity of being never enough—a freeloader until proven otherwise. By high school, the accumulated hurt of this had become an anger that informed everything.

Yes, it should scare you that that's all it took. That dehumanization can be so banal, yet, for all its normalcy, wreck so much. We need not be monsters to practice neoliberalism well—but training the recruits, enforcing the rules, manning the business, this is still its dirty work. We who are its prototypes have been fabulous proof of concept. And in no small part because of what we have willingly clear-cut from ourselves, what toxins proudly absorbed into family and community life. The uncle who sneers, "What do you think you're going to do with that?" The auntie who rubs mom's face in humblebrags. The little ones used for showing off before they can walk (they learn quickly what they're valued for, and not). From her desk at Harvard, an undergrad acknowledges what her life means: "Harvard [being] *the* marker of success for first-generation immigrants," she has redeemed her parents' sacrifices, and they have outcompeted everyone. But what this trophy child asks of the universe is that in thirty years, "my daughter stays far away from here"—stays free to "dream . . . independent of duty," and "there not [be] one more life placed upon the altar to burn." Not one more, that is, after the writer's own.[168] In this culture of competition, dreams are an encumbrance to ambition: better never had than forcibly removed. But what *does* happen to a dream deferred?

> Does it dry up
> like a raisin in the sun?
> Or fester like a sore—
> And then run?

Does it stink like rotten meat?
Or crust and sugar over—
like a syrupy sweet?

Maybe it just sags
like a heavy load.

*Or does it explode?**

I borrow Langston Hughes's drift to say, assembling "the ideal neoliberal subject"[169] is volatile business. Any investor must accept some risk, but no mom-and-pop model-minority shop is truly prepared for what can happen when wayward futures are trimmed from the bone.

Asked what lesson to take from his story, Robert addresses parents, bidding them to ensure that children know they are loved beyond their achievements, are safe beyond their mistakes. There's hope in this, that (however immense the global economy, however entrenched a racialization) it matters who the people next to us are. Do they see the jeopardy in success-frame life, and try with us to abate it? Or do they like prisms gather and focalize the heat? Robert has grown close with his mother, even as his course left the orbit of model-minority life, and their relationship has been allowed so few of the standard mother-son milestones. He's done a lot of work in prison—walking himself away from hypermasculinity in a place where unlearning anger must be the hardest thing. Much of what he's done I think must make her proud: awards and leadership, yes; hopefully the years spent crocheting beanie caps for newborns in the children's hospital, too. To this day, though, there hangs in a frame on her bedroom wall

---

* "Harlem [2]" from *The Collected Poems of Langston Hughes* by Langston Hughes, edited by Arnold Rampersad with David Roessel, Associate Editor, copyright © 1994 by the Estate of Langston Hughes. Used by permission of Alfred A. Knopf, an imprint of the Knopf Doubleday Publishing Group, a division of Penguin Random House LLC. All rights reserved.

the letter that came for Robert from the Harvard-Radcliffe Club of Southern California, weeks after his arrest. She has kept his invitation to interview, form and envelope and all, like saint's relics of the son she lost, or proof to the outside world that her son matters—that keeping him alive is not a waste—in the only currency it recognizes.

I asked Kirn after a screening of *BLT* what he'd change about the movie, if just one thing. The ending, he said, because they don't actually get away with it. Prison and what follows are a dimension of Asian American life that he wants the community to have to face.[170] That's an important answer; for most of the passers in this book, prison is the unintended but direct consequence of that community's fixations. If I could, though, I'd reinstate the director's-cut ending, for Ben's explanation that he *had* to snap out of the funk of killing Steve: he still had to get into college.[171] The theatrical-release version is less piercing. Wrapping with, "For the first time in my life, I don't know what my future will hold," it lets viewers ride off into a vague sunset with the glow of identification mostly intact: They've seen themselves in Ben, won by proxy as he beat the racist and won the girl, and cringed as he lost control, but are permitted to leave still wanting this overachieving nice guy to beat the system. At the Sundance debut, though, Lin's original punch line made people squirm. The gratification of seeing their doppelgangers as badass collided with Ben's stark self-talk: Self-serving, single-track minded, this wasn't a guy flipping stereotypes on their heads; this was a guy buying in, and what it said about the model-minority brand was damning, pathological. Clearly, that's not the ending we wanted, but I think it's the ending we need: one that gives Asian Americans due credit for dominating the SAT, the IB/AP/GPAs, and now the competition for varsity and extracurriculars, too, in two generations or less, sometimes against epic odds. That shit is not easy, and it doesn't come cheap. But give me also that ending that pulls us up short, for a cold, hard look at what all the work is for.

Last Words

A confession: this book actually makes now three renditions, not two. The same year my academic monograph came out, I launched "Ask a Model-Minority Suicide," hoping with an online column to reach different readers, or reach readers differently. I suppose they'll be there for as long as *Hyphen* magazine pays its web server: the essays about my own suicide attempt, the mandatory psych hold that followed, the family life that made it all possible. I sealed in alias there a few pieces of backstory that speak to why, from this side of a studiously respectable living, I'd recognize stories like Azia's, Jennifer's, and Robert's as versions of my own. Even bent on having no future, I was passing: my GPA, credit score, and Body Mass Index unimpeachable. (You can't judge this intimate public by its cover.) I have felt tasked with this story to keep telling—until it's heard or I run out of ways to word it. I hope this book proves to be the former, suspect it is the latter, but either way, have done.

As of this writing, it has been a year and a half since I last spoke to my parents or my sister. For decades, I had kept them in my life, at a careful distance. Because family life has the genre to beat all genres: from the baby pictures to the graduation photos, from wedding dances to beaming grandparents, family reunions. . . . Its cruel optimism is virtuoso, its plot points stringing along the hopeful on possibilities of the good love that could be ours someday. What I learned from my first book had given me the wherewithal to call harms by their rightful names. This made for a useful allergy: devices of sacrifice and guilt gall me instantly, even when folded in smiles and cloying concern. So those relations had never stopped feeling unsafe, precarious. Yet, I was attached to being a daughter or sister, at least to the extent that I did not know how to narrate myself as someone who could quit these things. *What kind of person does that?* Surely, only those dealt monstrous trauma, or who are monsters themselves. To quit the genre simply because its crisis is perfectly ordinary—everyday toxic beyond any actual sustenance—is unthinkable.

I think it would not have been possible to write this book while still hooked up to that matrix. What reader could I have looked in the eye and said, "Those who'd sooner mourn your death than grant you terms you can live with? Their approval is junk in your veins. Habits like that you are allowed to quit." And so came one ordinary crisis too many, and I preferred not to continue.* The first weeks were wrenching: waking hours overlaid with panicked self-talk, second-guessing, vividly furnished mental projections of what was being felt and said by my former family. But, as the new absence asserted itself, it has become mostly remarkable for its placidity. A calm not untroubled, of course, from time to time, but reminders of those relations, ultimately, reinforce what they were—and weren't. In my teens and twenties, there were nights I'd sob myself awake, from nightmares that one or the other of my parents had died and I'd not yet found a way to reach them.

---

* A nod to the Bartleby character Berlant herself cites (*Cruel Optimism*, 28), who confounds and infuriates all around him by opting out of productivity: "I would prefer not to."

And so I'd supposed that severing the family entirely could only be catastrophic, an amputation of the heart. But I would liken the actuality, instead, to a surcease, an ease: when a thing hurts, and hurts, and hurts, and then stops hurting. It turns out, the people for whom you stage yourself compulsively are not the ones you are stricken without.

As of this writing, it has been six months of a pandemic not ordinary at all. Cast against these life-and-death proportions, what it means to forsake all the people I come from has been made stark, unmistakable. I choose it still. The deathbed is the last plot point of the family genre, and I will not be made to bargain with it. Agency, after all, is outlaw. So be it.

Acknowledgments

I wish there were many different words for "thanks," in moments like these: some fit for small courtesies, others for acts of generosity that bond people together. Maybe seventeen precise shades, like a lattice of informal and formal modes of address: a memorandum-blue for cashiers at the register; a summer–blue sky for friends whose gifts are bounty.

But like "love," *thank you* holds such jealous monopoly. So, please excuse the word count below, which is directly proportional to nothing. Please know you are fully remembered, when I call your name.

For Robert Chan, I wish a multiverse in which your long-ago
   selves roam free.
Fair winds to Kirn Kim, whose new story is his own.
For Grace, watchful sister: refuge.
To Bert Yun: that the world follow in your kindness.
Takeo Rivera, may ever your causes win the day.
For Patrick and Fran Lampman: the laurels of keeping faith.

To Hannah Kim, Trent Walker, Anne Takemoto, Charlie Praphatanandam, Amy Chen: that doors you feared closed always open for you.

Eric Lai, Betty Kershner, may generous strangers make such time.

Dr. William Mynster, Lt. Karla Graves, Heather Nisen, may someone care enough to find the key.

This book has two North Stars.

★ To a brilliant counselor and utter neurotic: Jim Lee, may we always get to say, "I told you so."
★ To Miliann Kang, the wise and good: rooting for you in every scene.

Dearest Sau-ling, may we who look to you always find you there.

For Viet Nguyen, Leslie Bow: many reincarnations, for cashing in all your good karma.

Mindi Bagnall, Stefanie Liang Chung, may you always know whom to turn to.

Assistants someday for Catt Phan and Kristie Nguyen, as wonderful as mine.

Veronica Castillo-Munoz, may the worst roads be rather wonderful, after all.

For Lisa Park, Diane Fujino: help, when you need it.

For Sameer Pandya: honest company, great drinks.

With Mimi Khúc, true coven.

Lan Duong, Linda Võ, and Tu-Uyen, Thuy, and Tram of the CPG: may the postpandemic futures we dream of come to be.

With Oliver Wang, Cindy Lin, Crystal Baik: someday, friends who get to be neighbors again.

For Melissa Hung, Han Wang: good advice and true friends, wherever you go.

To Mom, Mark, and Janelle, if I could: FaceTime in a bottle,
    because those parts of this year I'd so keep.
To Scott and our Philip, love that sees you, every day.

I won't presume to make wishes for those who grant them, so I have only thanks for Susan Derwin and everyone at the Interdisciplinary Humanities Center at UC Santa Barbara, for the early support that made this research possible. Likewise, the yearlong research fellowship from UCLA's Institute of American Cultures is three wishes in one: the time, the means, and the confidence to make a book come true. And being at the Asian American Studies Center did feel like unbelievably good fortune—from the warm welcome of IAC's Fall Forum, to the serendipity of AASC's *Better Luck Tomorrow* screening just days before COVID-19 swept all calendars clean. Listing them here in descending quantity of emails they fielded from me, I thank Melany De La Cruz-Viesca, Irene Suico Soriano, Karen Umemoto, Victor Bascara, Janet Chen, David Yoo, Marji Lee, Tom Nguyen, and Betty Leung, for my temporary home.

For me, the worst grind of writing a crossover book has been the second-guessing—regular panics about the foolhardiness of making a thing neither fish nor fowl. So, it's meant a lot to have the full-throated support of Temple University Press. Sarah Munroe and Rick Bonus greeted this project with instant recognition, and though she has since moved on from Temple, I hope Sarah knows that her faith was instrumental. I thank Shaun Vigil for his careful support through the tricky parts.

If I may wish for Azia, Jennifer, and Audley: people who love you for who you are.

Notes

Introduction: The Strange Case of the College Impostor

1. "Virtually nothing beyond the anecdotal is known about the magnitude or distribution of actual race passing in the United States at any time. . . . The very condition of possibility for passing is secrecy, making it an extremely difficult object for traditional empirical study." Samira Kawash, *Dislocating the Color Line: Identity, Hybridity, and Singularity in African-American Narrative* (Stanford, CA: Stanford University Press, 1997), 126.

2. Likewise, again, with racial passing: Legal scholar Cheryl Harris reports in her article on postbellum passing and white privilege that "when I began to relate the subject matter of my research to Black friends and colleagues, in nearly every instance I was told, 'I had an uncle. . . . I had a great aunt. . . . My grandfather's brother left Alabama to go North as a white man and we never saw or heard from him again' or other similar stories." Cheryl Harris, "Whiteness as Property," *Harvard Law Review* 106, no. 8 (June 1993): 1712n.

3. Aimee Picchi, "Harvard Doesn't Discriminate against Asian-American Applicants, Judge Rules," CBS News, October 1, 2019, available at https://www.cbsnews.com/news/harvard-university-admissions-case-harvard-doesnt-discriminate-against-asian-american-applicants-judge-rules/.

4. Jennifer Lee and Min Zhou, *The Asian American Achievement Paradox* (New York: Russell Sage Foundation, 2015), 6.

5. Ibid., 4, emphases added.

6. Diane Wolf, "Family Secrets: Transnational Struggles among Children of Filipino Immigrants," *Sociological Perspectives* 40, no. 3 (1997): 458.

7. Sarah Willie and Bakirathi Mani, "Becoming South Asian in America," Communications Office, Swarthmore.edu, available at https://www.swarthmore.edu/news-events/becoming-south-asian-america.

8. Wolf, "Family Secrets," 465.

9. Pawan Dhingra, *Hyper Education: Why Good Schools, Good Grades, and Good Behavior Are Not Enough* (New York: New York University Press, 2020), 24.

10. Wolf, "Family Secrets," 463.

11. R. Duschinsky and E. Wilson, "Flat Affect, Joyful Politics and Enthralled Attachments: Engaging with the Work of Lauren Berlant," *International Journal of Politics, Culture, and Society* 28, no. 3 (2015): 179, emphasis added.

12. See John Howard Griffin, *Black Like Me* (Boston: Houghton Mifflin, 1977).

13. P. Gabrielle Foreman and Cherene Sherrard-Johnson quoted in Allyson Hobbs, *A Chosen Exile: A History of Racial Passing in American Life* (Cambridge: Harvard University Press, 2014), 29.

14. Hobbs, *Chosen Exile*, 5, 32.

15. Hobbs, *Chosen Exile*, 29; Samira Kawash, "*The Autobiography of an Ex-Coloured Man*: (Passing for) Black Passing for White," in *Passing and the Fictions of Identity*, ed. Elaine K. Ginsberg (Durham, NC: Duke University Press, 1996), 62.

16. Harris, "Whiteness as Property," 1711.

17. Hobbs, *Chosen Exile*, 13, 14, emphasis added.

18. Valerie Rohy, "Displacing Desire: Passing, Nostalgia, and *Giovanni's Room*," in *Passing and the Fictions of Identity*, ed. Elaine K. Ginsberg (Durham, NC: Duke University Press, 1996), 226.

19. She sees impersonation, her central concept, not as chicanery but as the everyday business of people "performing into existence their [given identities] as Asian Americans" (Tina Chen, *Double Agency: Acts of Impersonation in Asian American Literature and Culture* [Stanford, CA: Stanford University Press, 2005], xx). This she contrasts to racial imposture, which she writes off as acts of deception: performances meant to "fool others" by assuming a public identity not their own. It's not that she's stumbled across a cache of Asian people "imposturing whiteness" (7); the object of her concern is the robust mainstream imagination of Asians as counterfeit Americans: To be Asian in America is to look to one's countrymen like a spy, or at least at heart a foreigner, faking loyalty and love of country. (See, historically, J. Burton et al., "A Brief History of Japanese American Relocation during World War II," National Park Service, last modified April 1, 2016, available at https://www

.nps.gov/articles/historyinternment.htm; famously, Matthew Purdy, "The Making of a Suspect: The Case of Wen Ho Lee," *New York Times*, February 4, 2011, available at https://www.nytimes.com/2001/02/04/us/the-making -of-a-suspect-the-case-of-wen-ho-lee.html; or, recently, Brendan O'Malley, "'End Racial Profiling,' Say Chinese-American Scientists," *University World News*, March 29, 2019, available at https://www.universityworldnews.com /post.php?story=20190329073927844.) Were such deceit the case, Chen cedes, that would indeed be terrible, but the actuality is otherwise: Asian Americans as neither spies nor foreigners but impersonators all—made so, ironically, by that same racist thinking that says we can never be the real deal. The catch-22 is such that even if we do our best impression of loyalty and compliance, we will still only look like impressionists—impersonators—of Americanness, to the ruling ideology that *wants* us not truly to belong. No surprise, given our assigned racial placement in the social hierarchy as the model minority: "hardworking and high-achieving" (time-honored Ameri-can qualities), but "hyper-competitive, rigid, and singularly goal-oriented—automatons or robots" (thus unfairly good, artificial: Stacey J. Lee and Kevin K. Kumashiro, "Bias against Asian-American Students Is Real. Affirmative Action Isn't the Problem," *Vox*, June 27, 2018, available at https://www.vox .com/the-big-idea/2018/6/27/17509140/admissions-bias-personalities-har vard-affirmative-action).

20. T. Chen, *Double Agency*, xx, emphasis added.

21. Kristina Wong, "I Thought Being Miserable Was Just Part of Being Chinese American," kristinawong.com, May 15, 2014, available at http:// kristinawong.com/blog/2019/10/13/i-thought-being-miserable-was-just-part -of-being-chinese-american/?fbclid=IwAR2FYseJ_Fgmz4vdcQdIgzu9mzEu kcG_wEMvGFvSb3T0vIN1bcuMP2rP_Z4.

22. See their chap. 2. Lee and Zhou find that ethnic concentrations seed ethnic resources: from entrepreneurial, "after-school ethnic academic acade-mies—classes, tutoring, college preparation, and enrichment programs," to social networks, "which provide [even] working-class coethnics with the rele-vant knowledge about high school rankings, AP classes, and the college admis-sions process." Moreover, they "argue that [these] resources and strategies—*rather than* strict 'Tiger Mother' parenting practices—are key to *achieving* the success frame" (*AAAP*, 18, emphases added). But this should not be construed as striking parenting from relevance. The authors go on to show the success frame as a communal consensus to which immigrant parents subscribe, and its actualization as a family project to which they enroll their children. *AAAP*'s point is that "simply adopting a success frame does not ensure the desired outcome"—that is, those who wish to replicate these gains in grades and scores would do better to emulate the "reinforcement mechanisms" of choosing good schools or after-school academies, say, than relying on "relentless, demeaning parenting practices" (69, xiv). Point well taken. *Passing for Perfect* makes no

claims about relative efficacy but does take aim at model-minority subject formation across both familial and educational spaces.

23. Wolf, "Family Secrets," 478, 463, 480.

24. Shalini Shankar, *Desi Land: Teen Culture, Class, and Success in Silicon Valley* (Durham, NC: Duke University Press 2008), 37.

25. Dhingra, *Hyper Education*, 24, 267.

26. Lee and Zhou, *AAAP*, 52, 53.

27. Dhingra, *Hyper Education*, 14.

28. In the early twentieth century, to be sure, Asian aspirations took very much the form of whiteness, as immigrants quite literally sued to be considered white. This came of laws of the era that made them *ineligible* for citizenship and its rights, on the basis of race. (See Susan Koshy, "Morphing Race into Ethnicity: Asian Americans and Critical Transformations of Whiteness," *boundary 2* 28, no. 1 [Spring 2001]: 153–194.) It would be unwise, however, to assume that model minority ambitions of the early twenty-first century are locked on the same sights.

29. *Crazy Rich Asians*, directed by Kevin Kwan (Burbank, CA: Warner Bros. Home Entertainment, 2018).

30. See "strategic adaption" or the related "relative functionalism" in Yu Xie and Kimberly Goyette, "Social Mobility and the Educational Choices of Asian Americans," *Social Science Research* 32, no. 3 (2003): 478, 473.

31. See Harris, "Whiteness as Property"; George Lipsitz, "The Possessive Investment in Whiteness: Racialized Social Democracy and the 'White' Problem in American Studies," *American Quarterly* 47, no. 3 (September 1995): 378.

32. Margaret Jane Radin quoted in Harris, "Whiteness as Property," 1730, 1734.

33. Robbie Duschinsky and Emma Wilson, "Flat Affect, Joyful Politics and Enthralled Attachments: Engaging with the Work of Lauren Berlant," *International Journal of Politics, Culture, and Society* 28, no. 3 (2015), 179.

chapter one: Gen(i)us

1. Sam Blum, "The Mysterious Heir of Extreme Travel," *Rolling Stone*, May 16, 2018, available at https://www.rollingstone.com/culture/culture-features/the-mysterious-heir-of-extreme-travel-630274/.

2. Kyle Swensen, "He Convinced People He Was a Rich 'Saudi Prince.' He Was Really a Poor Street Kid from Bogota," *Washington Post*, May 30, 2018, available at https://www.washingtonpost.com/news/morning-mix/wp/2018/05/30/he-convinced-people-he-was-a-rich-saudi-prince-he-was-really-a-poor-street-kid-from-bogota/?noredirect=on&utm_term=.b0763eb07832.

3. Jessica Pressler, "Maybe She Had So Much Money She Just Lost Track of It," TheCut, May 28, 2018, available at https://www.thecut.com/2018/05/how-anna-delvey-tricked-new-york.html.

4. Melissa Chadburn and Carolyn Kellogg, "Who Is Anna March?" *Los Angeles Times*, July 26, 2018, available at http://www.latimes.com/projects /la-ca-jc-anna-march/.

5. See Julie Zauzmer, *Conning Harvard: Adam Wheeler, the Con Artist Who Faked His Way into the Ivy League* (Guilford: Lyons, 2012).

6. David Samuels, "The Runner: He Woke Up One Morning and Decided to Become Someone Else," *New Yorker*, September 3, 2001, available at https://www.newyorker.com/magazine/2001/09/03/the-runner.

7. Mark Goodman, "Bright and Athletic, He Seemed Perfect for Princeton, but This Paper Tiger's Stripes Came from the Jailhouse," *People*, March 18, 1991, available at http://www.people.com/people/archive/article/0,,20114695,00 .html.

8. Brigitte Greenberg, "Alleged Con Man Dupes Yale University for Nearly Two Years," APNewsArchive.com, April 11, 1995, available at http:// www.apnewsarchive.com/1995/Alleged-Con-Man-Dupes-Yale-University-for -Nearly-Two-Years/id-41cfb73ac54c41c094944ec72d9ffd61.

9. Ed Pilkington, "Student Who Conned His Way into Harvard Says Sorry," *The Guardian*, December 17, 2010, available at https://www.theguardian .com/world/2010/dec/17/student-conned-harvard-sorry.

10. "'He was a good guy who didn't talk about his academics or his life history much, but he came off as very smart. We just allowed him his privacy,' [said] a source close to Wheeler, who did not wish to be named," from Xi Yu and Julie M. Zauzmer, "Former Harvard Student Indicted for Falsified Applications, Identity Fraud," *Harvard Crimson*, May 17, 2010, available at https://www.thecrimson.com/article/2010/5/17/wheeler-harvard-wheelers -applications. See also Tracy Jan and Milton J. Valencia, "This Can't Be Our Adam Wheeler," Boston.com, May 30, 2010, available at http://archive.boston .com/news/local/massachusetts/articles/2010/05/30/this_cant_be_our_adam _wheeler/.

11. John Ellement and Tracy Jan, "Ex-Harvard Student Accused of Living a Lie," *The Boston* Globe, May 18, 2010, available at http://archive.boston .com/news/education/higher/articles/2010/05/18/ex_harvard_student_accused _of_living_a_lie/?page=2; emphasis added.

12. Maria Konnikova, *The Confidence Game: Why We Fall for It . . . Every Time* (New York: Viking, 2016), 23, 22.

13. Jim Newell, "Adam Wheeler Went to Harvard," *The Baffler*, no. 20 (2012), available at http://thebaffler.com/salvos/adam-wheeler-went-to-har vard.

14. Jan and Valencia, "This Can't Be Our Adam Wheeler," 3.

15. Konnikova, *Confidence Game*, 24, 11.

16. Newell, "Adam Wheeler Went to Harvard."

17. Greg Kesich, "Harvard Scam Artist Had the University's Cooperation: The Only Person Who Wants the Con Man's Story to Be True More Than

the Con Man Is His Victim," *Portland Press Herald*, May 26, 2010, available at https://www.pressherald.com/2010/05/26/commentary_2010-05-26/.

18. Konnikova, *Confidence Game*, 33.

19. Samantha Schmidt, "This Con Man Lied His Way into Princeton. Decades Later, He Was Found Squatting in Mountain Shack," *Washington Post*, February 10, 2017, available at https://www.washingtonpost.com /news/morning-mix/wp/2017/02/10/this-con-man-lied-his-way-into-prince ton-decades-later-he-was-found-squatting-in-mountain-shack/?utm_term= .20e3c4741269.

20. Samuels, "The Runner."

21. Isaac Arnsdorf, "The Man Who Duped the Ivy League," *Yale Daily News*, September 10, 2008, available at http://yaledailynews.com/blog/2008 /09/10/the-man-who-duped-the-ivy-league/.

22. Zauzmer, *Conning Harvard*, 163.

23. Arnsdorf, "Man Who Duped."

24. Newell, "Adam Wheeler Went to Harvard."

25. Daniel LeDuc, "Princeton Impostor's Next Term Is Jail: Still Dressing the Part, James Hogue Pleaded Guilty to Theft by Deception," Philly. com, February 11, 1992, available at http://articles.philly.com/1992-02-11 /news/26040419_1_alexi-indris-santana-alexi-indris-santana-princeton-police.

26. See Kathleen Pfeiffer, *Race Passing and American Individualism* (Amherst: University of Massachusetts Press, 2003); Laura Browder, *Slippery Characters: Ethnic Impersonators and American Identities* (Chapel Hill: University of North Carolina Press, 2000).

27. Anna Tong, "Murky Past Trails Man to Harvard," *Harvard Crimson*, April 11, 2007, available at http://www.thecrimson.com/article/2007/4/11 /murky-past-trails-man-to-harvard/.

28. Isaac Arnsdorf, "Yale No Stranger to Application Fraud," *Yale Daily News*, April 10, 2008, available at https://yaledailynews.com/blog/2008 /04/10/yale-no-stranger-to-application-fraud/.

29. "Abe Liu," Internet Archive: Wayback Machine, available at http:// web.archive.org/web/20050413154203/http://www.abeliu.com/index.html.

30. Amy Friedman and Justin C. Worland, "Weld Visitor Abe Liu: I Was Lonely," *Harvard Crimson*, December 14, 2011, available at http://www.the crimson.com/article/2011/12/14/Harvard-Abe-Liu-Extension/.

31. Lauren Landry, "Lonely 27-Year-Old Addicted to Posing as Harvard Freshman Finally Caught and Memed," *Bostinno*, December 14, 2011, available at https://www.americaninno.com/boston/lonely-27-year-old-addicted -to-posing-as-harvard-freshmen-finally-gets-caught-meme/. There is also, in this piece, word of "various crimes" in Abe's history, "including identity and credit card theft"—which if true would tip him into "scammer" status instead. However, that morsel appears in this solitary article—strange given

its sensational quality and the faithfulness with which *other* details are replicated and repeated across publications—and the original source cited can no longer be traced, making it both questionable and unverifiable. Given the circumstances, I have categorized Abe according to his characterization in the press aside from this instance.

32. Phil Yu, "'Lonely' 27-Year-Old Posed as Harvard Freshman for Months," *Angry Asian Man* (blog), December 14, 2011, available at http://blog.angryasianman.com/2011/12/lonely-27-year-old-posed-as-harvard.html.

33. Finn Vigeland, "2012–13 in Review: Campus Impostor Arrested after Posing as Student," *Columbia Spectator*, August 26, 2014, available at https://www.columbiaspectator.com/news/2013/05/13/2012-13-review-campus-impostor-arrested-after-posing-student/.

34. "Gujarat: One Birva Patel Held for Posing as Fake Student of Columbia University," DailyBhaskar.com, September 14, 2012, available at http://daily.bhaskar.com/article/GUJ-AHD-gujarat-one-birva-patel-held-for-posing-as-fake-student-3786098-NOR.html.

35. Vigeland, "2012–13 in Review."

36. Linette Lopez, "A Young Woman Was Arrested for Allegedly Posing as a Columbia Freshman for Two Weeks," *Business Insider*, September 10, 2012, available at http://www.businessinsider.com/rhea-shen-arrested-for-allegedly-posing-as-a-columbia-freshman-for-two-weeks-2012-9.

37. Doug Barry, "Columbia University Impostor Arrested after Two Weeks of Being Creepy to Actual Freshman," Jezebel.com, September 10, 2012, available at https://jezebel.com/5942095/columbia-university-impostor-arrested-after-two-weeks-of-being-creepy-to-actual-freshman.

38. Amit Arora and Daniel Novinson, "Physics Lab Squatter Banned from Campus," *Stanford Daily*, May 29, 2007, available at http://stanforddailyarchive.com/cgi-bin/stanford?a=d&d=stanford20070529-01.2.5&e=-------en-20--1--txt-txIN-------.

39. Julia Erlandson, "Increasingly Erratic Behavior Gives Away Impostor Student Using Campus Facilities," *Daily Bruin*, October 1, 2007, available at http://dailybruin.com/2007/10/01/increasingly_erratic_behavior_gives_away_impostor_/.

40. Annette Lee, "All of the Fun and None of the Work," *Hyphen* 13, January 1, 2008, available at http://hyphenmagazine.com/magazine/issue-13-hybrid-winter-2007/all-fun-and-none-work.

41. Michaela Hulstyn, "Man, 36, Allegedly Posed as Student," *Daily Bruin*, January 29, 2007, available at http://dailybruin.com/2007/01/29/man-36-allegedly-posed-as-stud/.

42. David Lazar, "Students, or Smoke and Mirrors?" *Daily Bruin*, February 5, 2007, available at http://dailybruin.com/2007/02/05/istudents_or_smoke_and_mirrorsi/.

43. Ibid.

44. Hulstyn, "Man, 36."

45. Marian Meyers, *News Coverage of Violence against Women: Engendering Blame* (Thousand Oaks: Sage, 1997), 22.

46. Teun A. van Dijk, *News as Discourse* (Hillsdale, NJ: L. Erlbaum, 1988), 86; Tony Harcup, *Journalism: Principles and Practice* (Thousand Oaks: Sage, 2004), 30, emphasis added.

47. "Korean 'Prodigy' a Serial Fabricator," *Chosunilbo*, January 14, 2016, available at http://english.chosun.com/site/data/html_dir/2015/06/12/2015061201525.html; Kiddy_days, "'Math Genius' Claiming Joint Admission to Both Harvard and Stanford Revealed to Be a Hoax," *Soompi*, June 11, 2015, available at http://www.soompi.com/2015/06/11/korean-math-genius-claiming-joint-admission-to-both-harvard-and-stanford-revealed-to-be-a-hoax/.

48. Brian Ashcraft, "The Harvard + Stanford Genius Story Is Bullshit [Update]," *Kotaku*, June 11, 2015, available at http://kotaku.com/hoax-allegations-over-the-harvard-stanford-math-genius-1710566649.

49. Jeff Yang, "Do Asian Students Face Too Much Academic Pressure?" CNN, Opinion, July 2, 2015, available at http://www.cnn.com/2015/07/02/opinions/yang-genius-girl/; T. Rees Shapiro, "How the Harvard-Stanford Admissions Hoax Became an International Scandal," *Independent*, June 19, 2015, available at http://www.independent.co.uk/news/world/americas/how-the-harvard-stanford-admissions-hoax-became-an-international-scandal-10332368.html.

50. Soompi, Facebook, June 11, 2015, available at https://www.facebook.com/permalink.php?id=12642315906&story_fbid=10153292607215907.

51. Liz Farmer, "Koreans, Indians Lead Northern Virginia's Asian Population Boom," *Washington Examiner*, July 21, 2011, available at https://www.washingtonexaminer.com/koreans-indians-lead-northern-virginias-asian-population-boom and https://www.census.gov/quickfacts/va.

52. Shapiro, "Harvard-Stanford Admissions Hoax," emphasis added.

53. Dhingra, *Hyper Education*, 26.

54. Chang May Choon, "The Great Pretenders," *Straits Times*, June 21, 2015, available at https://webcache.googleusercontent.com/search?q=cache:ZNmNqqrJYp4J:https://www.straitstimes.com/asia/east-asia/the-great-pretenders+&cd=1&hl=en&ct=clnk&gl=us&client=firefox-b-1-ab.

55. Rachel Bertsche, "'Genius Girl' Fakes Admission to Harvard, Stanford as Part of Elaborate Hoax," *Yahoo Parenting*, September 21, 2015, available at http://yahooparenting-us.tumblr.com/post/129608821502/genius-girl-fakes-admission-to-harvard-stanford?is_related_post=1; Shapiro, "Harvard-Stanford Admissions Hoax"; Kiddy_days, "'Math Genius' Claiming Joint Admission."

56. J. Yang, "Do Asian Students Face."

57. Lee and Zhou, *AAAP*, 6, 63–64.

58. "Korean girl and family go through insane lengths to convince everyone she was accepted to Harvard and Stanford (and will attend both, simultaneously). Plan backfires horribly, news calls them out on their bullshit in both Korea and America," Reddit 2016, available at https://www.reddit.com/r/korea/comments/399sfc/korean_girl_and_family_go_through_insane_lengths/.

59. The Marmot's Hole, "Harvard-Stanford Math Prodigy Hoax," Disqus, 2015, available at https://disqus.com/home/discussion/themarmotshole/harvard_stanford_math_prodigy_hoax/;

60. "Stanford Dorm Squatter (Stanford Daily Article)," *College Confidential*, TooRichforAid, May 25, 2007, at 6:07 P.M., available at http://talk.collegeconfidential.com/parents-forum/349023-stanford-dorm-squatter-stanford-daily-article-p3.html.

61. See the following discussion threads: "27 Year Old Man Lives in Harvard Freshman Yard Dorm for 2 Months," *College Confidential*, available at http://talk.collegeconfidential.com/harvard-university/1257843-27-year-old-man-lives-in-harvard-freshman-yard-dorm-for-2-months.html; Max Read, "Creepy 27-Year-Old Posed as Harvard Frosh Because He 'Was Lonely,'" *Gawker*, December 14, 2011, available at http://gawker.com/5868055/creepy-27-year-old-posed-as-harvard-frosh-because-he-was-lonely. Of the ninety-five comments on the latter site, two do mention race but in offhand ways that do not bear discernibly on Abe or his behavior: "Oh he'll probably just write a book and sell the movie rights only when they do the movie instead of an Asian person starring it will be a White dude," and "To the Crimson's defense, the dude is Asian."

62. See comment threads on the following pages: Lopez, "Young Woman Was Arrested." A single commenter wondered about Birva's immigration status as well as (nonsensically) whether she had a "legal guardian" (see Vigeland, "2012–13 in Review," Anonymous posted on November 14, 10:37 P.M.), but both these inquiries pertain to her vulnerability, not the intensity of her parenting.

63. Erlandson, "Increasingly Erratic Behavior"; Arora and Novinson, "Physics Lab Squatter Banned." It's worth noting that the Third World woman as gold digger *is* a racial trope, but I'd maintain that the specificity of "professor's wife" connotes more Stepford wife than mail-order bride.

64. Lee and Zhou, *AAAP*, 56, emphasis added.

65. TrailDog, "Not so SmaHt," Amazon.com, October 17, 2012, available at https://www.amazon.com/Conning-Harvard-Wheeler-Artist-League/product-reviews/0762780029/ref=cm_cr_arp_d_paging_btm_next_2?pageNumber=2.

66. David Samuels, *The Runner: A True Account of the Amazing Lies and Fantastical Adventures of the Ivy League Impostor James Hogue* (New York: New Press, 2008), 155.

67. Also Tonica Jenkins, whose mother was arrested for attempted cocaine trafficking alongside her, and Esther Reed, described by friends to the *New York Post* as "once an obese teenage dropout so abused by her loved ones that she wanted to scrap her entire life" (Marianne Garvey, "Ivy Gal Fled Her Past," *New York Post*, January 12, 2007, available at https://nypost.com/2007/01/12 /ivy-gal-fled-.her-past/). But each of these instances stands alone as true exceptions rather than forming a meaningful variant.

68. Christine Yano, and Neal Akatsuka, *Straight A's: Asian American College Students in Their Own Words* (Durham, NC: Duke University Press, 2018), 193–194.

69. Shapiro, "Harvard-Stanford Admissions Hoax"; Ashcraft, "Harvard + Stanford Genius Story."

70. "Father of 'Math Prodigy' Issues Apology," *Korea Times*, People, June 11, 2015, available at http://www.koreatimesus.com/father-of-math-prodigy -issues-apology/.

71. Chris Gabel, "Nevada Lineman Comes Clean: He Made Up Recruiting Story," *USA Today*, Sports, February 7, 2008, available at http://usatoday30 .usatoday.com/sports/preps/football/2008-02-06-reno-confession_N.htm; Chris Gabel, "Football: Fernley's Hart Commits to Cal in Late Switch," RGJ .com, February 2, 2008, available at http://blogs.rgj.com/preps/2008/02/02 /football-fernleys-hart-commits-to-cal-in-late-switch/; Josh Barr, "This Recruit Is Unreal," *Washington Post*, February 6, 2008, available at http://www.wash ingtonpost.com/wp-dyn/content/article/2008/02/05/AR2008020503672 .html?sid=ST2008020600092.

72. Mitch Albom, "This Is What Happens When We Turn College Sports Recruitment into Entertainment," *Jewish World Review*, February 11, 2008, available at http://www.jewishworldreview.com/0208/albom021108.php3.

73. Tom Friend, "The Boy Who Cried Cal," ESPN.com, March 10, 2009, available at http://sports.espn.go.com/espn/eticket/story?page=kevinhart.

74. Ibid.

75. Lee and Zhou, *AAAP*, 149.

76. Shapiro, "Harvard-Stanford Admissions Hoax," emphasis added.

77. Martin Conboy, *The Language of the News* (New York: Routledge, 2007), 38.

78. van Dijk, *News as Discourse*, 121, 122.

79. Lauren Berlant, *The Female Complaint: The Unfinished Business of Sentimentality in American Culture* (Durham, NC: Duke University Press, 2008), 4.

80. Duschinsky and Wilson, "Flat Affect," 179.

81. Berlant, *Female Complaint*, 18.

82. Ibid., 19.

83. See John Morreall, *Comedy, Tragedy, and Religion* (Albany: State University of New York Press, 1999).

chapter two: Exemplary

1. Daniel Novinson, "Impostor Caught," *Stanford Daily*, May 24, 2007, available at https://www.stanforddaily.com/2007/05/24/imposter-caught/.

2. Takeo Rivera, "Takeo Rivera—Azia Kim: An RA's Reflection," *communicASIANS* xii, no. 1 (Fall 2007), 14, available at http://www.scribd.com /doc/2369461/CommunicASIANS-Fall-2007.

3. John Coté and Jill Tucker, "Wannabe Freshman Outwits Stanford," *SFGate*, May 25, 2007, available at http://www.sfgate.com/education/article /Wannabe-freshman-outwits-Stanford-2591998.php.

4. Lisa M. Krieger, "Stanford Impostor Fools ROTC, Too," *San Jose Mercury News*, May 30, 2007, available at http://www.mercurynews.com/news /ci_6018365?nclick_check=1. The sole exception to a decidedly unpathological portrait of Azia also comes from the *San Jose Mercury News*, which reports rumors of prior misconduct—but without benefit of attribution or apparent corroboration: "[Some f]ormer classmates at Fullerton's Troy High School . . . allege that she was disciplined for dishonesty while at Troy, and that her parents were informed." This loose end was, however, neither repeated nor corroborated elsewhere; my own interviewees had no knowledge of such incidents. Though such a history would certainly be pertinent, given its status as gossip it is perhaps best set aside.

5. In a "DC Moms and Dads" forum on (admittedly) Sara's case (but the point remains), one participant's succinct, if partly mistaken, response minced no words:

> "Anonymous: An Asian student got into Harvard and Stanford? This is news? Like, happens every day.
> Next."

("Amazing Story: Korean Student Gets Chance to Attend Both Harvard and Stanford," DCUrbanMomsandDads.com, June 7, 2015, 21:06, available at http://www.dcurbanmom.com/jforum/posts/list/15/476545.page.)

6. Harcup, *Journalism*, 30.

7. Novinson, "Impostor Caught."

8. Meyers, *News Coverage*, 22.

9. Because of this industry standard (the more "reputable" the publication, the more likely to practice this reticence), a number of our impostors must be presumed non-Asian by name and lack of other indicators, but cannot be definitively identified here by race. It is most likely that Patrick

McDermit, Lon Grammer, and Edward Meinert are white, if only because articles tend to find *some* fashion of signaling racial otherness. It is mentioned, for example, that Kenneth Foster hung around the African American theme floor at the USC dorms. This is, of course, not definitive information, but it is an example of the kind of oblique referencing that traditional journalism is given to.

10. Coté and Tucker, "Wannabe Freshman."

11. Jay Mathews, "Overachieving Students under Pressure," *Washington Post*, August 16, 2006, available at http://www.washingtonpost.com/wp-dyn /content/discussion/2006/08/11/DI2006081101178.html.

12. Jay Mathews, *Harvard Schmarvard: Getting Beyond the Ivy League to the College that Is Best for You* (New York: Three Rivers Press, 2009).

13. Conboy, *Language of the News*, 38.

14. Catherine Squires and Daniel Brouwer, "In/discernible Bodies: The Politics of Passing in Dominant and Marginal Media," *Critical Studies in Media Communication* 19, no. 3 (2002): 285.

15. Daniel Novinson, "Imposter Caught," *Stanford Daily*, May 24, 2007, available at https://www.stanforddaily.com/2007/05/24/imposter-caught/.

16. "A Sad Charade," Mothertalkers, May 25, 2007, available at http://www.mothertalkers.com/2007/05/25/1726/a-sad-charade/.

17. C. N. Le, "Asian American Pretends to Be a Stanford Student," *Asian-Nation* (blog), May 31, 2007, available at http://www.asian-nation.org /headlines/2007/05/asian-american-pretends-to-be-a-stanford-student/; Jen Wang, "Oh Azia I Hate to Say Goodbye," *Disgrasian* (blog), May 29, 2007, available at http://disgrasian.com/tag/azia-kim/; Mike Lee, "Push to Achieve Tied to . . . Deception?" *8Asians* (blog), May 26, 2007, available at https:// www.8asians.com/2007/05/26/push-to-achieve-tied-to-deception/.

18. Berlant, *Female Complaint*, viii–x.

19. Ibid., 5, emphases added.

20. "Asian Girl Pretended to Be Stanford Student for 8 Months," Polykarbon Art Forum, available at http://www.polykarbonbbs.com/archive/index .php/t-19027.html; Wang, "Oh Azia." Palo Alto being, of course, the location of Stanford and ground zero of Silicon Valley, with an Asian American population of around 27 percent in the late 2000s.

21. Berlant, *Female Complaint*, 5.

22. Lee and Zhou call the field's stance "antiquated": stalled at the 1960s. I agree that scholars who "flippantly [reject] the model minority" trope as political fiction (*AAAP*, 118, 11) must then ignore material realities that *accompany* discursive racialization and also the internalization of those realities and discourses as normal. See Ellen Wu's *The Color of Success: Asian Americans and the Origins of the Model Minority* (Princeton, NJ: Princeton University Press, 2014) and Madeline Hsu's *The Good Immigrants: How the*

Yellow Peril Became the Model Minority (Princeton, NJ: Princeton University Press, 2015) for more historically calibrated accounts.

23. Lee and Zhou, *AAAP*, 56, 61.

24. Judith Butler, "Performative Acts and Gender Constitution," *Theatre Journal* 40, no. 4 (December 1988): 531.

25. Ibid., 520.

26. *Men Are from Mars, Women Are from Venus: How to Get What You Want in Your Relationships*, Amazon.com, available at https://www.amazon.com/Mars-Women-Venus-Communication-Relationships/dp/0007152590.

27. Butler, "Performative Acts," 520.

28. Guofang Li, "Other People's Success: Impact of the 'Model Minority' Myth on Underachieving Asian Students in North America," *KEDI Journal of Educational Policy* 2, no. 1 (2005): 72.

29. Min Song, *The Children of 1965: On Writing, and Not Writing, as an Asian American* (Durham, NC: Duke University Press, 2013), 43.

30. Paul Wong et al., "Asian Americans as a Model Minority: Self-Perceptions and Perceptions by Other Racial Groups," *Sociological Perspectives* 41, no. 1 (March 1, 1998): 113.

31. Candace West and Don H. Zimmerman, "Doing Gender," *Gender and Society* 1, no. 2 (June 1987): 130.

32. Butler, "Performative Acts," 528.

33. C. N. Le, "Asian American Pretends."

34. Vanessa Hua, "Accepted," in *Deceit and Other Possibilities* (Detroit: Willow Books, 2016), 82.

35. A Harvard senior whose visiting relatives insult her plans to pursue something other than medicine relates being told to "Just nod and smile." Rather than insist on defending what they disparage as her failure, she acquiesces, and "perform[s] the silence that was expected of me." Yano and Akatsuka, *Straight A's*, 141.

36. Vanessa Hua, interview with author, May 5, 2018.

37. See, for example: Jonathan Haidt, *The Righteous Mind: Why Good People Are Divided by Politics and Religion* (New York: Pantheon Books, 2012); Leda Cosmides and John Tooby, "Cognitive Adaptations for Social Exchange," in *The Adapted Mind: Evolutionary Psychology and the Generation of Culture*, ed. J. H. Barkow et al. (New York: Oxford University Press, 1992), 163–228; Jonathan Gottschall, *The Storytelling Animal: How Stories Make Us Human* (Boston: Houghton Mifflin Harcourt, 2012).

38. Duschinsky and Wilson, "Flat Affect," 179.

39. George Ritzer and Douglas J. Goodman, *Sociological Theory* (Boston: McGraw-Hill, 2008), 376, 377. Admittedly, "success frame" as it appears in *AAAP* does not necessarily do all this. Though Lee and Zhou (53) refer to

Erving Goffman's use of "frame" as an analytical, interpretive tool, syntax usually suggests a much more modest function: as an inflexible set of requirements. For example: "Even those Asian Americans whose outcomes *match the success frame* do not feel as successful as they would like" (8, emphasis added), or "Not only was a specific educational track critical to the success frame from the perspective of immigrant parents, but parents also strongly disapproved of and admonished *any deviation from it*" (56, emphasis added).

40. Duschinsky and Wilson, "Flat Affect," 179.

41. Lee and Zhou, *AAAP*, 112, 61.

42. Ruth Samuelson, "Faking College," *Houston Press*, October 12, 2006, available at http://www.houstonpress.com/news/faking-college-6576745.

43. Richard C. Paddock, "Living a Lie on Campus," *Los Angeles Times*, col. 1, June 13, 2007, 1, emphasis added, available at http://articles.latimes.com/2007/jun/13/local/me-impostor13.

44. Ian Lamont, "College Imposters, Part II: Azia Kim Exposed at Stanford," *Harvard Extended* (blog), May 26, 2007, available at http://harvardextended.blogspot.com/2007/05/college-imposters-part-ii-azia-kim.html; CS Staff, "Non-Student Lives at Stanford Dorm for 8 Months," *Campus Safety*, May 29, 2007, available at http://www.campussafetymagazine.com/article/non-student-lives-at-stanford-dorm-for-8-months/technology#; Jennifer Delson and Richard Paddock, "California Woman Fakes Her Way into Elite Stanford," *Seattle Times*, Education/Nation and World, May 27, 2007, available at http://www.seattletimes.com/nation-world/california-woman-fakes-her-way-into-elite-stanford/.

45. Paddock, "Living a Lie," 1.

46. Samuelson, "Faking College."

47. Ibid.

48. An arrangement for Stanford students, who have no ROTC on campus.

49. Takeo Rivera, interview with author, March 31, 2018; Trent Walker, interview with author, May 7, 2018.

50. Ju Yon Kim, *The Racial Mundane: Asian American Performance and the Embodied Everyday* (New York: New York University Press, 2015), 10, 3, 12. Per one premed Harvard undergrad, she spent high school going "through the motions. I took notes in class, I aced tests, I joined clubs, I became a leader on campus." At college? More of the same. Yano and Akatsuka, *Straight A's*, 138.

51. Gary Okihiro cited in Ju Yon Kim, *Racial Mundane*, 179.

52. Frosh FAQs, Program in Human Biology, Stanford University, available at https://humanbiology.stanford.edu/academicsadvising-declaring/frosh-faqs; emphasis added.

53. Rivera, interview.

54. Walker, interview; Rivera, interview.

55. Like Sara's charade, Azia's implies the kind of remote and extensive audience characteristic for Harvard undergrads, whose achievements yield "bragging rights" for "immediate and extended families that can go all the way back to Asia, schools and school districts, hometowns and counties, even friends and acquaintances." Yano and Akatsuka, *Straight A's*, 20.

56. Resident assistant, interview with author, October 5, 2018.

57. Rivera, interview; "Honor Code," Office of Community Standards, Stanford University, available at https://communitystandards.stanford.edu /policies-and-guidance/honor-code.

58. Valli Kalei Kanuha, "The Social Process of 'Passing' to Manage Stigma: Acts of Internalized Oppression or Acts of Resistance?" *Journal of Sociology and Social Welfare* 26, no. 4 (2015): 28.

59. Pfeiffer, *Race Passing*, 7.

60. Catherine Rottenberg, "Passing: Race, Identification, and Desire," *Criticism* 45, no. 4 (2003): 438, 439.

61. Stephanie Findlay and Nicholas Kohler, "Too Asian: Some Frosh Don't Want to Study at an Asian University" [retitled "The Enrollment Controversy: Worries That Efforts in the U.S. to Limit Enrollment of Asian Students in Top Universities May Migrate to Canada"], *Maclean's* (November 10, 2010), available at http://www.macleans.ca/news/canada/too-asian/.

62. Lee and Zhou, *AAAP*, 63, 60, 62, 53.

63. Yano and Akatsuka, *Straight A's*, 183.

64. Ibid., 6, original emphasis removed.

65. A blind reader for an early version of this chapter was so confident of the culprits to Azia's story that she dismissed the prospect of interviews as pointless: Why bother when such could uncover nothing surprising about the family, nothing we did not already "know."

66. Bert Yun, interview with author, May 18, 2018.

67. During her time at Stanford, he may have found his own ministry elsewhere; they were no longer at Cornerstone Church when the news broke. Yun, interview; Hannah Kim, interview with author, June 15, 2018.

68. Vivian S. Louie, *Compelled to Excel: Immigration, Education, and Opportunity among Chinese Americans* (Stanford, CA: Stanford University Press, 2004), 57.

69. Delson and Paddock, "California Woman."

70. Erica Perez, "O.C. Teens Win $40,000 at Science Contest," *Orange County Register*, December 6, 2005, available at https://www.ocregister.com /2005/12/06/oc-teens-win-40000-at-science-contest/ and https://www.link edin.com/in/huy-v-nguyen-bb21a22/.

71. *Troy High School Yearbook 2004*, 245. I was not able to access the 2003 edition and, though these are public materials, I have elected not to delve into Huy's yearbook records beyond his senior year, in order to limit his exposure.

72. Sherry B. Ortner, "'Burned Like a Tattoo': High School Social Categories and 'American Culture,'" *Ethnography* 3, no. 2 (June 1, 2002): 117.

73. Penelope Eckert, *Jocks and Burnouts: Social Categories and Identity in the High School* (New York: Columbia University, 1989), 2.

74. David A. Kinney, "From Nerds to Normals: The Recovery of Identity among Adolescents from Middle School to High School," *Sociology of Education* 66, no. 1 (January 1993): 27.

75. Grace Kao, "Group Images and Possible Selves among Adolescents: Linking Stereotypes to Expectations by Race and Ethnicity," *Sociological Forum* 15, no. 3 (2000): 417.

76. "San Marino High School," GreatSchools.org, available at https://www.greatschools.org/california/san-marino/2917-San-Marino-High-School/.

77. Lee and Zhou, *AAAP*, 60–64.

78. Twenty of the twenty-four varsity sports teams at Troy in 2006 included Asian American athletes; nearly every extracurricular club (barring the very liberal-arts leaning ones) had all but exclusively Asian American memberships. *Troy High School Yearbook 2006*, 94–129.

79. *Troy Yearbook 2006*, 400–403. For a quick snapshot of San Marino High's "leading crowd," see the local paper: "San Marino High School" tag, *San Marino Tribune*, available at https://sanmarinotribune.com/tags/san-marino-high-school/.

80. Eckert, *Jocks and Burnouts*, 3.

81. Average size of an entire public school in the United States in 2018 was 503; in California, 596. "Average Public School Student Size," Public School Review, accessed November 10, 2018, available at https://www.publicschoolreview.com/average-school-size-stats/national-data. These numbers have stayed fairly flat nationally since 2005. "Enrollment trends," Fast Facts, National Center for Education Statistics, available at https://nces.ed.gov/fastfacts/display.asp?id=65.

82. 2018–2019 Troy Tech / International Baccalaureate Programs Applicant Instructions for Current Eighth Grade Students available at https://www.fjuhsd.org/cms/lib/CA02000098/Centricity/Domain/235/Application%20Instructions%20and%20FAQ%20January%202019.pdf.

83. William Mynster, email message to author, December 3, 2018.

84. "Honor Roll," Troy High School, available at https://www.fjuhsd.org/Page/408.

85. See Lee and Zhou, *AAAP*, 4; the present "Introduction"; and my book *Ingratitude: The Debt-Bound Daughter in Asian American Literature* (New York: New York University Press, 2011), 3–15.

86. Lee and Zhou, *AAAP*, 59.

87. Kim, interview.

88. T. Chen, *Double Agency*, 4.

89. Krieger, "Stanford Impostor Fools ROTC."

90. Lauren Smiley, "Elite College Hoaxer Showdown: Stanford vs. Harvard," *SF Weekly*, May 20, 2010, available at https://archives.sfweekly.com/thesnitch/2010/05/20/elite-college-hoaxer-showdown-stanford-vs-harvard.

91. Yun, interview.

chapter three: Limit Case

1. Karen K. Ho, "Jennifer Pan's Revenge: The Inside Story of a Golden Child, the Killers She Hired, and the Parents She Wanted Dead," *Toronto Life*, July 22, 2015, available at http://torontolife.com/city/crime/jennifer-pan-revenge/.

2. Alyshah Hasham, "Murder Trial Opens for Daughter Accused of Planning Parents' Death," *Toronto Star*, Crime, March 19, 2014, available at http://www.thestar.com/news/crime/2014/03/19/crown_outlines_case_against_daughter_accused_of_planning_parents_death.html.

3. Rosie DiManno, "Pan's Unspeakable Crimes Done for Love and Lucre: DiManno," *Toronto Star*, December 14, 2014, available at http://www.thestar.com/news/gta/2014/12/14/pans_unspeakable_crimes_done_for_love_and_lucre_dimanno.html.

4. Ho, "Pan's Revenge," emphasis added.

5. DiManno, "Pan's Unspeakable Crimes," emphasis added.

6. Gordon Pon, "Importing the Asian Model Minority Discourse into Canada: Implications for Social Work and Education," *Canadian Social Work Review* 17, no. 2 (2000): 283.

7. Eleanor Rose Ty, *Asianfail: Narratives of Disenchantment and the Model Minority* (Urbana: University of Illinois Press, 2017), 5.

8. The "decoder ring" section of the present "Introduction" and my book *Ingratitude*, 3–15; see also Lee and Zhou, *AAAP*, 4.

9. The two are noted as twin causes here, for instance: "intense parental expectations . . . as well as the extremely high standard set by the 'model minority' stereotype . . . contribute to students' psychological distress and alienation from parents and peers." Catherine Costigan et al., "Living Up to Expectations: The Strengths and Challenges Experienced by Chinese Canadian Students," *Canadian Journal of School Psychology* 25, no. 3 (September 2010): 223.

10. Duschinsky and Wilson, "Flat Affect," 179.

11. Tim Kelly, "York Crime Reporter Jeremy Grimaldi Wins National Book Award," YorkRegion.com, May 29, 2017, available at https://www.yorkregion.com/whatson-story/7340360-york-crime-reporter-jeremy-grimaldi-wins-national-book-award/.

12. "Jennifer Pan's Revenge," Toronto Life, Disqus, July 22, 2015, available at https://disqus.com/home/discussion/tlife/jennifer_pans_revenge_the_inside_story_of_a_golden_child_the_killers_she_hired_and_the_parents_she_w/.

13. Jeremy Grimaldi, *A Daughter's Deadly Deception: The Jennifer Pan Story* (Toronto: Dundurn, 2016), 279.

14. Grimaldi, *Deadly Deception*, 179, 180.

15. Ho, "Pan's Revenge."

16. Grimaldi, *Deadly Deception*, 192, 180, 181, 185, 179.

17. Ibid., 178, 180, 187.

18. Ho, "Pan's Revenge," emphasis added.

19. Ibid., emphases added: these terms speak volumes to Ho's view of the matter.

20. In this instance, the success-framed intimate public veers closer to Lauren Berlant's definition, having been conjured by a mass-market publishing interest for coin.

21. See my "Amy Chua and the Externalized Cost of Book Sales" at either *Hyphen* magazine or *Huffington Post*, and "Advice on How Not to Misread the Tiger Mother," *Amerasia Journal* 37, no. 2 (2011): 123–129.

22. Amy Chua, "Kavanaugh Is a Mentor to Women," *Wall Street Journal*, Opinion/Commentary, July 12, 2018, available at https://www.wsj.com/arti cles/kavanaugh-is-a-mentor-to-women-1531435729; Sara Boboltz and Emily Peck, "Yale Students to Prof Who Denies Coaching Kavanaugh Clerks: You're Lying," *Huffington Post*, Politics, September 22, 2018, available at https:// www.huffingtonpost.com/entry/yale-students-to-prof-who-denies-coaching -kavanaugh-clerks-youre-lying_us_5ba685dde4b069d5f9d369e6.

23. This is the vein of cause-effect claim that Lee and Zhou refute, arguing that what works isn't Tiger strictness but material strategies and resources— that is, that Chao takes correlation for causation. See *AAAP*, chap. 4.

24. Ruth K. Chao, "Beyond Parental Control and Authoritarian Parenting Style: Understanding Chinese Parenting through the Cultural Notion of Training," *Child Development* 65, no. 4 (August 1994): 1111–1119.

25. Linda P. Juang et al., "Deconstructing the Myth of the 'Tiger Mother': An Introduction to the Special Issue on Tiger Parenting, Asian-Heritage Families, and Child/Adolescent Well-Being," *Asian American Journal of Psychology* 4, no. 1 (2013): 1–6.

26. Ray Kwong, "How This Golden Child Became a Tiger from Hell," Ejinsight.com, July 30, 2015, available at http://www.ejinsight.com/20150730 -how-this-golden-child-became-a-tiger-from-hell/; u/Belaire, "The Story of Jennifer Pan," Reddit.com, July 22, 2015, available at https://www.reddit .com/r/toronto/comments/3e9smx/the_story_of_jennifer_pan/.

27. Dhingra, *Hyper Education*, 14, emphasis added.

28. Ty, *Asianfail*, 57.

29. Grimaldi, *Deadly Deception*, 129.

30. Nadia Sorkhabi and Ellen Middaugh, "How Variations in Parents' Use of Confrontive and Coercive Control Relate to Variations in Parent– Adolescent Conflict, Adolescent Disclosure, and Parental Knowledge: Ado-

lescents' Perspective," *Journal of Child and Family Studies* 23, no. 7 (2014): 1231, 1233, 1236.

31. Amy Tan, *The Joy Luck Club* (New York: Putnam's, 1989), 173.

32. Sorkhabi and Middaugh, "How Variations," 1239.

33. Sorkhabi and Middaugh, "Domain-Specific Parenting Practices and Adolescent Self-Esteem, Problem Behaviors, and Competence," *Journal of Child and Family Studies* 28 (2019): 506.

34. Amy Chua, *Battle Hymn of the Tiger Mother* (New York: Penguin, 2011), 3.

35. A young woman at Harvard recalls her mother's swift retribution and threats of disownment over her high school "efforts at rebellion": "buying tickets to a nonclassical music concert," purchasing "jeans that rest too low on the hips . . . or watching an R-rated movie." Yano and Akatsuka, *Straight A's*, 45.

36. Jenny P. Yau et al., "Disclosure to Parents about Everyday Activities among American Adolescents from Mexican, Chinese, and European Backgrounds," *Child Development* 80, no. 5 (September 2009): 1483, emphasis added.

37. Ibid., 1498.

38. Ibid., 1485.

39. Vivian Louie, "'Being Practical' or 'Doing What I Want': The Role of Parents in the Academic Choices of Chinese Americans," in *Becoming New Yorkers: Ethnographies of the New Second Generation*, ed. Philip Kasinitz et al. (New York: Russell Sage, 2004), 95, emphasis added.

40. Ho, "Pan's Revenge," emphasis added.

41. u/Belaire, "Story of Jennifer Pan."

42. Yau et al., "Disclosure to Parents," 1482, emphases added.

43. Ho, "Pan's Revenge," emphasis added.

44. F. James Davis, quoted in Adrian Piper, "Passing for White, Passing for Black," *Transition* 58 (1992): 13.

45. Piper, "Passing for White," 12.

46. Sara Lee, "Class Matters," in *Becoming New Yorkers: Ethnographies of the New Second Generation*, ed. Philip Kasinitz et al. (New York: Russell Sage, 2004), 314, 331, 317, 331.

47. Ibid., 333.

48. "High Expectations Asian Father," KnowYourMeme.com, available at https://knowyourmeme.com/photos/232168-high-expectations-asian-father; Jukebox 9, "Meme Spotlight: High Expectations Asian Father," Wordpress.com, August 3, 2015, available at https://jukebox9.wordpress.com/2015/08/03/meme-spotlight-high-expectations-asian-father/; "Your Sister Get B on Math Test," Meme, available at https://me.me/i/your-sister-get-bon-math-test-congratulation-you-only-child-6638413; "Asian Grading Scale," Frenys, available at http://frenys.com/post/6027634-asian-grading-scale/.

49. Kate M. Miltner, "There's No Place for Lulz on LOLCats: The Role of Genre, Gender, and Group Identity in the Interpretation and Enjoyment of an Internet Meme," *First Monday* 19, no. 8 (August 4, 2014), available at https://journals.uic.edu/ojs/index.php/fm/article/view/5391/4103,

50. "[M]emes precipitate the collective, . . . they rely on such processes and call them into being." This article on online behavior describes the performance of *High Expectations Asian Father* in particular as "social constitution . . . as the constitution of self by relying on the network (and here Judith Butler is evoked), a performance of well-established discursive formations (such as those recently made more visible through The Tiger Mother publication and its publicity campaign . . .)." Olga Goriunova, "The Force of Digital Aesthetics. On Memes, Hacking, and Individuation," *Nordic Journal of Aesthetics* 24, no. 47 (2015): 65, 66. And Ty's book, in fact, opens with an image from *High Expectations*, as prime example of a meme "successful and funny only because there is an audience with a shared knowledge and understanding of the stereotypes, expectations, and issues of diasporic Asians." Ty, *Asianfail*, 18.

51. Goriunova, "Force of Digital Aesthetics," 65.

52. Maxine Hong Kingston, *The Woman Warrior: Memoirs of a Girlhood among Ghosts* (New York: Vintage International, 1989), 7.

53. Kenji Yoshino, "Covering," *Yale Law Journal* 111, no. 4 (2002): 772.

54. Ibid., 885.

55. Jean Shin, "The Asian American Closet," *Asian American Law Journal* 11, no. 1 (2004): 1.

56. In her interviews, Sara Lee found that middle-class Korean Americans, better positioned to approximate the success frame, "felt no conflict in self-identifying and being identified as Asian, as Korean American, and also as model minority" ("Class Matters," 321).

57. Lee and Zhou, *AAAP*, 161, 166, 167, 168.

58. Lauren Berlant, *Cruel Optimism* (Durham, NC: Duke University Press, 2011), 1, 11, 24.

59. *Time Out* (*L'Emploi du Temps*), directed by Laurent Cantet (France: Haut et Court, 2001), DVD, 1.23.00.

60. Berlant, *Cruel Optimism*, 24, emphasis in original, 2, 199.

61. *L'Emploi du Temps*, 2:01:20.

62. Grimaldi, *Deadly Deception*, 227.

63. "Time Out (*L'Emploi du Temps*)," Rotten Tomatoes, available at https://www.rottentomatoes.com/m/time_out_l_emploi_du_temps.

64. Pollocabra, "Strict Parenting Can Lead to a Lifetime of Hardship," July 30, 2015, available at https://pollocabra.wordpress.com/2015/07/30/strict-parenting-can-lead-to-a-lifetime-of-hardship/.

65. Iscrewedupbadinto, "The Story of Jennifer Pan," Reddit, available at https://www.reddit.com/r/toronto/comments/3e9smx/the_story_of_jennifer_pan/ctdbo7l/.

66. Hua Hsu, "Affect Theory and the New Age of Anxiety," *New Yorker*, March 25, 2019, available at https://www.newyorker.com/magazine/2019/03/25/affect-theory-and-the-new-age-of-anxiety.

67. Emmanuel Carrère, *The Adversary: A True Story of Monstrous Deception* (New York: Henry Holt, 2000), 37, 42, 46–47.

68. "[N]eoliberalism becomes not just a government strategy but also a parenting strategy to create a particular kind of individual who should be able to weather life's storms alone." Dhingra, *Hyper Education*, 141.

69. Ruth Cain, "Bringing Up Neoliberal Baby: Post-austerity Anxieties about (Social) Reproduction," OpenDemocracy.net, July 14, 2016, available at https://www.opendemocracy.net/en/opendemocracyuk/bringing-up-neoliberal-baby-post-austerity-anxieties-about-social-repro/.

70. Berlant, *Cruel Optimism*, 15, 205.

71. Dhingra, *Hyper Education*, 117, 43.

72. Lee and Zhou, *AAAP*, 83, emphasis added. The latter set of numbers seems to be reversed in error: per the description, 27 percent of Asian Americans should disagree with that sentiment.

73. Ho, "Pan's Revenge," emphasis added.

74. Ibid., 167.

75. Piper, "Passing for White," 13, emphasis added.

76. Josephine Kim, "Afterword" in Yano and Akatsuka, *Straight A's*, 204.

77. Duschinsky and Wilson, "Flat Affect," 180.

78. Wolf, "Family Secrets," 468.

79. Lee and Zhou, *AAAP*, 166.

80. Hasham, "Murder Trial Opens."

81. Lee and Zhou, *AAAP*, 166.

82. Alysha Hasham, "I Tried to Have Myself Killed, Not Parents, Jennifer Pan Tells Murder Trial," *The Star*, August 19, 2014, available at https://www.thestar.com/news/crime/2014/08/19/i_tried_to_have_myself_killed_not_parents_jennifer_pan_tells_murder_trial.html.

83. See chapter one. There is also an argument made in chapter two worth refreshing here: That this paradoxical mindspace Garrett and Jennifer have come to inhabit is, looked at another way, not entirely so out of the ordinary. Model-minority identity is performed according to the same social script no matter whether its perfection is a little bit of a lie or a lot.

84. Berlant, *Female Complaint*, 4.

85. Hasham, "I Tried to Have Myself Killed."

86. P. D. James, *The Murder Room* (New York: A. A. Knopf, 2003), 12.

87. Grimaldi, *Deadly Deception*, 276, 280, 279.

88. "On occasion psychiatrists are asked for an opinion about an individual who is in the light of public attention or who has disclosed information about himself/herself through public media. In such circumstances, a psychiatrist may share with the public his or her expertise about psychiatric issues

in general. However, it is unethical for a psychiatrist to offer a professional opinion unless he or she has conducted an examination and has been granted proper authorization for such a statement." American Psychiatric Association, *The Principles of Medical Ethics with Annotations Especially Applicable to Psychiatry, 2013 Edition*, Section 7.3, 9, available at https://www.psychiatry.org/psychiatrists/practice/ethics. The American Psychological Association holds much the same. (Susan H. McDaniel, "Response to Article on Whether Therapists Should Analyze Presidential Candidates," American Psychological Association, March 14, 2016, available at https://web.archive.org/web/20160420031828/http://www.apa.org/news/press/response/presidential-candidates.aspx).

89. Chris Kolmar, "Connecticut Cities with the Largest Asian Population for 2020," HomeSnacks, December 26, 2019, available at https://www.homesnacks.net/most-asian-cities-in-connecticut-1214558/; "Toronto Population 2019," Canada Population, available at https://canadapopulation.org/toronto-population/; Grimaldi, *Deadly Deception*, 191.

90. See Cecilia Tasca et al., "Women and Hysteria in the History of Mental Health," *Clinical Practice and Epidemiology in Mental Health* 8 (2012): 110–119; Jack Drescher, "Out of DSM: Depathologizing Homosexuality," *Behavioral Sciences* 5, no. 4 (December 2015): 565–575.

91. Steven Hyman, "Diagnosing the DSM: Diagnostic Classification Needs Fundamental Reform," Dana Foundation, April 26, 2011, available at http://dana.org/Cerebrum/2011/Diagnosing_the_DSM__Diagnostic_Classification_Needs_Fundamental_Reform/.

92. Grimaldi, *Deadly Deception*, 280, emphasis added.

93. Jennifer Sarrett, "Is the Changing Definition of Autism Narrowing What We Think of as 'Normal'?" The Conversation, September 21, 2015, available at https://theconversation.com/is-the-changing-definition-of-autism-narrowing-what-we-think-of-as-normal-47310.

94. "*I have not met Jennifer Pan nor have I conducted a psychological assessment of her.* However, there are psychological factors and profiles generally associated with certain kinds of experiences—the sort of background, upbringing, family, and social life that Jennifer had. Based only on what is reported second- and third-hand, I can speculate about the personality and mental health associated with that kind of life and this kind of murder and how the situation might have developed. I cannot say specifically that this is what happened with Jennifer Pan: I do not know her or her family. *I can only offer informed speculation*" (Grimaldi, *Deadly Deception*, 315, emphasis added).

95. Betty Kershner, interview with author, October 5, 2018.

96. Grimaldi, *Deadly Deception*, 325.

97. Wolf, "Family Secrets," 459.

98. Janna Kim, "Asian American Women's Retrospective Reports of Their Sexual Socialization," *Psychology of Women Quarterly* 33, no. 3 (2009): 342.

99. Grimaldi, *Deadly Deception*, 327.

100. Kanuha, "Social Process," 33.

101. Grimaldi, *Deadly Deception*, 327.

102. Sara Ahmed, *The Promise of Happiness* (Durham, NC: Duke University Press, 2010), 61.

103. Dhingra, *Hyper Education*, 48.

104. Grimaldi, *Deadly Deception*, 328, 194, 328.

105. Sareeta Amute, "Learning from Stuart Hall: The Limit as Method," savageminds.org, December 10, 2014, available at https://savageminds.org /2014/12/10/learning-from-stuart-hall-the-limit-as-method/.

chapter four: Bad Boys

1. *Better Luck Tomorrow* (*BLT*), directed by Justin Lin (Hollywood, CA: Paramount, 2003), DVD; Brian Hu, "The 20 Best Asian American Films of the Last 20 Years," *Los Angeles Times*, October 4, 2019, available at https://www.latimes .com/entertainment-arts/movies/story/2019-10-04/asian-american-films-canon.

2. City News Service, June 12, 2008 Thursday, available at https:// advance-lexis-com.proxy.library.ucsb.edu:9443/api/document?collection =news&id=urn:contentItem:4SRK-HYS0-TX4S-91HN-00000-00&context =1516831.

3. "Police Link UCR Incident to Effort to Spare a Mother Disappointment" (originally published at *Press Enterprise* available at http://www.pe .com/localnews/inland/stories/PE_News_Local_D_yung21.3e8b628.html —cached at) UCR, Livejournal, June 21, 2007, available at https://ucr.live journal.com/606407.html.

4. City News Service, June 12, 2008.

5. Sara Lin, "Dropout Status Led to Bomb Threat, Police Say," *Los Angeles Times*, June 22, 2007, available at https://www.latimes.com/archives/la-xpm -2007-jun-22-me-ucr22-story.html.

6. "Police Link UCR Incident," Livejournal.

7. Phil Yu, "The Worst Way to Tell Your Mom You Dropped Out of School," *Angry Asian Man* (blog), June 25, 2007, available at http://blog.angryasianman .com/2007/06/worst-way-to-tell-your-mom-you-dropped.html (emphasis added).

8. Phil Yu, "UC Riverside Dropout Pleads Guilty to Bomb Scare," *Angry Asian Man* (blog), April 28, 2008, available at http://blog.angryasianman .com/2008/04/uc-riverside-dropout-pleads-guilty-to.html.

9. Steve Lowery, "Bomb Voyage," *OC Weekly*, August 11, 2005; Gustavo Arellano, "OC's 31 Scariest People," *OC Weekly*, October 27, 2005.

10. Arellano, "OC's 31."

11. Yano and Akatsuka, *Straight A's*, 12.

12. "The pain and resentment and anger of young men is so grand and vast and special that they can and will make others pay for it." (Monica Hes-

se, "We Need to Talk about Why Mass Shooters Are Almost Always Men," *Washington Post*, Style/Perspective, August 5, 2019, available at https://www .washingtonpost.com/lifestyle/style/we-need-to-talk-about-why-mass-shoot ers-are-almost-always-men/2019/08/05/dec0c624-b700-11e9-a091-6a96e 67d9cce_story.html.) The term for this "gendered emotion" is "aggrieved enti- tlement," and at military grade it erupts in mass shootings (Rachel Kalish and Michael Kimmel, "Suicide by Mass Murder: Masculinity, Aggrieved Enti- tlement, and Rampage School Shootings," *Health Sociology Review* 19, no. 4 [2010]: 451–464)—but its civilian counterpart can look like nothing more than an annoying comfort with making one's needs into everyone's problem.

13. After a letter was found in Audley's apartment "stating his hatred of all rich white and Chinese kids, and that he was going to kill them all," press coverage shifted momentarily to an intention to cause injury (Lin, "Dropout Status"). That does not seem to have borne out, as concluding coverage (and conviction) reverted to the original motive of avoiding exposure. In itself, however, the letter does suggest alienation from both whites . . . and model minorities.

14. "Harvard Student Accused of Bomb Threats to Avoid Final Exam Is Due in Court on Hoax Charge," Postmedia Breaking News, December 18, 2013, available at https://advance-lexis-com.proxy.library.ucsb.edu:9443/api /document?collection=news&id=urn:contentItem:5B34-FKJ1-F125-10VB-0 0000-00&context=1516831.

15. Nicholas Hartlep, "Eldo Kim and the Specter of Academic Failure," in *Asian/Americans, Education, and Crime: The Model Minority as Victim and Perpetrator*, ed. Daisy Ball and Nicholas Hartlep (Lanham: Lexington Books, 2017), 49.

16. Mariel Klein, "Analysis: Kim Secured 'Extraordinary' Bargain, Experts Say," *Harvard Crimson*, October 22, 2014, available at https://www .thecrimson.com/article/2014/10/22/eldo-kim-legal-analysis/.

17. Hartlep, "Eldo Kim," 51.

18. Matthew Clarida and Nicholas Fandos, "Substantiating Fears of Grade Inflation, Dean Says Median Grade at Harvard College Is A-, Most Common Grade Is A," *Harvard Crimson*, December 3, 2013, available at https://www.thecrimson.com/article/2013/12/3/grade-inflation-mode-a/.

19. Hartlep, "Eldo Kim," 54.

20. Eldo Kim, "A Statement from Eldo Kim," *Harvard Crimson*, Novem- ber 25, 2014, available at https://www.thecrimson.com/article/2014/11/25 /statement-from-eldo-kim/.

21. Phil Yu, "Harvard Student Charged in Bomb Threat Hoax," *Angry Asian Man* (blog), December 17, 2013, available at http://blog.angryasian man.com/2013/12/harvard-student-charged-in-bomb-threat.html. Yu's account of Eldo twice calls his *actions* idiotic, not the person—and the overall tone is decidedly gentler than for Audley, without snark.

22. Alexander Lu and Y. Joel Wong, "Stressful Experiences of Masculinity among U.S.-Born and Immigrant Asian American Men," *Gender and Society* 27, no. 3 (June 2013): 360.

23. Phil Gollner, "Tay Killing's Ringleader Gets Life; COURTS: Victim's Mom Tells Court That Her Son's Death Has Left a 'Big, Gaping Hole in Our Hearts,'" *Orange County Register*, August 9, 1994.

24. Dan Froomkin, "The Honor Roll Murder; Stuart Tay's Shattered Life; Adolescence: Trouble on the Horizon," *Orange County Register*, January 16, 1993, available at https://advance-lexis-com.proxy.library.ucsb.edu:9443/api/document?collection=news&id=urn:contentItem:3S6N-20F0-00D3-84R4-00000-00&context=1516831.

25. Dan Froomkin, "New Year's Eve: Deadly Acquaintances," *Orange County Register*, January 17, 1993, available at https://advance-lexis-com.proxy.library.ucsb.edu:9443/api/document?collection=news&id=urn:contentItem:3S6N-2070-00D3-84JG-00000-00&context=1516831.

26. While these can be easily googled, the state of the internet in 1993 neither housed nor captured the kind of widespread, informal discussion of the case that social media has since made possible. But because *BLT*'s release in 2003 partially reanimated that earlier discussion, this chapter looks to Asian American responses to the film for a shared intimate public.

27. Cheryl Chen, "*Better Luck Tomorrow* Hits Too Close to Home," *Synapse* 47, no. 31, 22, available at https://cdnc.ucr.edu/?a=d&d=ucsf20030522-01.2.15&e=-------en--20--1--txt-txIN--------1.

28. Vanessa Hua, interview with author, May 5, 2018.

29. Daniel Yi, "They're the Bad Seeds? A Tale of Murderous Asian American Teens Didn't Set Out to Explode Stereotypes, but It May Hit the Bull's-Eye," *Los Angeles Times*, April 6, 2003, available at https://search.proquest.com/docview/421796036?accountid=14512.

30. Shirley Hune, "Demographics and Diversity of Asian American College Students," *New Directions for Student Services* 2002, no. 97 (Spring 2002): 14.

31. David Bell, "The Triumph of Asian-Americans," *New Republic*, July 14, 1985, available at https://newrepublic.com/article/76218/the-triumph-asian-americans.

32. Dana Takagi, "From Discrimination to Affirmative Action: Facts in the Asian American Admissions Controversy," *Social Problems* 37, no. 4 (November 1990): 578.

33. Helen Jun, *Race for Citizenship: Black Orientalism and Asian Uplift from Pre-Emancipation to Neoliberal America* (New York: New York University Press, 2011), 126, 128.

34. Bell, "Triumph of Asian-Americans."

35. Justin Lin, via assistant Jameson Hargear, email communication with author, July 31, 2020.

36. Logan Hill, "Meet Justin Lin, the Most Important Blockbuster Director You've Never Heard Of," *Wired*, May 19, 2016, available at https://www.wired.com/2016/05/justin-lin-star-trek-beyond/.

37. Jane Yong Kim, "How *Better Luck Tomorrow* Argued for Its Existence, 15 Years Ago," *The Atlantic*, Culture, August 21, 2018, available at https://www.theatlantic.com/entertainment/archive/2018/08/how-better-luck-tomorrow-argued-for-its-existence-15-years-ago/568045/.

38. John Powers, "The Dorky, the Docile and the Dead," *LA Weekly*, April 10, 2003, available at https://www.laweekly.com/the-dorky-the-docile-and-the-dead/.

39. Ruthann Lee, "Ambivalence, Desire and the Re-Imagining of Asian American Masculinity in *Better Luck Tomorrow*," in *Pimps, Wimps, Thugs and Gentlemen: Essays on Media Images of Masculinity*, ed. Elwood Watson (Jefferson, NC: McFarland, 2009), 51; Jane Yong Kim, "How *BLT* Argued."

40. Ju Yon Kim, *The Racial Mundane: Asian American Performance and the Embodied Everyday* (New York: New York University Press, 2015), 173.

41. *BLT*, 47:40; Jane Yong Kim, "How *BLT* Argued"; Charline Jao, "Why Justin Lin's Teen Crime Film *Better Luck Tomorrow* Still Resonates with Asian Americans," *The Mary Sue*, August 10, 2018, available at https://www.themarysue.com/better-luck-tomorrow-revisit/.

42. Laura Mulvey, "Visual Pleasure and Narrative Cinema," *Screen* 16, no. 3 (Autumn 1975): 6–18; Nary Kim, "Too Smart for His Own Good: The Devolution of a Model Asian American Student," *Asian American Law Journal* 20 (2013): 83.

43. Jao, "Why . . . *BLT*"; Ju Yon Kim, *Racial Mundane*, 184.

44. Jao, "Why . . . *BLT*."

45. *BLT*, 9:00–11:50.

46. Min Zhou and Carl L. Bankston III, "The Model Minority Stereotype and the National Identity Question: The Challenges Facing Asian Immigrants and Their Children," *Ethnic and Racial Studies* 43, no. 1 (2020): 247, emphasis added.

47. *BLT*, 11:55.

48. Lipsitz, "Possessive Investment in Whiteness," 371.

49. Ibid.

50. Tom Romero II, "War of a Much Different Kind: Poverty and the Possessive Investment in Color in the 1960s United States," *Chicano-Latino Law Review* 26 (2006): 72, 73.

51. Susan Koshy, "Category Crisis: South Asian Americans and Questions of Race and Ethnicity," *Diaspora: A Journal of Transnational Studies* 7, no. 3 (Winter 1998): 290, 304.

52. Romero, "War," 40.

53. Kevin Keller and Donald Lehmann, "Brands and Branding: Research Findings and Future Priorities," *Marketing Science* 25, no. 6 (November 2006): 740.

54. See for more brand associations: "Model Minority Stereotype for Asian Americans," Counseling and Mental Health Center, UT Austin, available at https://cmhc.utexas.edu/modelminority.html.

55. Hui Soo Chae, "Talking Back to the Asian Model Minority Discourse: Korean-Origin Youth Experiences in High School," *Journal of Intercultural Studies* 25, no. 1 (2004): 68.

56. Hu, "20 Best."

57. Lee and Zhou, *AAAP*, 130.

58. A study of five school sites in California's San Gabriel Valley found that, suggestively, in addition to 72 percent of gang members enrolled in high school, "almost 15% . . . indicated that they were currently attending college" (Glenn Tsunokai, "Beyond the Lenses of the 'Model' Minority Myth: A Descriptive Portrait of Asian Gang Members," *Journal of Gang Research* 12, no. 4 [Summer 2005]: 42). Alternatively, a study that set out to discover whether API youth with high GPAs might still be engaging in "delinquent behaviors (aggressive offenses, nonaggressive offenses, and gang initiation), sexual behaviors, and substance use" concluded this was not statistically the case (Yoonsun Choi, "Academic Achievement and Problem Behaviors among Asian Pacific Islander American Adolescents," *Journal of Youth and Adolescence* 36, no. 4 [May 2007]: 403–415). The latter is drawn, however, from a "nationally representative" data set so is not valid for contexts with Asian Americans in critical mass.

59. Brian Udoff, "Lin Beats Asian Trap," *Johns Hopkins News-Letter*, April 24, 2003, available at https://www.jhunewsletter.com/article/2003/04/lin-beats-asian-trap-95782.

60. *BLT*, 1:07:51.

61. Center for Demographic Research, "Components of Orange County's Population Growth: The Last Thirty Years," *Orange County Profiles* 5, no. 1 (March 2000): 2, available at http://www.fullerton.edu/cdr/products/profiles.aspx.

62. Derek Lu, "Searching for Stephanie: Negotiating Female Subjectivity in Justin Lin's Masculinist Feature *Better Luck Tomorrow*," Thinking Gender Papers, UCLA (April 1, 2016): 2, available at https://escholarship.org/content/qt30h7m423/qt30h7m423.pdf.

63. *BLT*, 37:10.

64. Lu, "Searching for Stephanie," 5.

65. *BLT*, 1:12:08.

66. *BLT*, 1:16:23.

67. *BLT*, 1:15:51. Another such pairing: when Steve follows up his "offer" to connect Ben to some internships, with a suggestion that Ben take Steph to the winter formal (24:24).

68. https://www.facebook.com/groups/1343933772408499/.

69. Nary Kim, "Too Smart," 83.

70. https://www.facebook.com/groups/1343933772408499/.

71. Robert Chan, "From Shackles to Square Hats: Higher Education and Lifer Prisoners," Past Year's Winners, 2015, The Elie Wiesel Foundation for Humanity, available at https://eliewieselfoundation.org/prize-ethics/winners/#1532981512334-b96fdd70-7239.

72. Robert Chan, interview with author, January 11, 2020.

73. Patrick Lampman, letter of recommendation, 1992, emphases added.

74. Gebe Martinez and De Tran, "Friends Can't See Suspect as Mastermind in Murder," *Los Angeles Times*, January 12, 1993, available at https://www.latimes.com/archives/la-xpm-1993-01-12-mn-1340-story.html.

75. R. Chan, interview.

76. Teri Sforza, "New Year, New Image for Sunny Hills," *Orange County Register*, Education, October 22, 1993; Chan, interview.

77. R. Chan, interview.

78. Patrick and Fran Lampman, interview with author, January 30, 2020.

79. Sforza, "New Year"; Lampman, interview.

80. Kirn Kim, interview with author, January 23, 2020.

81. Kathie Bozanich, "Asian Population in Orange County," *Los Angeles Times*, June 16, 1991, available at https://www.latimes.com/archives/la-xpm-1991-06-16-me-1456-story.html.

82. R. Chan, interview; Lampman, interview.

83. Jodi Wilgoren, "School Stands Out for Better, for Worse," *Los Angeles Times*, November 27, 1994, available at https://www.latimes.com/archives/la-xpm-1994-11-27-mn-2175-story.html; emphasis added.

84. Ibid., emphasis added.

85. Wendy Cheng, *The Changs Next Door to the Díazes: Remapping Race in Suburban California* (Minneapolis: University of Minnesota Press, 2013), 75. Cheng makes an argument quite close to what I call "possessive investment in the model minority," in fact, but because the school she studies is bifurcated between high-achieving Asians and Latinx students on the noncollege track, the "racialized privilege" she observes doesn't have the same edge of having bested the entire field. Given that "model minority" is usually taken to mean a second-tier or manservant role to whiteness, *but does not mean that at SHHS*, this is an important difference.

86. R. Chan, letter 9, January 27, 2020; letter 12, January 31, 2020.

87. R. Chan, letter 9.

88. Wilgoren, "School Stands Out."

89. Dhingra, *Hyper Education*, 25.

90. R. Chan, letter 3, January 20, 2020.

91. "Finalist Southern California High School Teams Will Meet for 'Ambassadors to Singapore' Competition," *Business Wire*, February 7, 1992, Friday.

92. R. Chan, interview; Robert Chan's 1992 "résumé," a self-narrative provided to Lampman to assist in writing a thorough letter of recommendation.

93. Yano and Akatsuka, *Straight A's*, xii.

94. Kirn Kim, "The Silent Shame: My Experience Returning from Incarceration," Crushing the Myth, November 5, 2019, available at https://www.crushingthemyth.com/watch-videos/the-silent-shame-my-experience-returning-from-incarceration-kirn-kim.

95. Actual enrollment numbers were closer to three thousand for Peninsula ("Palos Verdes Peninsula High," SchoolDigger.com, available at https://www.schooldigger.com/go/CA/schools/2970010246/school.aspx?t=tbStudents) and two thousand for SHHS (Sforza, "New Year") in 1993, but the discrepancy—and Kirn's pride in it—stands.

96. R. Chan, interview.

97. Grace Chan, interview with author, February 7, 2020.

98. Kirn, interview.

99. Catherine Gewertz, "Image in Death Doesn't Match Stuart Tay's Life," *Los Angeles Times*, January 10, 1993, available at https://www.latimes.com/archives/la-xpm-1993-01-10-mn-1667-story.html.

100. R. Chan, "Who I Was Then," preinterview written statement to author, emphases added to highlight the active subjects in these decisions.

101. R. Chan, interview.

102. R. Chan, interview; R. Chan, letter 17, March 23, 2020.

103. R. Chan, letter 4, January 23, 2020; R. Chan interview.

104. R. Chan, letter 6, January 24, 2020.

105. SHHS yearbook 1990–1991, 176; R. Chan, letter 17.

106. Martinez and De Tran, "Friends Can't See."

107. R. Chan, letter 17.

108. R. Chan, interview.

109. See James Diego Vigil, "Gangs, Social Control, and Ethnicity: Ways to Redirect," in *Identity and Inner-City Youth*, ed. Shirley Brice Heath and Milbrey McLaughlin (New York: Teachers College Press, 1993), 94–119.

110. R. Chan, letter 17.

111. Grace Chan, interview.

112. R. Chan, letter 11, January 29, 2020.

113. "Writ of Petition for Writ of Habeas Corpus," G042317, Initial Parole Consideration Hearing, Orange County Superior Court, July 17, 2009, 110.

114. R. Chan, letter 4.

115. R. Chan, letter 11.

116. R. Chan, letter 12.

117. R. Chan, interview.

118. R. Chan, interview.

119. R. Chan, interview. (Or, in other words, "It reminds me of how homework, clubs, and studying in *Better Luck Tomorrow* feel like something

done in autopilot, achievements that are so naturally expected and taken for granted that they feel simultaneously like an inextricable part of your identity and not part of who you are at all." Jao, "Why . . . *BLT*")

120. R. Chan, letter 13, February 3, 2020.

121. R. Chan, letter 21, April 3, 2020.

122. Wilgoren, "School Stands Out."

123. For instance: Jenifer B. McKim, "As Student Suicides Rise, a Harvard Case Opens New Questions about Schools' Responsibility," WBGH News, Education, September 16, 2019, available at https://www.wgbh.org/news/education/2019/09/16/as-student-suicides-rise-a-harvard-case-opens-new-questions-about-schools-responsibility.

124. R. Chan, letter 21.

125. R. Chan, letter 12; letter 2, January 19, 2020.

126. Kim, interview; In re Kirn Kim, Petition for Writ of Habeas Corpus Filed on March 26, 2012, G042317, Orange County Superior Court, 38.

127. Martha Rogers, quoted in Steven Renfeldt, "Psychological Evaluation for the Board of Parole Hearings, August 2008," G042317, Forensic Assessment Division, R. J. Donovan State Prison, 3.

128. For an overview, see Eugene Lee Davids et al., "Decision Making Styles: A Systematic Review of Their Associations with Parenting," *Adolescent Research Review* 1, no. 1 (2016): 69–90.

129. *Heathers*, directed by Michael Lehmann (Burbank, CA: Anchor Bay Entertainment, 1989), DVD.

130. R. Chan, interview.

131. Nary Kim, "Too Smart," 89.

132. Ibid., 92.

133. R. Chan, interview.

134. R. Chan, letter 21. Stuart had claimed to be twenty, but was in actuality a year younger than Robert.

135. Dhingra, *Hyper Education*, 31, 47.

136. Chae, "Talking Back," 69.

137. H. C. Yoo et al., "A Preliminary Report on a New Measure: Internalization of the Model Minority Myth Measure and Its Psychological Correlates among Asian American College Students," *Journal of Counseling Psychology* 57, no. 1 (January 2010): 115, emphasis added.

138. Jun, *Race for Citizenship*, 129.

139. Duschinsky and Wilson, "Flat Affect," 179.

140. William Deresiewicz, "The Neoliberal Arts: How College Sold Its Soul to the Market," *Harper's Magazine*, September 11, 2015, 25, available at https://harpers.org/archive/2015/09/the-neoliberal-arts/2/.

141. Eric Mark Kramer, "Introduction: Assimilation and the Model Minority Ideology," in *The Emerging Monoculture: Assimilation and the Model Minority* (Westport, CT: Praeger, 2003), xii.

142. Franklin D. Roosevelt, "May 7, 1933: Fireside Chat 2: On Progress during the First Two Months," Miller Center, University of Virginia, available at https://millercenter.org/the-presidency/presidential-speeches/may-7-1933 -fireside-chat-2-progress-during-first-two-months.

143. Jun, *Race for Citizenship*, 128, 129.

144. Ibid., 135, emphasis added.

145. Ibid., 136.

146. *BLT*, 11:55. But where Jun argues the criminal turn exclusively as an extension of model-minority pathology (i.e., another forum of competitive self-interest), I think its more salient aspects in both *BLT* and the real-life Honor Roll Murder are as an alternative.

147. Ahmed, *Promise of Happiness*, 165.

148. Peter Demerath et al., "Dimensions of Psychological Capital in a U.S. Suburb and High School: Identities for Neoliberal Times," *Anthropology and Education Quarterly* 39, no. 3 (September 2008): 286, 284, emphases added.

149. Jeffrey Pfeffer and Dana Carney, "The Economic Evaluation of Time Can Cause Stress," *Academy of Management Discoveries* 4, no. 1 (2018): 85, 75; online only, available at https://doi.org/10.5465/amd.2016.0017.

150. Deresiewicz, "Neoliberal Arts," 28.

151. Dhingra, *Hyper Education*, 21–22.

152. Deresiewicz, "Neoliberal Arts," 28.

153. Jennifer Hamer and Clarence Lang, "Race, Structural Violence, and the Neoliberal University: The Challenges of Inhabitation," *Critical Sociology* 41, no. 6 (September 2015): 902; Yu Xie and Kimberly Goyette, "Social Mobility and the Educational Choices of Asian Americans," *Social Science Research* 32, no. 3 (2003): 467–498.

154. Shankar, *Desi Land*, 73, 144, 149.

155. Lampman, interview.

156. Wilgoren, "School Stands Out."

157. Wade Pyun, "Let Tay Killing Mark an End to Parents' State of Denial," *Orange County Register*, February 17, 1993.

158. "Seniors Receive Early Acceptances," *Accolade* 34, no. 8 (January 22, 1993): 2.

159. Shankar, *Desi Land*, 151.

160. Joe Brunoli, "This Is Neoliberalism, Part I: The 10 Tenets of Neoliberalism," *Medium*, June 24, 2017, available at https://medium.com/@EuroY ankeeBlog/10-tenets-of-neoliberalism-ea90f34e51f9.

161. See Joel Bakan, *The Corporation: The Pathological Pursuit of Profit and Power* (New York: Free Press, 2004).

162. See James Kyung-Jin Lee's *Pedagogies of Woundedness: Illness, Memoir, and the Ends of the Model Minority* (forthcoming, Temple University Press).

163. Yano and Akatsuka, *Straight A's*, 35.

164. Wolf, "Family Secrets," 464, 467.

165. Dhingra, *Hyper Education*, 48, 69.

166. R. Chan, letter 17.

167. Joy Kogawa, *Obasan* (New York: Anchor, 1994), 67.

168. Yano and Akatsuka, *Straight A's*, 57.

169. Stacey Lee, *Unraveling the "Model Minority" Stereotype: Listening to Asian American Youth* (New York: Teachers College Press, 2009), 11.

170. *Better Luck Tomorrow* Q&A, Hammer Museum, UCLA, March 7, 2020, available at https://hammer.ucla.edu/programs-events/2020/better-luck-tomorrow.

171. Ibid. Per Jason Tobin, who played Virgil; also interviewed following above screening.

Selected Bibliography

Ahmed, Sara. *The Promise of Happiness*. Durham, NC: Duke University Press, 2010.

Bakan, Joel. *The Corporation: The Pathological Pursuit of Profit and Power*. New York: Free Press, 2004.

Baumrind, Diana. "Current Patterns of Parental Authority." *Developmental Psychology* 4, no.1, (January 1971): 1–103.

Bell, David A. "The Triumph of Asian-Americans." *New Republic*, July 14, 1985. Available at https://newrepublic.com/article/76218/the-triumph-asian-americans.

Berlant, Lauren. *Cruel Optimism*. Durham, NC: Duke University Press, 2011.

———. *The Female Complaint: The Unfinished Business of Sentimentality in American Culture*. Durham, NC: Duke University Press, 2008.

Browder, Laura. *Slippery Characters: Ethnic Impersonators and American Identities*. Chapel Hill: University of North Carolina Press, 2000.

Butler, Judith. "Performative Acts and Gender Constitution." *Theatre Journal* 40, no. 4 (December 1988): 519–531.

Cain, Ruth. "Bringing Up Neoliberal Baby: Post-austerity Anxieties about (Social) Reproduction." OpenDemocracy.net, July 14, 2016. Available at https://www.opendemocracy.net/en/opendemocracyuk/bringing-up-neoliberal-baby-post-austerity-anxieties-about-social-repro/.

Cantet, Laurent, dir. *Time Out (L'Emploi du Temps)*. France: Haut et Court, 2001. DVD.

Carrère, Emmanuel. *The Adversary: A True Story of Monstrous Deception*. New York: Henry Holt, 2000.

Chae, Hui Soo. "Talking Back to the Asian Model Minority Discourse: Korean-Origin Youth Experiences in High School." *Journal of Intercultural Studies* 25, no. 1 (2004): 59–73.

Chan, Robert. "From Shackles to Square Hats: Higher Education and Lifer Prisoners." Past Year's Winners, 2015, Elie Wiesel Foundation for Humanity. Available at https://eliewieselfoundation.org/prize-ethics/winners/#1532981512334-b96fdd70-7239.

Chao, Ruth K. "Beyond Parental Control and Authoritarian Parenting Style: Understanding Chinese Parenting through the Cultural Notion of Training." *Child Development* 65, no. 4 (August 1994): 1111–1119.

Chen, Tina. *Double Agency: Acts of Impersonation in Asian American Literature and Culture.* Stanford, CA: Stanford University Press, 2005.

Cheng, Wendy. *The Changs Next Door to the Díazes: Remapping Race in Suburban California.* Minneapolis: University of Minnesota Press, 2013.

Chin, Frank, Jeffery Paul Chan, Lawson Fusao Inada, and Shawn Wong, eds. "Introduction: Fifty Years of Our Whole Voice—An Introduction to Chinese and Japanese American Literature." In *Aiiieeeee! An Anthology of Asian-American Writers*, 3rd ed. Seattle: University of Washington Press, 2019.

Choi, Yoonsun. "Academic Achievement and Problem Behaviors among Asian Pacific Islander American Adolescents." *Journal of Youth and Adolescence* 36, no. 4 (May 2007): 403–415.

Chua, Amy. *Battle Hymn of the Tiger Mother.* New York: Penguin, 2011.

Conboy, Martin. *The Language of the News.* New York: Routledge, 2013.

Cosmides, Leda, and John Tooby. "Cognitive Adaptations for Social Exchange." In *The Adapted Mind: Evolutionary Psychology and the Generation of Culture*, edited by J. H. Barkow, Leda Cosmides, and John Tooby, 163–228. New York: Oxford University Press, 1992.

Costigan, Catherine et al. "Living Up to Expectations: The Strengths and Challenges Experienced by Chinese Canadian Students." *Canadian Journal of School Psychology* 25, no. 3 (September 2010): 223–245.

Davids, Eugene Lee et al. "Decision Making Styles: A Systematic Review of Their Associations with Parenting." *Adolescent Research Review* 1, no. 1 (2016): 69–90.

Demerath, Peter et al. "Dimensions of Psychological Capital in a U.S. Suburb and High School: Identities for Neoliberal Times." *Anthropology and Education Quarterly* 39, no. 3 (September 2008): 270–292.

Deresiewicz, William. "The Neoliberal Arts: How College Sold Its Soul to the Market." *Harper's Magazine*, September 11, 2015. Available at https://harpers.org/archive/2015/09/the-neoliberal-arts/2/.

Dhingra, Pawan. *Hyper Education: Why Good Schools, Good Grades, and Good Behavior Are Not Enough.* New York: New York University Press, 2020.

Drescher, Jack. "Out of DSM: Depathologizing Homosexuality." *Behavioral Sciences* 5, no. 4 (December 2015): 565–575.

Duldulao, Aileen. "Proof." *Open in Emergency: A Special Issue on Asian American Mental Health, Asian American Literary Review* 7, no. 2 (Fall/Winter 2016): 68–70.

Duschinsky, Robbie, and Emma Wilson. "Flat Affect, Joyful Politics and Enthralled Attachments: Engaging with the Work of Lauren Berlant." *International Journal of Politics, Culture, and Society* 28, no. 3 (2015): 179–190.

Eckert, Penelope. *Jocks and Burnouts: Social Categories and Identity in the High School*. New York: Columbia University, 1989.

Eng, David. *Racial Castration: Managing Masculinity in Asian America*. Durham, NC: Duke University Press, 2001.

Findlay, Stephanie, and Nicholas Kohler. "Too Asian: Some Frosh Don't Want to Study at an Asian University" [retitled "The Enrollment Controversy*"]. *Maclean's*, November 10, 2010. Available at http://www.macleans.ca/news /canada/too-asian/.

Ginsberg, Elaine K., ed. *Passing and the Fictions of Identity*. Durham, NC: Duke University Press, 1996.

Goriunova, Olga. "The Force of Digital Aesthetics: On Memes, Hacking, and Individuation." *Nordic Journal of Aesthetics* 24, no. 47 (2015): 54–75. Available at https://tidsskrift.dk/nja/article/view/23055/20143.

Gottschall, Jonathan. *The Storytelling Animal: How Stories Make Us Human*. Boston: Houghton Mifflin Harcourt, 2012.

Graham, Ian. *The Ultimate Book of Impostors: Over 100 True Stories of the Greatest Phonies and Frauds*. Naperville, IL: Sourcebooks, 2013.

Griffin, John Howard. *Black Like Me*. Boston: Houghton Mifflin, 1977.

Grimaldi, Jeremy. *A Daughter's Deadly Deception: The Jennifer Pan Story*. Toronto: Dundurn, 2016.

Haidt, Jonathan. *The Righteous Mind: Why Good People Are Divided by Politics and Religion*. New York: Pantheon Books, 2012.

Hamer, Jennifer, and Clarence Lang. "Race, Structural Violence, and the Neoliberal University: The Challenges of Inhabitation." *Critical Sociology* 41, no. 6 (September 2015): 897–912.

Harcup, Tony. *Journalism: Principles and Practice*. Thousand Oaks: Sage, 2004.

Harris, Cheryl. "Whiteness as Property." *Harvard Law Review* 106, no. 8 (June 1993): 1707–1791.

Hartlep, Nicholas. "Eldo Kim and the Specter of Academic Failure." In *Asian/ Americans, Education, and Crime: The Model Minority as Victim and Perpetrator*, edited by Daisy Ball and Nicholas Hartlep, 49–64. Lanham: Lexington Books, 2017.

Ho, Karen K. "Jennifer Pan's Revenge: The Inside Story of a Golden Child, the Killers She Hired, and the Parents She Wanted Dead." *Toronto Life*, July 22, 2015. Available at https://torontolife.com/city/jennifer-pan-revenge/?utm _source=thenextmeme.

Hobbs, Allyson Vanessa. *A Chosen Exile: A History of Racial Passing in American Life*. Cambridge: Harvard University Press, 2014.

Hsu, Hua. "Affect Theory and the New Age of Anxiety." *New Yorker*, March 25, 2019. Available at https://www.newyorker.com/magazine/2019/03/25 /affect-theory-and-the-new-age-of-anxiety.

Hsu, Madeline Yuan-yin. *The Good Immigrants: How the Yellow Peril Became the Model Minority*. Princeton, NJ: Princeton University Press, 2015.

Hu, Brian. "The 20 Best Asian American Films of the Last 20 Years." *Los Angeles Times*, October 4, 2019. Available at https://www.latimes.com/entertainment-arts/movies/story/2019-10-04/asian-american-films-canon.

Hua, Vanessa. "Accepted." In *Deceit and Other Possibilities*, 82–93. Detroit: Willow Books, 2016.

Hune, Shirley. "Demographics and Diversity of Asian American College Students." *New Directions for Student Services* 2002, no. 97 (Spring 2002): 11–20.

James, P. D. *The Murder Room*. New York: A. A. Knopf, 2003.

Jao, Charline. "Why Justin Lin's Teen Crime Film *Better Luck Tomorrow* Still Resonates with Asian Americans." *The Mary Sue*, August 10, 2018. Available at https://www.themarysue.com/better-luck-tomorrow-revisit/.

Juang, Linda P. et al. "Deconstructing the Myth of the 'Tiger Mother': An Introduction to the Special Issue on Tiger Parenting, Asian-Heritage Families, and Child/Adolescent Well-Being." *Asian American Journal of Psychology* 4, no. 1 (2013): 1–6.

Jun, Helen. *Race for Citizenship: Black Orientalism and Asian Uplift from Pre-Emancipation to Neoliberal America*. New York: New York University Press, 2011.

Kalish, Rachel, and Michael Kimmel. "Suicide by Mass Murder: Masculinity, Aggrieved Entitlement, and Rampage School Shootings." *Health Sociology Review* 19, no. 4 (2010): 451–464.

Kanuha, Valli Kalei. "The Social Process of 'Passing' to Manage Stigma: Acts of Internalized Oppression or Acts of Resistance?" *Journal of Sociology and Social Welfare* 26, no. 4 (2015): 27–46.

Kao, Grace. "Group Images and Possible Selves among Adolescents: Linking Stereotypes to Expectations by Race and Ethnicity." *Sociological Forum* 15, no. 3 (2000): 407–430.

Kawash, Samira. "*The Autobiography of an Ex-Coloured Man*: (Passing for) Black Passing for White." In *Passing and the Fictions of Identity*, edited by Elaine K. Ginsberg, 59–74. Durham, NC: Duke University Press, 1996.

———. *Dislocating the Color Line: Identity, Hybridity, and Singularity in African-American Narrative*. Stanford, CA: Stanford University Press, 1997.

Keller, Kevin, and Donald Lehmann. "Brands and Branding: Research Findings and Future Priorities." *Marketing Science* 25, no. 6 (November 2006): 740–759.

Kim, Jane Yong. "How *Better Luck Tomorrow* Argued for Its Existence, 15 Years Ago." *The Atlantic*, Culture, August 21, 2018. Available at https://www.theatlantic.com/entertainment/archive/2018/08/how-better-luck-tomorrow-argued-for-its-existence-15-years-ago/568045/.

Kim, Janna. "Asian American Women's Retrospective Reports of Their Sexual Socialization." *Psychology of Women Quarterly* 33, no. 3 (2009): 334–350.

Kim, Ju Yon. *The Racial Mundane: Asian American Performance and the Embodied Everyday*. New York: New York University Press, 2015.

Kim, Kirn. "The Silent Shame: My Experience Returning from Incarceration." Crushing the Myth, November 5, 2019. Available at https://www.crush

ingthemyth.com/speakers-page/the-silent-shame-my-experience-returning-from-incarceration-kirn-kim.

Kim, Nary. "Too Smart for His Own Good: The Devolution of a Model Asian American Student." *Asian American Law Journal* 20 (2013): 82–107.

Kingston, Maxine Hong. *The Woman Warrior: Memoirs of a Girlhood among Ghosts*. New York: Vintage International, 1989.

Kinney, David A. "From Nerds to Normals: The Recovery of Identity among Adolescents from Middle School to High School." *Sociology of Education* 66, no. 1 (January 1993): 21–40.

Kogawa, Joy. *Obasan*. New York: Anchor, 1994.

Konnikova, Maria. *The Confidence Game: Why We Fall for It . . . Every Time*. New York: Viking, 2016.

Koshy, Susan. "Category Crisis: South Asian Americans and Questions of Race and Ethnicity." *Diaspora: A Journal of Transnational Studies* 7, no. 3 (Winter 1998): 285–320.

———. "Morphing Race into Ethnicity: Asian Americans and Critical Transformations of Whiteness." *boundary 2* 28, no. 1 (Spring 2001): 153–194.

Kramer, Eric Mark. "Introduction: Assimilation and the Model Minority Ideology." In *The Emerging Monoculture: Assimilation and the Model Minority*, xi–xxi. Westport, CT: Praeger, 2003.

Le, C. N. "Asian American Pretends to Be a Stanford Student." *Asian-Nation* (blog), May 31, 2007. Available at http://www.asian-nation.org/headlines/2007/05/asian-american-pretends-to-be-a-stanford-student/.

Lee, Annette. "All of the Fun and None of the Work." *Hyphen* 13, January 1, 2008. Available at http://hyphenmagazine.com/magazine/issue-13-hybrid-winter-2007/all-fun-and-none-work.

Lee, Christopher. *The Semblance of Identity*. Stanford, CA: Stanford University Press, 2012.

Lee, Erika. "The 'Yellow Peril' and Asian Exclusion in the Americas." *Pacific Historical Review* 76, no. 4 (2007): 537–562.

Lee, Jennifer, and Min Zhou. *The Asian American Achievement Paradox*. New York: Russell Sage Foundation, 2015.

Lee, Mike. "Push to Achieve Tied to . . . Deception?" *8Asians* (blog), May 26, 2007. Available at https://www.8asians.com/2007/05/26/push-to-achieve-tied-to-deception/.

Lee, Ruthann. "Ambivalence, Desire and the Re-Imagining of Asian American Masculinity in *Better Luck Tomorrow*." In *Pimps, Wimps, Thugs and Gentlemen: Essays on Media Images of Masculinity*, edited by Elwood Watson, 51–67. Jefferson, NC: McFarland, 2009.

Lee, Sara. "Class Matters." In *Becoming New Yorkers: Ethnographies of the New Second Generation*, edited by Philip Kasinitz et al., 313–338. New York: Russell Sage, 2004.

Lee, Stacey. *Unraveling the "Model Minority" Stereotype: Listening to Asian American Youth*. New York: Teachers College Press, 2009.

Lee, Stacey J., and Kevin K. Kumashiro. "Bias against Asian-American Students Is Real. Affirmative Action Isn't the Problem." *Vox*, June 27, 2018.

Available at https://www.vox.com/the-big-idea/2018/6/27/17509140 /admissions-bias-personalities-harvard-affirmative-action.

Lehmann, Michael, dir. *Heathers*. Burbank, CA: Anchor Bay Entertainment, 2008.

Li, Guofang. "Other People's Success: Impact of the 'Model Minority' Myth on Underachieving Asian Students in North America." *KEDI Journal of Educational Policy* 2, no. 1 (2005): 69–86.

Lin, Justin, dir. *Better Luck Tomorrow*. Hollywood, CA: Paramount, 2003. DVD.

Lipsitz, George. "The Possessive Investment in Whiteness: Racialized Social Democracy and the 'White' Problem in American Studies." *American Quarterly* 47, no. 3 (September 1995): 369–387.

Louie, Vivian S. "'Being Practical' or 'Doing What I Want': The Role of Parents in the Academic Choices of Chinese Americans." In *Becoming New Yorkers: Ethnographies of the New Second Generation*, edited by Philip Kasinitz et al., 79–110. New York: Russell Sage, 2004.

———. *Compelled to Excel: Immigration, Education, and Opportunity among Chinese Americans*. Stanford, CA: Stanford University Press, 2004.

Lu, Alexander, and Y. Joel Wong. "Stressful Experiences of Masculinity among U.S.-Born and Immigrant Asian American Men." *Gender and Society* 27, no. 3 (June 2013): 345–371.

Lu, Derek. "Searching for Stephanie: Negotiating Female Subjectivity in Justin Lin's Masculinist Feature *Better Luck Tomorrow*." Thinking Gender Papers, UCLA, April 1, 2016. Available at https://escholarship.org/content /qt30h7m423/qt30h7m423.pdf.

Mar, M. Elaine. *Paper Daughter*. New York: HarperCollins, 1999.

Meyers, Marian. *News Coverage of Violence against Women: Engendering Blame*. Thousand Oaks: Sage, 1997.

Miltner, Kate M. "There's No Place for Lulz on LOLCats: The Role of Genre, Gender, and Group Identity in the Interpretation and Enjoyment of an Internet Meme." *First Monday* 19, no. 8 (August 4, 2014). Available at https:// journals.uic.edu/ojs/index.php/fm/article/view/5391/4103.

Morreall, John. *Comedy, Tragedy, and Religion*. Albany: State University of New York Press, 1999.

Mudambi, Anjana. "South Asian American Discourses: Engaging the Yellow Peril-Model Minority Dialectic." *Howard Journal of Communications* 30, no. 3 (October 2018): 284–298.

Mulvey, Laura. "Visual Pleasure and Narrative Cinema." *Screen* 16, no. 3 (Autumn 1975): 6–18.

Ngo, Bic, and Stacey J. Lee. "Complicating the Image of Model Minority Success: A Review of Southeast Asian American Education." *Review of Educational Research* 77, no. 4 (December 2007): 415–453.

Ninh, erin Khuê. "Advice on How Not to Misread the Tiger Mother." *Amerasia Journal* 37, no. 2 (2011): 123–129.

———. "Amy Chua and the Externalized Cost of Book Sales." *Hyphen* (blog), January 19, 2011. Available at https://hyphenmagazine.com/blog/2011 /1/19/amy-chua-and-externalized-cost-book-sales.

————. "Amy Chua's Recipe for Disaster and the Externalized Cost of Book Sales." *Huffington Post*, January 18, 2011. Available at https://www.huff post.com/entry/amy-chuas-recipe-for-disa_b_810607?guccounter=1.

————. *Ingratitude: The Debt-Bound Daughter in Asian American Literature.* New York: New York University Press, 2011.

Omi, Michael, and Howard Winant. *Racial Formation in the United States.* New York: Routledge/Taylor and Francis, 2015.

Ortner, Sherry B. "'Burned Like a Tattoo': High School Social Categories and 'American Culture.'" *Ethnography* 3, no. 2 (June 1, 2002): 115–148.

Pellerin, Lisa. "Applying Baumrind's Parenting Typology to High Schools: Toward a Middle-Range Theory of Authoritative Socialization." *Social Science Research* 34, no. 2 (June 2005): 283–303.

Petersen, William. "Success Story, Japanese-American Style." *New York Times*, January 9, 1966.

Pfeffer, Jeffrey, and Dana Carney. "The Economic Evaluation of Time Can Cause Stress." *Academy of Management Discoveries* 4, no. 1 (2018): 74–93. Online only. Available at https://doi.org/10.5465/amd.2016.0017.

Pfeiffer, Kathleen. *Race Passing and American Individualism.* Amherst: University of Massachusetts Press, 2003.

Piper, Adrian. "Passing for White, Passing for Black." *Transition* 58 (1992): 4–32.

Pon, Gordon. "Importing the Asian Model Minority Discourse into Canada: Implications for Social Work and Education." *Canadian Social Work Review* 17, no. 2 (2000): 277–291.

Reiner, Rob, dir. *Stand by Me.* Culver City, CA: Columbia Pictures, 2000.

Ritzer, George, and Douglas J Goodman. *Sociological Theory.* Boston: McGraw-Hill, 2008.

Rohy, Valerie. "Displacing Desire: Passing, Nostalgia, and *Giovanni's Room.*" In *Passing and the Fictions of Identity*, edited by Elaine K. Ginsberg, 218–233. Durham, NC: Duke University Press, 1996.

Romero II, Tom I. "War of a Much Different Kind: Poverty and the Possessive Investment in Color in the 1960s United States." *Chicano-Latino Law Review* 26 (2006): 69–237.

Rottenberg, Catherine. "Passing: Race, Identification, and Desire." *Criticism* 45, no. 4 (2003): 435–452.

Samuels, David. *The Runner: A True Account of the Amazing Lies and Fantastical Adventures of the Ivy League Impostor James Hogue.* New York: New Press, 2008.

Shankar, Shalini. *Desi Land: Teen Culture, Class, and Success in Silicon Valley.* Durham, NC: Duke University Press, 2008.

Shin, Jean. "The Asian American Closet." *Asian American Law Journal* 11, no. 1 (2004): 1–30.

Song, Min. *The Children of 1965: On Writing, and Not Writing, as an Asian American.* Durham, NC: Duke University Press, 2013.

Sorkhabi, Nadia, and Ellen Middaugh. "Domain-Specific Parenting Practices and Adolescent Self-Esteem, Problem Behaviors, and Competence." *Journal of Child and Family Studies* 28 (2019): 505–518.

————. "How Variations in Parents' Use of Confrontive and Coercive Control Relate to Variations in Parent–Adolescent Conflict, Adolescent Disclosure, and Parental Knowledge: Adolescents' Perspective." *Journal of Child and Family Studies* 23, no. 7 (2014): 1227–1241.

Squires, Catherine, and Daniel Brouwer. "In/discernible Bodies: The Politics of Passing in Dominant and Marginal Media." *Critical Studies in Media Communication* 19, no. 3 (2002): 283–310.

"Success Story of One Minority Group in U.S." *U.S. News and World Report.* December 26, 1966.

Takagi, Dana. "From Discrimination to Affirmative Action: Facts in the Asian American Admissions Controversy." *Social Problems* 37, no. 4 (November 1990): 578–592.

Tan, Amy. *The Joy Luck Club.* New York: Putnam's, 1989.

Tasca, Cecilia et al. "Women and Hysteria in the History of Mental Health." *Clinical Practice and Epidemiology in Mental Health* 8 (2012): 110–119.

Tsunokai, Glenn T. "Beyond the Lenses of the 'Model' Minority Myth: A Descriptive Portrait of Asian Gang Members." *Journal of Gang Research* 12, no. 4 (Summer 2005): 37–58.

Ty, Eleanor Rose. *Asianfail: Narratives of Disenchantment and the Model Minority.* Urbana: University of Illinois Press, 2017.

van Dijk, Teun A. *News as Discourse.* Hillsdale, NJ: L. Erlbaum, 1988.

Vigil, James Diego. "Gangs, Social Control, and Ethnicity: Ways to Redirect." In *Identity and Inner-City Youth,* edited by Shirley Brice Heath and Milbrey McLaughlin, 94–119. New York: Teachers College Press, 1993.

Wang, Jen. "Oh Azia I Hate to Say Goodbye." *Disgrasian* (blog), May 29, 2007. Available at http://disgrasian.com/tag/azia-kim/.

West, Candace, and Don H. Zimmerman. "Doing Gender." *Gender and Society* 1, no. 2 (June 1987): 125–151.

Wolf, Diane. "Family Secrets: Transnational Struggles among Children of Filipino Immigrants." *Sociological Perspectives* 40, no. 3 (1997): 457–482.

Wong, Kristina. "I Thought Being Miserable Was Just Part of Being Chinese American." kristinawong.com, May 15, 2014. Available at http://kristina wong.com/blog/2019/10/13/i-thought-being-miserable-was-just-part-of -being-chinese-american/?fbclid=IwAR2FYseJ_Fgmz4vdcQdIgzu9mzEu kcG_wEMvGFvSb3T0vIN1bcuMP2rP_Z4.

————. *Wong Flew Over the Cuckoo's Nest.* Directed by Mike Closson. Los Angeles, CA: Flying Wong Productions, 2011. DVD.

Wong, Paul et al. "Asian Americans as a Model Minority: Self-Perceptions and Perceptions by Other Racial Groups." *Sociological Perspectives* 41, no. 1 (March 1, 1998): 95–118.

Wong, Y. Joel et al. "Asian American Male College Students' Perceptions of People's Stereotypes about Asian American Men." *Psychology of Men and Masculinity* 13, no. 1 (January 2012): 75–88.

Wu, Ellen D. *The Color of Success: Asian Americans and the Origins of the Model Minority.* Princeton, NJ: Princeton University Press, 2014.

Xie, Yu, and Kimberly Goyette. "Social Mobility and the Educational Choices of Asian Americans." *Social Science Research* 32, no. 3 (2003): 467–498.

Yang, Jeff. "Do Asian Students Face Too Much Academic Pressure?" CNN, Opinion, July 2, 2015. Available at http://www.cnn.com/2015/07/02/opin ions/yang-genius-girl/.

Yang, Wesley. "Paper Tigers." *New York Magazine*, May 6, 2011. Available at http://nymag.com/news/features/asian-americans-2011-5/.

Yano, Christine Reiko, and Neal Akatsuka. *Straight A's: Asian American College Students in Their Own Words*. Durham, NC: Duke University Press, 2018.

Yau, Jenny P. et al. "Disclosure to Parents about Everyday Activities among American Adolescents from Mexican, Chinese, and European Back-grounds." *Child Development* 80, no. 5 (September 2009): 1481–1498.

Yoo, H. C. et al. "A Preliminary Report on a New Measure: Internalization of the Model Minority Myth Measure and Its Psychological Correlates among Asian American College Students." *Journal of Counseling Psychology* 57, no. 1 (January 2010): 114–127.

Yoshino, Kenji. "Covering." *Yale Law Journal* 111, no. 4 (2002): 769–793.

Yu, Phil. "Harvard Student Charged in Bomb Threat Hoax." *Angry Asian Man* (blog), December 17, 2013. Available at http://blog.angryasianman .com/2013/12/harvard-student-charged-in-bomb-threat.html.

———. "'Lonely' 27-Year-Old Posed as Harvard Freshman for Months." *Angry Asian Man* (blog), December 14, 2011. Available at http://blog.angryasian man.com/2011/12/lonely-27-year-old-posed-as-harvard.html.

———. "UC Riverside Dropout Pleads Guilty to Bomb Scare." *Angry Asian Man* (blog), April 28, 2008. Available at http://blog.angryasianman.com /2008/04/uc-riverside-dropout-pleads-guilty-to.html.

———. "The Worst Way to Tell Your Mom You Dropped Out of School." *Angry Asian Man* (blog), June 25, 2007. Available at http://blog.angryasian man.com/2007/06/worst-way-to-tell-your-mom-you-dropped.html.

Yuan, Jada. "From *Twilight* to *Gook*: How Justin Chon Found His Voice in His Own Painful Racial Past." Vulture.com, August 25, 2017. Available at https://www.vulture.com/2017/08/from-twilight-to-gook-how-justin -chon-found-his-voice.html.

Zauzmer, Julie. *Conning Harvard: Adam Wheeler—The Con Artist Who Faked His Way into the Ivy League*. Guilford: Lyons, 2012.

Zhou, Min, and Carl L. Bankston III. "The Model Minority Stereotype and the National Identity Question: The Challenges Facing Asian Immigrants and Their Children." *Ethnic and Racial Studies* 43, no. 1 (2020): 233–253.

Index

The letter *t* following a page number denotes a table.

erin Khuê Ninh is an Associate Professor of Asian American Studies at the University of California, Santa Barbara. She is the author of *Ingratitude: The Debt-Bound Daughter in Asian American Literature*, which won the Literary Studies Book Award from the Association for Asian American Studies in 2013.

Also in the series *Asian American History and Culture*

Shirley Geok-lin Lim and Amy Ling, eds., *Reading the Literatures of Asian America*

Karen Isaksen Leonard, *Making Ethnic Choices: California's Punjabi Mexican Americans*

Gary Y. Okihiro, *Cane Fires: The Anti-Japanese Movement in Hawaii, 1865–1945*

Sucheng Chan, *Entry Denied: Exclusion and the Chinese Community in America, 1882–1943*